IT'S NOT AS IT SEEMS

A Game of Hide and Seek

Randall and Angelia Barton

It's Not as It Seems®

A Game of Hide and Seek

by Randall Barton
Title and editing by Angelia Barton
Copyright © 2022 by Randall Barton
itsnotasitseems.com

Like the Wind Press
An Imprint of Like the Wind Publishing
Medford, Oregon
likethewindpress.com

Cover design graphics and interior layout by Chris Molé Design
www.chrismoledesign.com

Like the Wind Press
Born of the Spirit, Born of Dreams

Printed in the United States of America
Library of Congress Control Number: 2022906014
ISBN: 979-8-9860194-0-6 (Hardcover)
ISBN: 979-8-9860194-1-3 (Paperback)
ISBN: 979-8-9860194-2-0 (ebook)
First Edition

It's Not as It Seems

It will never look the same again

Once you have seen
What you have never been able to see before
You will never be able to see again
What you were only able to see before

It will never look the same again

This is the end of a time
The beginning of something new

It will become a "Once Upon a Time"
And this is what I know
Though it was something you once knew
They will not believe you

This is the end of "Once Upon a Time"
This is the start of something new
And if you try to tell the story of "Once Upon a Time"
They will not believe you

It will never look the same again
It will never be the same again

It's Not as It Seems

by Randall Barton

Description of Design

Book Design

Every chapter, paragraph, stanza, diagram, table, list, sentence and individual word in *It's Not as It Seems - A Game of Hide and Seek* has been arranged and formatted to complement the written text to help visually illustrate and *show*, the meaning of what is being, *said*.

Chapter Design

The chapters are titled as would be seen in a theatrical play. Example: Act 1, Act 2, etc. Each chapter begins with a short introductory scene, titled as a 'Vignette.' Example: Opening Vignette, Act 2 Vignette, etc.

Scripture Text

All Scripture text is shown indented and italicized. For every first use or mention of a Scripture, the Scripture address along with the Bible version being quoted will be listed immediately following and shown as right justified on the page. Addresses have also been listed as needed for supplemental reference. For example an address will be listed again if the Scripture text had not been recently mentioned.

The use of the Scripture addresses will also include vertical side bars to identify the Scripture text from the surrounding narrative. There are a few exceptions to the use of the side bars due to textual formatting and layout styles.

Example: The Scripture text below is shown with preceding narrative, vertical side bar, Scripture address and Bible version.

Jesus said to those standing nearby,

> *"Loose him, and let him go."*
>
> John 11:44 NKJV

Some Scripture addresses will be listed as *"See Scripture address."* This is used when there has not been a direct quotation of Scripture, yet is being used as a reference for the reader.

Abbreviations

e.a.   Emphasis Added   Used when bolding or special formatting has been applied to highlight sections of Scripture text.

par.   Paraphrased   Used when Scripture text has been modified.

Punctuation Use

Parentheses ()   Used for insertion of additional words into Scripture text. Example:
I speak with him (Moses) face to face

Also used to highlight specific words or sections in narrative.

Square Brackets []   Used for word substitution in Scripture text. Example:
When [Jesus] got into the boat

The name Jesus was substituted for the pronoun He.

Quotation Marks ""

Scripture text has been copied as presented from its respective Bible version. Quotation marks have not been added if not present in original text. If a selection of text begins with an opening quotation mark, that mark is copied along with the text. If there is no quotation mark at either the beginning or the end of the selected text, no quotation mark is added. A selection of text may show an opening quotation mark with no closing mark due to a portion of the sentence being listed, or the placement of the closing mark on a following sentence within the original text.

Example: Shown with opening quotation mark only.

"The kingdom of heaven is like a treasure hidden in the field
Matthew 13:44 NASB

Example: Shown without opening or closing quotation mark.

the kingdom of heaven is like a merchant seeking fine pearls
Matthew 13:45 NASB

Main Program

Program of Events

OPENING VIGNETTE

A GAME OF HIDE AND SEEK

It is the glory of God to conceal a matter,
But the glory of kings is to search out a matter.

Proverbs 25:2 NKJV

HIDE AND SEEK; A GAME CHILDREN PLAY. We have all played it, some of us still do. Everyone enjoys finding something hidden. What you are about to read tells the story of a masterful game of Hide and Seek; a story of secrets, riddles and clues. Secrets have been hidden by the Lord, with riddles and clues given so we might search and find them.

This book is about the pursuit of those things that have been hidden. And more importantly, the discovery of... *what has been found!*

Jesus said,

> *"I praise You, Father, Lord of heaven and earth, that You have hidden these things from the wise and intelligent and have revealed them to infants.*

Matthew 11:25 NASB

If the Lord has indeed hidden something, shouldn't we at least be curious as to what it might be?

Hide and Seek, it's just a child's game, surely we can play.

Jesus also said,

> *"Truly I say to you, unless you are converted and become like children, you will not enter the kingdom of heaven.*

Matthew 18:3 NASB

So let's play this game of Hide and Seek.
Let's uncover what the Lord has hidden.

Welcome to Act 1 – Hidden Things

Act 1

Hidden Things

THE PROPHECIES

PROPHECIES; EVERYONE LOVES A GOOD PROPHECY. People yearn to know what the future holds and what tomorrow will bring. Prophecies are intriguing; they capture the attention of even the most ardent skeptic. The Old Testament is literally filled, beginning to end, with prophecies speaking of our future.

What is a prophecy?

Simply stated, it is a word or message from the Lord, which many times tells of something that will happen in the future.

When we think of prophecies, we wouldn't think of them as hiding something. Rather, we naturally think of them as *revealing* something; they are telling us what is going to happen. This would be a logical assumption and, in some cases, would be entirely correct.

Look at this example of the Lord telling Abraham his wife Sarah will have a child.

The Lord said to Abraham,

> *"I will surely return to you at this time next year;*
> *and behold, Sarah your wife will have a son."*
>
> *Genesis 18:10 NASB*

Then the following year,

> *Then the LORD took note of Sarah as He had said, and the LORD did for Sarah as He had promised. So Sarah conceived and bore a son to Abraham in his old age, at the appointed time of which God had spoken to him. Abraham called the name of his son who was born to him, whom Sarah bore to him, Isaac.*
>
> *Genesis 21:1-3 NASB*

This prophetic word from the Lord to Abraham clearly said, what would happen, to whom it would happen, and when.

> *Sarah will have a son next year*

7

Some prophecies however, unlike this first example, are not so clear, and not so easily understood.

Look at this next prophecy. The Lord speaks to the prophet Ezekiel and gives him a prophetic message for King Zedekiah.

> Say to them, 'Thus says the Lord GOD: "This burden concerns the prince in Jerusalem and all the house of Israel who are among them."'
>
> Say, 'I am a sign to you. As I have done, so shall it be done to them; they shall be carried away into captivity.' And the prince who is among them shall bear his belongings on his shoulder at twilight and go out. They shall dig through the wall to carry them out through it. He shall cover his face, so that he cannot see the ground with his eyes. I will also spread My net over him, and he shall be caught in My snare.
>
> I will bring him to Babylon, to the land of the Chaldeans; **yet he shall not see it, though he shall die there**.
>
> *Ezekiel 12:10-13 NKJV e.a.*

Notice this prophecy takes on the form of a riddle. It says the king will go into captivity in Babylon,

> yet he shall not see it, though he shall die there.

How can he go to Babylon and yet not see it?

Look at the record in the book of Jeremiah regarding King Zedekiah when Nebuchadnezzar the king of Babylon attacked Jerusalem and captured the city.

> So it was, when Zedekiah the king of Judah and all the men of war saw them, that they fled and went out of the city by night, by way of the king's garden, by the gate between the two walls. And he went out by way of the plain. But the Chaldean army pursued them and overtook Zedekiah in the plains of Jericho. And when they had captured him, they brought him up to Nebuchadnezzar king of Babylon, to Riblah in the land of Hamath, where he

> *pronounced judgment on him. Then the king of Babylon killed the*
> *sons of Zedekiah before his eyes in Riblah; the king of Babylon also*
> *killed all the nobles of Judah.*
>
> **Moreover he put out Zedekiah's eyes, and bound him with**
> **bronze fetters to carry him off to Babylon.**
>
> *Jeremiah 39:4-7 NKJV e.a.*

This prophetic word was fulfilled exactly as it had been told. King
Zedekiah did go into captivity in Babylon, but he did not see it.

His eyes had been put out.

The full meaning of this prophecy would not be understood by King
Zedekiah, or anyone else, until *after* it came to pass. The meaning of this
prophecy remained a mystery and riddle to the king.

Look at this next example. The Lord speaks to the prophet Isaiah and
gives him a message for King Ahaz.

The Lord said,

> *"Therefore the Lord Himself will give you a sign: Behold, a virgin*
> *will be with child and bear a son, and she will call His name*
> *Immanuel.*
>
> *Isaiah 7:14 NASB*

This is a difficult prophecy. Who is this referring to? When will this
happen?

How can a virgin be with child?

Today we may take this prophecy for granted because we have heard the
story of Mary conceiving a child by the Holy Spirit while still a virgin
and giving birth to Jesus.

But that story wasn't known when Isaiah's prophecy was given. That
story wouldn't be told for another 700 years. To put that length of time
into perspective, the United States has been a nation for less than 250
years. For almost three times longer than the United States has been in
existence, no one knew the meaning of this prophecy.

After this prophecy was given to King Ahaz, 700 years later, the angel Gabriel tells Mary she is going to have a baby. Watch how Mary reacts when she is told, her question is the same as ours.

> *The angel said to her,*
> *"Do not be afraid, Mary; for you have found favor with God. "And behold, you will conceive in your womb and bear a son, and you shall name Him Jesus.*
>
> *"He will be great and will be called the Son of the Most High; and the Lord God will give Him the throne of His father David; and He will reign over the house of Jacob forever, and His kingdom will have no end."*

Mary does not understand and asks,

> **"How can this be, since I am a virgin?"**

Now, notice this next detail. When Mary asked, *"How can this be?"* Gabriel then explained the prophecy.

> *The angel answered and said to her,*
> *"The Holy Spirit will come upon you, and the power of the Most High will overshadow you; and for that reason the holy Child shall be called the Son of God.*
>
>

Luke 1:30-35 NASB e.a.

Gabriel explained the prophecy given to Mary. But there was no explanation given to King Ahaz; he was given only the prophecy. The meaning of the prophecy remained a mystery and riddle to the king.

A virgin will be with child

The prophetic word given to King Ahaz was fulfilled exactly as had been told, a virgin was found to be with child. But the meaning of this prophecy would not be understood by anyone until again, *after,* it had come to pass. More than seven centuries later, the angel Gabriel gave Mary a prophetic message that it was she who would conceive and give birth to a son.

The Meanings of the Prophecies

The prophecy in the first example was clear and its meaning was understood.

> *Sarah will have a son next year*

The prophecies in the second and third examples however, were not clear and their meanings were not understood.

> *How will he not see it, though he will die there?*
> *How can a virgin be with child?*

These latter prophecies took on the form of riddles; their meanings were hidden.

To summarize what we have just seen:

- Some prophecies are *clear* and their meanings are understood.
- Some prophecies are *riddles* and their meanings are hidden.

Hidden Meanings

Here are three other examples of Old Testament Scriptures that also have hidden meanings.

After the Israelites had fled Egypt, while still in the desert, they complained to Moses that there was no water.

The Lord said to Moses,

> *"Take the rod; you and your brother Aaron gather the congregation together. Speak to the rock before their eyes, and it will yield its water; thus you shall bring water for them out of the rock, and give drink to the congregation and their animals."*
>
> *Numbers 20:8 NKJV*

Here is a Scripture from the Old Testament that contains a hidden meaning, which we only now know because the apostle Paul explained it in the New Testament.

Paul said,

> *Moreover, brethren, I do not want you to be unaware that all our*
> *fathers were under the cloud, all passed through the sea, all were*
> *baptized into Moses in the cloud and in the sea, all ate the same*
> *spiritual food, and all drank the same spiritual drink.*
>
> *For they drank of that spiritual Rock that followed them,*
> ***and that Rock was Christ.***
>
> *1 Corinthians 10:1-4 NKJV e.a.*

This Old Testament Scripture in the book of Numbers is hiding the fact it is speaking of the Messiah.

The rock that followed the children of Israel through the wilderness and the rock that provided water for them to drink was their Messiah; it was Jesus Christ. The Lord had Moses speak to the rock to bring forth water for the people, as a prophetic act which spoke of the coming Messiah.

The Messiah is being hidden in this Scripture.

Here is a second example. Later, the people were again complaining about the lack of food and water. So the Lord sent serpents among them, and some of the people were dying from having been bitten.

The Lord said to Moses,

> *"Make a fiery serpent, and set it on a pole; and it shall be that*
> *everyone who is bitten, when he looks at it, shall live."*
>
> *So Moses made a bronze serpent, and put it on a pole; and so it*
> *was, if a serpent had bitten anyone, when he looked at the bronze*
> *serpent, he lived.*
>
> *Numbers 21:8-9 NKJV*

This is another Scripture from the Old Testament with a hidden meaning. And again, we only know this because Jesus Himself explained it in the New Testament.

Jesus spoke of this serpent and said,

> And **as Moses lifted up the serpent** in *the wilderness,* **even so must the Son of Man be lifted up**, *that whoever believes in Him should not perish but have eternal life.*

John 3:14-15 NKJV e.a.

This too, is an Old Testament Scripture that we now know speaks of the Messiah.

The Lord had Moses make a fiery serpent and set it on a pole as a prophetic act that spoke of the coming Messiah. Jesus Christ, the Messiah, was lifted up and hung on a cross, and all who look to Him, *shall live!*

The Messiah is being hidden in this Scripture.

Now for one final example.

While the Israelites were still slaves, as God was preparing them to leave Egypt, He said this to Moses about the Passover lamb.

The Lord said,

> *Speak to all the congregation of Israel, saying: 'On the tenth of this month* **every man shall take for himself a lamb,** *according to the house of his father,* **a lamb for a household**.
>
> *Your lamb shall be without blemish, a male of the first year. You may take it from the sheep or from the goats. Now you shall keep it until the fourteenth day of the same month. Then the whole assembly of the congregation of Israel shall kill it at twilight. And they shall take some of the blood and put it on the two doorposts and on the lintel of the houses where they eat it.*
>
> *'For I will pass through the land of Egypt on that night, and will strike all the firstborn in the land of Egypt, both man and beast; and against all the gods of Egypt I will execute judgment: I am the LORD. Now the blood shall be a sign for you on the houses where*

> *you are. And when I see the blood, I will pass over you; and the*
> *plague shall not be on you to destroy you when I strike the land*
> *of Egypt.*
>
> *Exodus 12:3, 5-7, 12-13 NKJV e.a.*

The Lord then told Moses they were to perpetually celebrate a yearly feast to remember what the Lord had done when He delivered them out of the hands of the Egyptians.

And He said of the Passover lamb,

> *"It is to be eaten in a single house; you are not to bring forth any*
> *of the flesh outside of the house,* **nor are you to break any bone**
> **of it.**
>
> *Exodus 12:46 NASB e.a.*

Again, from the New Testament, we see these Old Testament Scripture verses are hiding that they are speaking of the Messiah.

There was a man referred to as John the Baptist, who, when he first saw Jesus, proclaimed of Him,

> *"Behold! The Lamb of God who takes away the sin of the world!*
>
> *John 1:29 NKJV*

And then on the *very day* of this permanent yearly feast when the Jews were celebrating the feast of Passover with the Passover lamb, Jesus was crucified, being lifted up and hung from a cross for all the nation to see.

And because it was a holy feast day, the Jewish elders came and asked the Roman governor to break the legs of all those who had been crucified to speed their death so they might be taken down. The Roman soldiers then went and broke the legs of the first two prisoners who had been crucified with Jesus. But when they came to Jesus, they found He had already died. Therefore, they did not break His legs. But instead, they thrust a spear into His side and water and blood poured out.

One of Jesus' disciples, John, wrote of this and said,

> For these things were done that **the Scripture should be fulfilled,**
> **"Not one of His bones shall be broken."** And again another
> Scripture says, "They shall look on Him whom they pierced."
>
> John 19:36-37 NKJV e.a.

When the Lord gave Moses these instructions regarding the Passover lamb, He was actually having Moses and the Jewish people perform a prophetic act that spoke of the future sacrifice of the coming Messiah of Israel.

Today, as Christians, we know Jesus is the Lamb of God who takes away the sins of the world. We know the Passover lamb spoken of in Exodus is a prophetic reference to Jesus.

Jesus, the Messiah of Israel, was hidden in this Old Testament Scripture of the Passover lamb.

We have just seen three Scriptures that all have hidden references to the Messiah. No one knew what these Scriptures actually meant, *until after* they came to pass or were explained for us.

So we see the *meanings* of these Scriptures are hidden. Even so, there is something else also hidden in each of these three Scriptures. There is something more, common to each of them, that is also being concealed.

Something More Is Hidden

In each of those Scriptures, the Lord was giving Moses instructions on what he was to do for the people. Those "instructions" were for their current, present, situation.

The Lord said, *speak to the rock, lift up the serpent,* and *kill the lamb,* as instructions for the people, *for that day,* for their immediate circumstance.

There was no statement made, there was no indication given, that these instructions were in any way prophetic. Neither Moses, nor the Jewish people, ever recognized these instructions as being prophetic. They were simply thought of, and known as, instructions given for that day.

These "instructions" however, were actually prophecies that spoke forward of the coming Messiah. These instructions were not known to be prophecies. These prophecies were in fact *concealed*. It is the prophecies themselves we find that are also being hidden.

The prophecies were hidden!

Two Things Are Hidden

A clarification and distinction must be made at this point. There are two different things being hidden here. They are related, yet they are distinct, individual and separate items.

The first item hidden is the *prophecy* itself.
We have to find the prophecy.

The second item hidden is the *meaning* of the prophecy.
We have to find the prophecy's meaning.

Two things, the prophecies, and their meanings, are being hidden.

The Prophecies Are Hidden

Here is further evidence showing these prophecies are indeed hidden. To this very day, thousands of years after these events took place, the Jewish people still do not recognize the story of the Passover lamb as speaking prophetically of their Messiah. Each year, for thousands of years, they have celebrated this feast of Passover in remembrance of what God has done, but not in anticipation of what God said prophetically *He will do!* Presently, these Scriptures have only historical significance for the Jewish people. However…,

That is about to change!

Recognizing and making an intentional distinction that these Scripture verses are actually *hidden prophecies* is extremely important. This is not an insignificant detail. This point makes all the difference to those looking for their Messiah!

Let's see just how important this detail truly is.

They Did Not Know

The Lord had specifically instructed Moses to *speak* to the rock. Yet, because Moses was angry at the people for complaining, he struck the rock instead!

It says,

> So Moses took the rod from before the LORD as He commanded him. And Moses and Aaron gathered the assembly together before the rock;
>
> and he said to them,
> "Hear now, you rebels! Must we bring water for you out of this rock?" Then Moses lifted his hand and struck the rock twice with his rod; and water came out abundantly, and the congregation and their animals drank.

The Lord then said to Moses,

> "Because you did not believe Me, to hallow Me in the eyes of the children of Israel, therefore you shall not bring this assembly into the land which I have given them."
>
> *Numbers 20:9-12 NKJV*

Because Moses did this…,

this same Moses who boldly led the people of Israel out of slavery in Egypt, because he struck the rock, and did not simply speak to the rock as the Lord had clearly instructed him, was not allowed to enter into the land along with the people of Israel.

After all Moses had accomplished and endured for his people, he would not be allowed to enter the new land with them. Moses could not go home! This had to be a devastating punishment for Moses. Something like this would break the greatest of men.

If Moses had known…,
these "instructions" were speaking prophetically of the coming Messiah,

If Moses had known…,
he was acting out a prophecy speaking of the Messiah of Israel,

If Moses had known the rock was Christ,

> *He would not have struck the rock!*

It may seem perfectly clear to us now, these "instructions" were actually prophecies, because we as Christians have the benefit of looking back on them through time. But when the Lord gave these instructions to the Jewish people, *they did not know* they were prophetic. The Lord hid these prophecies from them!

If you are wondering why the Lord would hide these prophecies about the Messiah from His people, here is one reason. The apostle Paul commented on another significant event, where a similar thing happened to the Jewish people as had earlier happened to Moses.

Paul wrote,

> *But we speak the wisdom of God in **a mystery, the hidden wisdom** which God ordained before the ages for our glory, **which none of the rulers of this age knew; for had they known, they would not have crucified the Lord of glory**.*
>
> *1 Corinthians 2:7-8 NKJV e.a.*

If Moses had known the rock was Christ,
he never would have struck the rock!

If the people had known Jesus was the Christ,
they never would have crucified their king!

> *They did not know!*

These prophecies were hidden because, had the people known and understood, they never would have crucified Jesus. This was God's plan and purpose for them from the very beginning. This was not a mistake, nor was it the fault of the Jewish people. It was planned, it was intentional, and…,

It was hidden!

The Prophecy Was Hidden
The Meaning Was Hidden

In the first three examples we looked at, the words spoken to Abraham and Sarah, King Zedekiah, and King Ahaz, were all clearly known to be prophecies.

With the latter examples of the rock, the serpent and the Passover lamb however, those prophecies were unknown. No one knew they were prophecies; they were only known to be instructions.

Because it was unknown, the prophecy was hidden. With the prophecy being hidden, we see this has the added effect of also hiding its meaning. Here is a principle to make note of: If any prophecy is hidden, the meaning of that prophecy will be hidden as well. We cannot know the meaning of a prophecy, if we first do not know it is actually a prophecy. Therefore, the meanings of these prophecies were also hidden.

The prophecy was hidden and the meaning was hidden!

The Hidden Prophecies Are Riddles

As we saw with our first examples of "known prophecies," those with hidden meanings took on the form or type of a riddle. Even so, it is the same with the "hidden prophecies." Because their meanings will always be hidden, the hidden prophecies can also be considered as riddles.

The hidden prophecies are riddles!

We have to find the meaning of the prophecy; we have to find the answer to the riddle. To find a hidden meaning to a hidden prophecy, we have to do the following:

We have to find the prophecy, and we have to find its meaning.
We have to find both, but…,

We have to find the prophecy first!

Concealed here is a subtle yet important point. Because we have to find the prophecy to be able to unlock its meaning, we discover the hidden prophecy is no longer just a type of riddle, but is actually part of the riddle itself.

To solve the riddle, you have to find the riddle.
To solve *this*… riddle, you have to find the prophecy.

The prophecy being hidden is part of the riddle!

We have now seen the following:
- Prophecies that are known, with meanings that are known and understood.
- Prophecies that are known, with meanings that are unknown or hidden.
- Prophecies that are unknown or hidden, always have meanings that are also unknown or hidden.
- Prophecies with unknown or hidden meanings are riddles.

And lastly,
- The hiding of the prophecy is part of the riddle itself.

So, where do we go from here? As Christians, we recognize these Scriptures are prophecies. But how do we help the Jewish people see this? They only recognize these Scriptures as historical records of what God has done. We need to be able to identify these Scriptures as prophecies.

How to Identify a Prophecy

There are several ways a Scripture verse can be identified as being a prophecy. The first two methods are simple and obvious.

The first method is from the Scripture text itself. Within the text, it will say what *will* happen in the future.

> *Sarah **will**... have a son next year*
> *He **will not**... see it, though he **will**... die there*
> *A virgin **will**... be with child*

In the second method, the Lord Himself identifies what He is saying is a prophecy. There are numerous verses such as this one, where the Lord gives a message to someone and tells them to prophesy.

The Lord spoke to the prophet Ezekiel and said,

> *"Son of man, prophesy against the shepherds of Israel,*
> *prophesy and say to them, 'Thus says the Lord GOD ...*
> *Ezekiel 34:2 NKJV par.*

The Lord tells the prophet to prophesy, then gives him a message to speak to the people.

We have seen two methods:
1. The text clearly shows it as a prophecy.
2. The Lord Himself says, *"Prophesy!"*

Now we will see a third.

In our opening vignette we described this as a game of Hide and Seek, a game the Lord Himself has set out; a game of secrets, riddles and clues. Thus far, we have seen secrets, and we have seen riddles, now we are going to see the clues! Just like the prophecies and their meanings are being concealed, there are clues that are being concealed as well. We can use these clues as a third method to identify a prophecy. However...,

We have to find the clues first!

Finding the Clues

Clues to "hidden prophecies," can be found by searching through, "known prophecies." The book of Isaiah records a message from the Lord which is very clearly a prophetic word about the future.

This is part of that message,

> *For unto us a Child is born,*
> *Unto us a Son is given;*
> *And the government will be upon His shoulder.*
> *And His name will be called*
> *Wonderful, Counselor, Mighty God,*
> *Everlasting Father, Prince of Peace.*
> *Of the increase of His government and peace*
> *There will be no end,*
> *Upon the throne of David and over His kingdom,*
> *To order it and establish it with judgment and justice*
> *From that time forward, even forever.*
> *The zeal of the Lord of hosts will perform this.*
>
> *Isaiah 9:6-7 NKJV*

This Scripture in Isaiah is a critical, primary prophecy regarding the Messiah. It is well known and not hidden. It is clearly evident from the text that this speaks prophetically of the future.

> *And the government **will**… be upon His shoulder*
> *And His name **will**… be called Wonderful, Counselor, Mighty God*
> *Of the increase of His government and peace there **will**… be no end*

It is also clearly evident this is referring to the coming King and Messiah of Israel; this is not hidden either. However, only a few details of the Messiah are given.

We need to find more; we need to find the Messiah!

Finding the Messiah

Mentioned within this prophecy are details that have been stated in another prophecy. It mentions, "a Child is born" and "a Son."

> *Unto us **a Child is born***
> *Unto us **a Son** is given*

It also states this Son's name will be called, "Mighty God."

> *And **His name will be called**,*
> *Wonderful, Counselor, **Mighty God***

These three items were all spoken of in an earlier prophecy we had seen. That prophecy also speaks of a child being born, a son, and His name as God.

> *"Therefore the Lord Himself will give you a sign: Behold, a virgin will be with **child** and **bear a son**, and she will call **His name Immanuel**.*
>
> *Isaiah 7:14 NASB e.a.*

(Immanuel translated means, ***"God with us."***)

See Matthew 1:23

From this we can identify a clear correlation between these two prophecies.

In Isaiah 7:14, we see a virgin is to *give birth* to *a son* and she will *name Him Immanuel*, (God with us).

In Isaiah 9:6-7, we see *this son*, who is to *be born*, will also *be named Mighty God*.

It is not clear from the Isaiah 7 Scripture alone, that it refers to the Messiah; there is not enough detail given. However, we do know the Isaiah 9 Scripture speaks of the Messiah. And because the details found in Isaiah 9 can also be found in Isaiah 7, we can then make the determination that Isaiah 7:14 speaks of the Messiah as well. The common references found in both Scriptures identify Isaiah 7 as a prophecy of the Messiah.

One prophecy, Isaiah 9, helped identify the subject of another prophecy, Isaiah 7. And these two prophecies together, help in identifying the Messiah.

These two prophecies are complementary of each other. When read together, they provide a clearer insight into the identity of the coming Messiah. Each prophecy gives further clarity to the meaning of the other prophecy.

Known Prophecies and Clues

These two Scriptures, Isaiah 7 and 9, are known prophecies; they are not hidden. Within these two "known prophecies" we find common details. Within one prophecy we find some piece of information, some detail, that makes a connection to a similar detail in another prophecy.

These common details are clues.

Let's look at one other example of a "known prophecy" that also contains these same details of the Messiah. This is a prophecy we had looked at previously with the angel Gabriel speaking to Mary.

> *The angel said to her,*
> *"Do not be afraid, Mary; for you have found favor with God. "And behold, you will conceive in your womb and **bear a son**, and you shall name Him Jesus.*
>
> *"He will be great and will be called the Son of the Most High; and the Lord God will give Him **the throne of His father David**; and He will reign over the house of Jacob **forever**, and **His kingdom will have no end.**"*
>
> Luke 1:30-33 NASB e.a.

This is another clearly prophetic message. In this prophecy we see details that are common within the Isaiah prophecies.

The Gabriel prophecy states,

> *you will conceive in your womb and **bear a son***

Mary was still a virgin at the time she received this prophecy. This prophecy directly points to both Isaiah 7 and 9.

> *A virgin will be with child and bear a son*

And,

> *For unto us a Child is born,*
> *Unto us a Son is given*

The Gabriel prophecy also states,

> *The Lord God will give Him the throne of His father David*
> *He will reign over the house of Jacob forever*
> *His kingdom will have no end*

These details tie directly in with Isaiah 9.

> *Of the increase of His government and peace*
> *There will be no end,*
> *Upon the throne of David and over His kingdom,*
> *To order it and establish it with judgment and justice*
> *From that time forward, even forever.*

The Gabriel prophecy has direct, clear pointers to these prophecies.

Notice now, with this latest Gabriel prophecy, we are given more information about, *this Son,* who is, *to be born.* He is now called by *other names.*

> *You shall name Him Jesus*
> *He will be called the Son of the Most High*

Although these names are not mentioned or common to the other two Scriptures, they point to the Isaiah prophecies by way of this particular phrase,

> *His name will be called...*

Isaiah 9 and 7,

> *His name will be called...*
> *Wonderful, Counselor, Mighty God*

And,

> *She will call His name... Immanuel*

Now add in this new prophecy from Gabriel,

> **You shall name Him**... *Jesus*
> **He will be called**... *the Son of the Most High*

With each successive "known prophecy," we are given further insight into their meanings. Or, in this case specifically, we are given more information on the identity of the Messiah.

Each known prophecy contains certain references that point to similar details found within other prophecies. We must pay close attention to the use of these pointers; these are clues.

There is one more significant detail that needs to be highlighted about this last example. The Isaiah Scriptures had been recorded in the scrolls of the Hebrew Bible. The Jewish scribes had made a permanent record of the prophetic words of Isaiah. *These prophecies were well known* to the Jewish people who were considerably familiar with the book of Isaiah.

The prophecy given by Gabriel would finally identify Mary's son as being, *'the Son,'* spoken of in the Isaiah prophecies. However, this was not a prophecy recorded by the Jewish scribes. This prophecy was not given or announced by God to the leadership of Israel. This prophecy was only given privately to Mary, a young, unmarried woman, thought to be of no significant importance among her people.

Although it would identify who the Son is to Mary, *this prophecy remained hidden* from the Jewish people as a whole. Because it is recorded in the New Testament, the Jewish people today do not recognize or accept this as a prophecy that speaks of their Messiah.

If we are to demonstrate to the Jewish people that Jesus is indeed their Messiah, we need to do it from their Old Testament Scriptures only.

An Old Testament Prophecy

In the book of Zechariah, the Lord gives a very strong message to the prophet for the nation of Israel. It is clearly a prophetic message and it states what most certainly, *is going to happen*, in the near future.

Here is that message.

> *Thus says the LORD, who stretches out the heavens, lays the foundation of the earth, and forms the spirit of man within him: "Behold, I will make Jerusalem a cup of drunkenness to all the surrounding peoples, when they lay siege against Judah and Jerusalem.*
>
> *And it shall happen in that day that I will make Jerusalem a very heavy stone for all peoples; all who would heave it away will surely be cut in pieces, though all nations of the earth are gathered against it. In that day," says the LORD, "I will strike every horse with confusion, and its rider with madness; I will open My eyes on the house of Judah, and will strike every horse of the peoples with blindness.*
>
> *And the governors of Judah shall say in their heart, 'The inhabitants of Jerusalem are my strength in the LORD of hosts, their God.' In that day I will make the governors of Judah like a firepan in the woodpile, and like a fiery torch in the sheaves; they shall devour all the surrounding peoples on the right hand and on the left, but Jerusalem shall be inhabited again in her own place — Jerusalem.*
>
> *"The LORD will save the tents of Judah first, so that the glory of the house of David and the glory of the inhabitants of Jerusalem shall not become greater than that of Judah. In that day the LORD will defend the inhabitants of Jerusalem; the one who is feeble among them in that day shall be like David, and the house of David shall be like God, like the Angel of the LORD before them.*
>
> *It shall be in that day that I will seek to destroy all the nations that come against Jerusalem.*
>
> Zechariah 12:1-9 NKJV

To the people of Israel, to the Jewish people, I say this, you know these Scriptures. You hold this Scripture in Zechariah dear to your heart. It gives you hope, it gives you comfort in the midst of the turmoil in which you live; God will defend you! It is a rallying cry for you. God has spoken and made you a promise, He will destroy those who seek your harm.

Yet, that very same prophecy you look to for hope, also goes on to say this…,

> *"I will pour out on the house of David and on the inhabitants of*
> *Jerusalem, the Spirit of grace and of supplication, so that they will*
> *look on Me whom they have pierced; and they will mourn for Him,*
> *as one mourns for an only son, and they will weep bitterly over*
> *Him like the bitter weeping over a firstborn.*
>
> *Zechariah 12:10 NASB*

God, who spoke about the nations of the world in the first part, also speaks about you, Israel, in the second. It is the same God, it is the same Scripture, it is the same message.

If you look to the first part for hope, then look to the second part for hope as well.

As we continue, you will begin to see and understand why your hope comes more from what God said about you, than it does from what God said about those who come against you.

Old Testament Clues

In this "known prophecy" of Zechariah 12, in verse 10, we find it speaks of a, "son" and a, "firstborn."

> *they will mourn for Him, as one mourns for an only **son**,*
> *and they will weep bitterly over Him like the bitter weeping over a*
> ***firstborn**.*

This would give us two connections to the Isaiah 7 and 9 prophecies that also speak of, "a son" and a son being, "born."

Isaiah 7 and 9,

> *A virgin will be with child and **bear a son***

And,

> *For unto us a **Child is born**,*
> *Unto us **a Son** is given*

Now remember, these references are not just simple details; they are clues. Clues can also be thought of as hints. These clues in Zechariah are hinting at something; something more is hidden here!

There is an amazing detail hidden in this Scripture. What does the Zechariah prophecy specifically say about this son? It describes Him as a, "firstborn."

> *they will weep bitterly over Him like the bitter weeping over a*
> ***firstborn**.*

In Isaiah 7, it mentions a son being born to a virgin.

> ***a virgin** will be with child and **bear a son***

Here is the hint; here is the question to ask: What would a child be called born to a woman who was still a virgin? She would have no other children. Therefore, a child born to her would be called her, *"firstborn."*

The child spoken of in Isaiah 7 is a, *firstborn child!*

What else, specifically, does Zechariah say about this son? It says He is an, "only son."

> *they will mourn for Him, as one mourns for an **only son***

Again, what would a son born to a virgin woman be called? She would have no other children. Therefore, a son born to her would be called her, *"only son."*

The son spoken of in Isaiah 7 is an, *only son!*

We now see, we do not have just one or two, or even three, but we have four connections to Isaiah 7 and Isaiah 9. Since Isaiah 7 and 9 both speak of the Messiah, we now know Zechariah 12 speaks of the Messiah as well.

We have these common clues, "a son" and "born." But, the "only son" and "firstborn" spoken of in Zechariah 12:10, also tie into Isaiah 7:14 by way of *'this son'* being born of a virgin.

> *Therefore the Lord Himself will give you a sign:*
> *Behold, a virgin will be with child and bear a son,*
> ***an only son, a firstborn son!***

Selah, wait, be still.

The Lord Himself

There is one more critical piece of information to see and consider; in Zechariah 12, it is the Lord Himself speaking.

> *Thus says the LORD, who stretches out the heavens, lays the foundation of the earth, and forms the spirit of man within him:*
>
> *Zechariah 12:1 NKJV*

The Lord, speaking in the first-person, says,

> *"I... will pour out on the house of David and on the inhabitants of Jerusalem, the Spirit of grace and of supplication,*

The Lord, again speaking in the first-person, goes on to say,

> *so that they will look on **Me**... whom they have pierced; and they will mourn for Him, as one mourns for an only son, and they will weep bitterly over Him like the bitter weeping over a firstborn.*
>
> *Zechariah 12:10 NASB e.a. par.*

In Zechariah 12, it is God Himself, speaking of, *Himself!*

Now notice the detail in Isaiah 7:14, it specifically says, *"the Lord **Himself**..."*

> *"Therefore the Lord **Himself**... will give you a sign..."*

In Zechariah 12, the Lord Himself, is speaking of *Himself.*
In Isaiah 7 it says, *"the Lord Himself will give you a sign..."*

The Lord is speaking of Himself and the Lord Himself will give us a sign.

So, Isaiah 7 and Zechariah 12 are connected by this clue of the, "Lord Himself." In addition to this, all three Scriptures, Isaiah 7, Isaiah 9, and Zechariah 12, are tied together by this same clue, as all three speak of God.

Isaiah 7 and 9,

> *she will call **His name Immanuel**. (**God with us**)*
> *His name will be called... **Mighty God***

Zechariah 12,

> **"I**... *will pour out..."*
> *they will look on* **Me**... **(God)**

All three prophecies speak of God, and in the Zechariah prophecy, it is God Himself, speaking of, *Himself!*

> *This is about... God!*

Zechariah 12

The person being spoken of, the person being referred to in Zechariah 12, is none other than the Lord. God, quite unmistakably, is identifying that, *He, Himself, will be pierced.* This prophecy states, the Jewish people will weep and mourn as for an only child, once they have recognized it was their Messiah, God Himself, whom they had pierced.

We know this prophecy speaks of the Messiah; we now also know the Messiah is God Himself. And now, through adding these details together, we begin to see an indication, the Messiah is in some way going to be injured; He will be pierced.

The Road to Messiah

These three "known prophecies" all speak of the Messiah. These three prophecies together make a triad; three prophecies, each having common connections to the other two prophecies. All three speak of "a child," and "a son" being "born." All three, speak of *'this child and son'* as, *"God."*

This diagram illustrates their relationship.

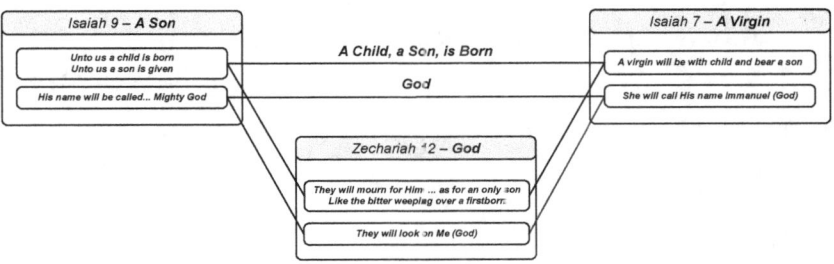

We find this Zechariah 12 Scripture, where the Lord is speaking of Himself, turns out to be a central prophecy. Like spokes on a wheel, there are connections that radiate out from Zechariah 12 to other Scriptures. There are clues in Zechariah with ties into yet another well-known prophecy from Isaiah.

They Will Look on Me

From this one individual sentence in Zechariah, we will see that several additional clues can be found. The phrase, *"look on Me,"* is a clue.

> they will **look on Me**... whom they have pierced
>
> *Zechariah 12:10 NASB e.a. par.*

In Isaiah 53, we find this similar phrase being used. Here is the first portion of that Scripture.

Isaiah 53:1-3,

> *Who has believed our message?*
> *And to whom has the arm of the LORD been revealed?*
> *For He grew up before Him like a tender shoot,*
> *And like a root out of parched ground;*
> *He has no stately form or majesty*
> *That we should **look upon Him**,*
> *Nor appearance that we should be attracted to Him.*
> *He was despised and forsaken of men,*

> *A man of sorrows and acquainted with grief;*
> *And like one from whom men hide their face*
> *He was despised, and we did not esteem Him.*
>
> *Isaiah 53:1-3 NASB e.a.*

Zechariah 12 says,

> *they will **look on Me***

Isaiah 53 says,

> *we should **look upon Him***

Whom They Have Pierced

Here is another clue from this one sentence in Zechariah; it speaks of one as being, *"pierced."* Isaiah 53, also speaks of one being pierced. Here is another small section of that Scripture.

Isaiah 53:4-5,

> *Surely our griefs He Himself bore,*
> *And our sorrows He carried;*
> *Yet we ourselves esteemed Him stricken,*
> *Smitten of God, and afflicted.*
> *But **He was pierced** through for our transgressions,*
> *He was crushed for our iniquities;*
> *The chastening for our well-being fell upon Him,*
> *And by His scourging we are healed.*
>
> *Isaiah 53:4-5 NASB e.a.*

The text in Zechariah 12 says,

> *They will look on Me **whom they have pierced***

This prophecy in Isaiah 53 says,

> ***He was pierced** through for our transgressions*

We now have five separate clues from just this one sentence in Zechariah, two of which point to Isaiah 53. There is now one more clue to show from that same section of Scripture in Zechariah 12:10.

I Will Pour Out

Zechariah 12:10 uses the phrase, *"pour out."*

> *"I will **pour out** on the house of David and on the inhabitants of Jerusalem, the Spirit of grace and of supplication, so that they will look on Me whom they have pierced;*
>
> Zechariah 12:10 NASB e.a.

We see this similar phrase is also used in Isaiah 53. This is another portion of that same Scripture.

Isaiah 53:11-12,

> *By His knowledge the Righteous One,*
> *My Servant, will justify the many,*
> *As He will bear their iniquities.*
> *Therefore, I will allot Him a portion with the great,*
> *And He will divide the booty with the strong;*
> *Because He **poured out** Himself to death,*
> *And was numbered with the transgressors;*
> *Yet He Himself bore the sin of many,*
> *And interceded for the transgressors.*
>
> Isaiah 53:11-12 NASB e.a.

The text in Zechariah 12 says,

> *I will **pour out**... on the house of David*

This text in Isaiah 53 says,

> *He **poured out**... Himself to death*

We now have three separate clues from Zechariah 12, that connect to Isaiah 53.

ZECHARIAH 12	ISAIAH 53
*they will **look on Me***	*we should **look upon Him***
*whom they have **pierced***	*He was **pierced***
*I will **pour out***	*He **poured out** Himself*

Isaiah 53 is a "known prophecy," but its meaning was hidden. Because we find Isaiah 53 mentions the same details spoken of in Zechariah 12, we now know it too, speaks of the Messiah.

Clues to Hidden Prophecies

We have now seen four known prophecies, Isaiah 7, 9, 53 and Zechariah 12, all containing related clues. If these known prophecies have clues to each other, it stands to reason they might have clues to hidden prophecies as well. Perhaps they can identify a prophecy of which we are not yet aware.

It so happens that finding this next set of clues is going to be quite easy. There are similar references to the last three clues from Isaiah 53, that can also be found in Psalm 22.

Psalm 22 is a song to the Lord, written by King David. Today we recognize that many of these songs or psalms David wrote, were prophetic. However, we need to keep in mind we know this today only because many of these prophecies have already been fulfilled.

If we read through Psalm 22, we see the author writes of his own personal despair and troubles. However, nowhere in this psalm is there any indication it is speaking prophetically of the Messiah.

In Psalm 22, King David cries out to the Lord,

> *My God, My God, why have You forsaken Me?*

Psalm 22:1 NKJV

In this song of despair, David writes,

> *Be not far from Me,*
> *For trouble is near;*
> *For there is none to help.*
> *Many bulls have surrounded Me;*
> *Strong bulls of Bashan have encircled Me.*
> *They gape at Me with their mouths,*
> *Like a raging and roaring lion.*
> *I am* **poured out** *like water,*
> *And all My bones are out of joint;*
> *My heart is like wax;*
> *It has melted within Me.*
> *My strength is dried up like a potsherd,*
> *And My tongue clings to My jaws;*
> *You have brought Me to the dust of death.*
> *For dogs have surrounded Me;*
> *The congregation of the wicked has enclosed Me.*
> *They* **pierced** *My hands and My feet;*
> *I can count all My bones.*
> *They* **look** *and stare* **at Me.**
> *They divide My garments among them,*
> *And for My clothing they cast lots.*

Psalm 22:11-18 NKJV e.a.

This song, this Scripture, contains three common references found in both Zechariah 12 and Isaiah 53. We again see the common words or phrases, *"poured out," "pierced"* and *"look at me."*

Psalm 22, verses 14, 16 and 17,

> *I am* **poured out** *like water*
> *They* **pierced** *My hands and my feet*

And,

> *They* **look** *and stare* **at Me**

Nothing in the song of Psalm 22 gave any indication it was speaking prophetically. The song was a cry to the Lord for help. Today, we as Christians clearly recognize this Scripture as prophetic. But it was, and to this day still is, a hidden prophecy to the Jewish people.

The fact that this "song" of King David contains clues also found in two well-known prophecies, means this is not simply a song.

If Zechariah 12 and Isaiah 53 speak of the Messiah, and Psalm 22 mentions those same details, Psalm 22 must then be speaking of the Messiah as well. And, if Zechariah 12 and Isaiah 53 are prophecies, then Psalm 22 must be a prophecy also. These clues have identified Psalm 22 as being a prophecy of the Messiah. It is a cry for help, written in a song.

The Messiah is crying for help!

These five Scriptures we have seen so far, Isaiah 7, 9, 53, Zechariah 12, and now Psalm 22, are all prophecies. When we view them together, we begin to see Who, and what, these prophecies are referring to.

As we add these latest clues about the Messiah into our diagram, we see the Zechariah prophecy has taken on a central position amongst the four other prophecies. Zechariah 12 is a central hub, that identifies God Himself at the center.

This is our diagram with these latest prophecies added.

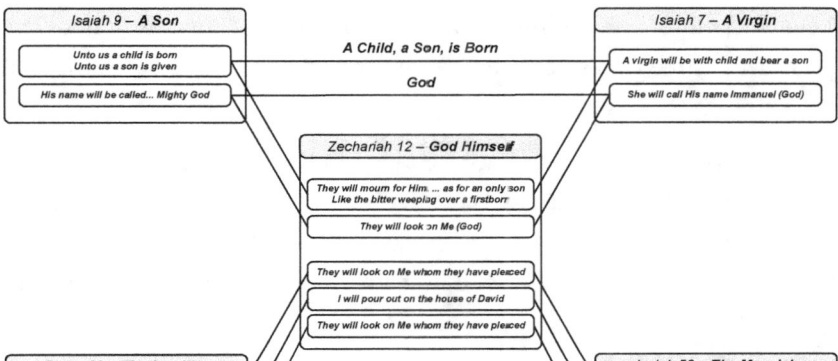

From these five separate, isolated prophecies, when brought together, we see the beginning of a story. A child, a son, is to be born. This child will be God Himself. He will be pierced; He will pour Himself out. And lastly, we will look upon Him!

Selah

Moses and the Rock

Let's find more clues to this intriguing story. Since those last clues were each used three times, let's see if there might be any other instances of their use.

In one of our first examples, we told part of the story of Moses and the rock. The story we looked at was referring to the *second* time God had spoken to Moses about the rock. The second time, God instructed Moses to simply speak to the rock. The first time however, God told Moses to strike it!

God said to Moses,

> *Behold, I will stand before you there on the rock in Horeb; and you shall strike the rock, and water will come out of it, that the people may drink.*
>
> Exodus 17:6 NKJV

Are you able to see any commonalities in this verse to clues we have already seen?

The clue, *"poured out,"* is used three other times in Scriptures that we know speak prophetically of the Messiah. In one of those uses it mentions another detail of something being poured out, 'water'; *"I am poured out like water."*

This verse in Exodus has two similarities with the verse, *"I am poured out like water."*

God said of the rock,

> *"water will come out of it"*

Though the word, "poured," is not actually used here, the phrases, "poured out" and "will come out," are similar, as both speak of water. Look at these two statements together.

Psalm 22 says, *"poured out like water."*
And this verse says, *"water will come out."*

This had been a hidden prophecy. The apostle Paul from the New Testament identified these "Scriptures," these "instructions," given about the rock, were actually speaking prophetically of the Messiah. We now see a connection of this verse into other prophecies that speak of the Messiah. Paul had identified this as a prophecy. But now, we can see a connection for ourselves!

This Scripture speaks of the Messiah, and now we need only look to the Old Testament to see it.

> *you shall strike the rock, and **water will come out** of it,*
>
> *Exodus 17:6 NKJV e.a.*

Moses and the Serpent

Here is another connection to one of those same three clues initially found between Zechariah 12 and Isaiah 53. This is again, another Scripture we had read earlier. God had given Moses instructions to set a bronze serpent on a pole.

The Lord said to Moses,

> *"Make a fiery serpent, and set it on a pole;*
> *and it shall be that everyone who is bitten, when he looks at it,*
> *shall live."*
>
> *Numbers 21:8 NKJV*

Are you able to see clues in this verse similar to clues previously seen?

In Zechariah 12, it says, *"look on Me."*
In Isaiah 53, it says, *"look upon Him."*

And now we see in this obscure verse about a serpent, it says, *"looks at it"!*

> *everyone who is bitten, when he **looks at it**, shall live*

Again, Jesus in the New Testament identified this act of lifting up the serpent in the wilderness was actually a prophetic reference to the Messiah. Jesus identified this as a prophecy. Now, through the use of these clues we can see a connection for ourselves. From the Old Testament only, we can see this "Scripture," this "instruction," given about the serpent, is actually a prophecy of the Messiah.

This prophecy had been hidden, but now a connection has been found and unveiled.

Hidden Prophecies

Because we first found clues or common connections in four well-known, clearly identifiable prophecies, we have now been able to identify three additional Scriptures as also being prophecies. We no longer have four, we now have seven prophecies with which to work! All of these Scriptures are in effect the same; they are all now, "known prophecies."

These prophecies are riddles; these prophecies are hiding clues. If the original four prophecies hid clues, then it stands to reason, the new prophecies may be hiding clues as well. That is in fact how we found them, from their use of hidden clues.

Now let's search these new prophecies to see if they might have any new clues. In Psalm 22, we see something that stands out by itself as being rather unusual. Psalm 22 twice, uses the phrase, *"all My bones."*

It says,

> *all **My bones** are out of joint*

And also,

> *I can count **all My bones***

Psalm 22:14, 17 NKJV e.a.

Having been used two separate times in this single Scripture, it seems this phrase is being highlighted; this may be a clue, to finding a clue! As we look for a similar use of this phrase, we find it in another one of the psalms, Psalm 34. It says, *"He guards all his bones."*

Psalm 34 is another song to the Lord written by King David. If we read through the psalm, we see that it is a prayer to the Lord. It sings the praises of how the Lord cares for His people. But again, as with Psalm 22, nowhere in the psalm is there any indication it speaks prophetically of the Messiah.

Here is a small section from Psalm 34.

> *Many are the afflictions of the righteous,*
> *But the LORD delivers him out of them all.*
> *He guards **all his bones**;*
> *Not one of them is broken.*

Psalm 34:19-20 NKJV e.a.

With Psalm 22 using this phrase, *"all My bones,"* twice, it has given us two connections to Psalm 34. There is still one more connection to see. And this connection, is a different type of clue.

In Psalm 22, verses 14, 16 and 17, if we look at what is written, and the order in which the sentences are written, we see a pattern emerge. Both of the first lines, point to the Zechariah 12 prophecy. Then both of the second lines that follow, point to the Psalm 34 prophecy.

Here is a diagram illustrating the pattern.

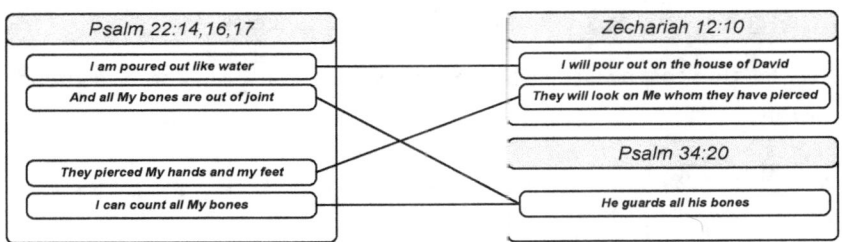

Psalm 22, verses 14, 16 and 17, in the order they are written:

Psalm 22:14 – *I am **poured out** like water*
Points to Zechariah 12:10 – *I will **pour out** on the house of David*

Psalm 22:14 – *And **all My bones** are out of joint*
Points to Psalm 34:20 – *He guards **all his bones***

Psalm 22:16 – *They **pierced** My hands and my feet*
Points to Zechariah 12:10 – *They will look on Me whom they have **pierced***

Psalm 22:17 – *I can count **all My bones***
Points to Psalm 34:20 – *He guards **all his bones***

What we see in this pattern is a demonstration of design; this did not happen by chance. Twice, the first statements in Psalm 22, point to Zechariah 12, and again twice, the second statements that immediately follow, point to Psalm 34.

This unmistakably establishes Psalm 34 as also speaking of the Messiah. Because Zechariah 12 and Psalm 22 are prophecies of the Messiah, Psalm 34 is then a prophecy of the Messiah as well. Another type of clue, and another prophecy, has been found!

As each clue is found, another prophecy is uncovered. With each successive prophecy found, the meaning of the prophecies and the identity of the Messiah become clearer. All of these prophecies, when taken together, paint a sharper picture of the Messiah.

There are still more clues to be found. Here is a principle to follow while searching for these clues: Use what is known to find what is unknown. This is the same principle we have been following since we began; we used known prophecies to find unknown prophecies.

Now let's look at the last clue we found; we used only part of the sentence for the last clue.

In Psalm 34 it says,

> *Many are the afflictions of the righteous,*
> *But the LORD delivers him out of them all.*
> ***He guards all his bones;***
> ***Not one of them is broken.***
>
> *Psalm 34:19-20 NKJV e.a.*

We have multiple references to, "all his bones," then we find this verse that says of, 'these bones,' "not one of them is broken." This detail is in fact a clue.

You Are Not to Break Any Bone of It

We find a similar description of, *bones not being broken,* in Exodus 12, the story of the Passover lamb.

In all the instructions the Lord gave to Moses and the people about what they were to do with the Passover lamb, the Lord gave very specific instructions that the bones of this lamb were not to be broken. It says of the Passover lamb,

> *"It is to be eaten in a single house;*
> *you are not to bring forth any of the flesh outside of the house,*
> **nor are you to break any bone of it.**
>
> *Exodus 12:46 NASB e.a.*

Psalm 34 says, *He guards all his bones, not one of them is broken.* Exodus 12 says, *nor are you to break any bone of it.*

The subject of Psalm 34 is definitely speaking of the Messiah. Exodus 12 is speaking specifically about the Passover lamb. The reference in Exodus 12 says the same thing about the Passover lamb, as we see Psalm 34 says prophetically about the Messiah; not one of His bones will be broken.

If Psalm 34 is a prophecy about the Messiah, and Exodus 12 mentions those same things, then Exodus 12 may be a prophecy about the Messiah also. What was written about the Passover lamb, might have been written about the Messiah.

You are not to break any bone of it!

Psalm 34 speaks of the Messiah. Exodus 12 speaks of a lamb, a Passover lamb. Back in Isaiah 53, a prophecy we know also speaks of the Messiah, we see that it too, speaks of a lamb.

The Lamb

We have looked at three sections of Isaiah 53, this is another small section of that prophecy.

Isaiah 53:6-7,

> *All of us **like sheep** have gone astray,*
> *Each of us has turned to his own way;*
> *But the LORD has caused the iniquity of us all*
> *To fall on Him.*
> *He was oppressed and He was afflicted,*
> *Yet He did not open His mouth;*
> ***Like a lamb** that is led to slaughter,*
> *And **like a sheep** that is silent before its shearers,*
> *So He did not open His mouth.*
>
> *Isaiah 53:6-7 NASB e.a.*

Here we see three similar phrases used: *"like sheep," "like a lamb,"* and, *"like a sheep."*

Of those three instances, one, refers to us.

> ***All of us… like sheep** have gone astray*

The other two instances however, refer to, *Him!*

> ***Like a lamb** that is led to slaughter,*
> *And **like a sheep** that is silent before its shearers,*
> *So **He…** did not open **His…** mouth.*

This Isaiah 53 prophecy, that we unquestionably know speaks of the Messiah, says of this Messiah, He is, *"like a lamb"*; He is, *"like a sheep."*

Here is part of the account again in Exodus that speaks of the Passover lamb.

The Lord said to Moses,

> *Speak to all the congregation of Israel, saying: 'On the tenth of this month **every man shall take for himself a lamb**, according to the house of his father, **a lamb for a household.***
>
> ***Your lamb shall be without blemish, a male of the first year.** **You may take it from the sheep or from the goats.***

> *Exodus 12:3, 5 NKJV e.a.*

Isaiah 53 says,

> ***Like a lamb** that is led to slaughter,*
> ***like a sheep** that is silent before its shearers,*

Exodus 12 says,

> *every man shall take for himself **a lamb**,*
> ***a lamb** for a household*
> ***Your lamb** shall be without blemish, a male of the first year.*
> *You may take it from **the sheep** or from the goats.*

Psalm 34, by speaking of His bones not being broken, gave the first clue that the Passover lamb spoken of here in Exodus 12, is a prophetic reference to the Messiah of Israel. Now we see from another prophecy, Isaiah 53, that it says of *the Messiah, He is like a lamb.*

The Prophecy Is No Longer Hidden

Psalm 34 and Isaiah 53 have opened up the prophecy held in Exodus 12. The "historical record," "the story," of the Passover lamb, is no longer only historical, it is no longer simply a story. The account written about the Passover lamb is a detailed, prophetic record, of what would happen to the Messiah of Israel.

The Messiah of Israel is… the Passover Lamb!

"It" Is Messiah

Look at the perspective of the writer and the pronouns used in some of these prophecies. In the clues for, "poured out," we see the writers speaking in both the first and third-person, using the pronouns, *'I'* and *'He.'*

> *I... will pour out on the house of David*
> *I... am poured out like water*
> *He... poured out Himself to death.*

But with the prophecy about the rock, the pronoun used changes to, *'it.'*

> *water will come out of... **it***

These are important details. These clues are all speaking about a person, the same person, the Messiah of Israel. But this last clue, while speaking about the rock, refers to this person as, *'it.'*

Here is another example. In the clues for, "look on Me," we see again the writers speaking in both the first and third-person, with the use of the pronouns, *'Me'* and *'Him.'*

> *look on... **Me***
> *look upon... **Him***
> *They look and stare at... **Me***

And then, with the prophecy about the serpent, the pronoun used changes to, *'it.'*

> *it shall be that everyone who is bitten, when he looks at... **it**, shall live.*

Again, these clues are all speaking about the person of the Messiah. But this last clue, while speaking about the serpent, refers to this person as, *'it.'*

> *Look at **it**!*

We see this very same thing in the references to, "all My bones." The writers speak in both the first and third-person, using the pronouns, *'I'* and *'He'* along with similar uses of, *'My'* and *'His.'*

> *I... can count all **my**... bones.*
> *all **my**... bones are out of joint*

And also,

> *He... guards all **his**... bones, not one of them is broken.*

And then, with this Scripture about the Passover lamb, the pronoun used changes to, *'it.'*

> *nor are you to break any bone of... **it**.*

The Messiah, in all of these Scriptures, is being referred to as, 'it.'

> The Rock: *Water will come out of... **it***
> The Serpent: *When he looks at... **it***
> The Lamb: *Nor are you to break any bone of... **it***

'It' is being used to refer to the Messiah. This is difficult; this is offensive to those of us who love God and love our Messiah. We would *never* refer to Jesus, or the Messiah, as an, 'It.' But that is exactly what God has done here. And as offensive as the use of this term may be, *this is nothing,* compared to what is coming next for the Messiah.

God Says, "Kill It!"

We have seen four individual sections from Isaiah 53, which speaks of the Messiah as a lamb. This is another small section from that Scripture.

Isaiah 53: A prophecy of the Messiah.

> *By oppression and judgment He was taken away;*
> *And as for His generation, who considered*
> *That **He was cut off out of the land of the living***
> *For the transgression of my people, to whom the stroke was due?*
> ***His grave** was assigned with wicked men,*
> *Yet He was with a rich man in **His death**,*
> *Because He had done no violence,*
> *Nor was there any deceit in His mouth.*
> *But the LORD was pleased*
> *To crush Him, putting Him to grief;*
> *If He would render Himself as a guilt offering,*
>
> Isaiah 53:8-10 NASB e.a.

Isaiah 53 says of the Messiah,

> ***Like a lamb** that is led to slaughter,*
> *And **like a sheep** that is silent before its shearers,*
> *So He did not open His mouth.*
>
> ***He was cut off out of the land of the living***
> ***His grave** was assigned with wicked men,*
> *Yet He was with a rich man in **His death***

Exodus 12 says of the Passover lamb,

> ***Your lamb shall be without blemish, a male of the first year.***
> *You may take it from the sheep or from the goats. Now you shall keep it until the fourteenth day of the same month.*
>
> *Then the whole assembly of the congregation of Israel shall... **kill it***

By God's own instructions, on God's own orders, for God's own purpose, God Himself said of the Messiah,

"*Kill it!*"

The Messiah has been killed; the Messiah has died.

The Messiah of Israel… is dead!

Selah, wait, be still.

We can now complete the diagram these prophecies reveal.

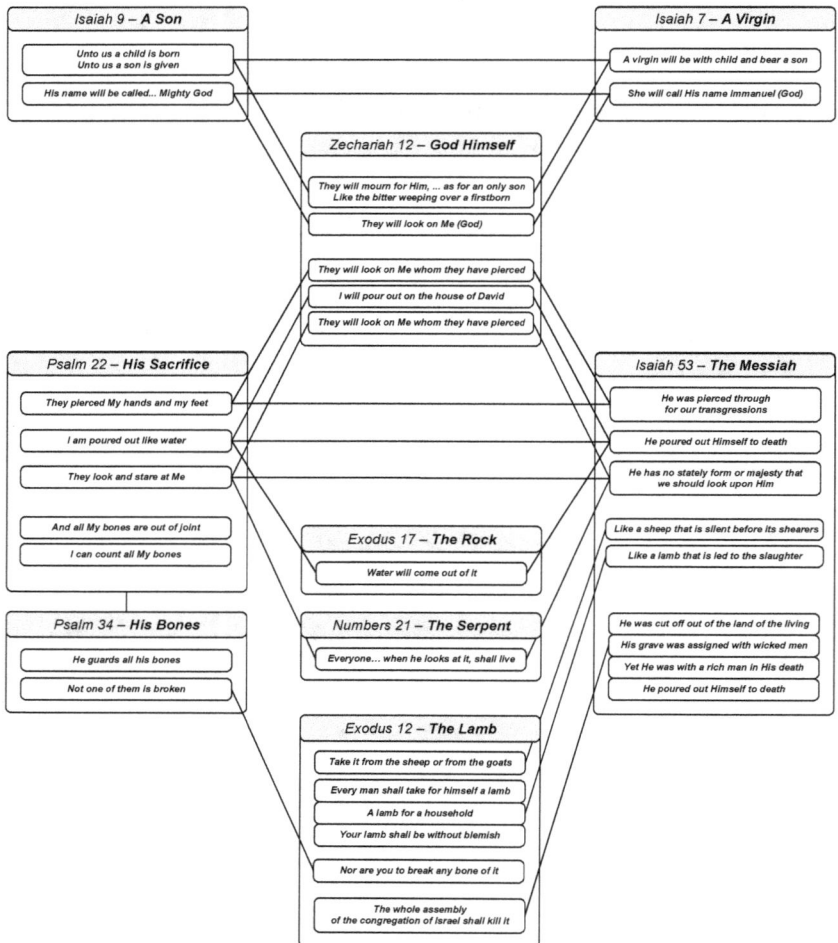

We see from this image two separate connections, two legs, from the Exodus 12 prophecy and story of the Passover lamb, that connect back to Zechariah 12, where God Himself is speaking.

The *"Passover lamb"* spoken of in Exodus 12, connects to the lamb spoken of in Isaiah 53; from there it connects to *"God Himself"* speaking in Zechariah 12.

The *'bones of the Passover lamb that were not to be broken,'* spoken of in Exodus 12, connect to Psalm 34, *"He guards all his bones, not one of them is broken."* Psalm 34 then connects to Psalm 22, and from there, it too connects back to *"God Himself"* speaking in Zechariah 12.

Two paths, two legs, tie "the story," "the prophecy," of the *"Passover lamb,"* back to *"God Himself."* And lastly, we see it is God Himself, who instructs the people of Israel regarding the Passover lamb, regarding their Messiah, to, *"Kill it!"*

> *The Lord Himself... will give you a sign!*
> *The Lord Himself... is the Passover Lamb!*

This completes our diagram, but this *does not* complete the story!

Although we see the death of the Messiah is spoken of in Isaiah 53, as we look further, we see it too, speaks of His life.

A Prophecy of the Messiah

This is now the last section of that Scripture; this will complete the Isaiah 53 prophecy.

Isaiah 53: *A prophecy of the Messiah.*

> *He will see His offspring,*
> *He will prolong His days,*
> *And the good pleasure of the LORD will prosper in His hand.*
> *As a result of the anguish of His soul,*
> *He will see it and be satisfied;*
>
> *Isaiah 53:10-11 NASB*

> *He will... see His offspring,*
> *He will... prolong His days,*
> *The good pleasure of the LORD will... prosper in His hand,*
> *He will... see it,*
> ***And He will be satisfied!***

The Messiah will live!
Our Messiah lives!

The Messiah of Israel… lives!

Rejoice O Israel! Your Messiah lives!
And again, I say to you, rejoice!

Oh, what a story; a story of a God who so loves His people that He gave His own life, so they may live!

Oh, what a story; a story told through prophecies, in secrets, riddles and clues. The story is told for those who will look for it. This story is found by those who search for it.

They Did Not Recognize the Prophecy

We have seen prophecies that were known and prophecies that were hidden. And here is a statement that is true of all prophecies:

A prophecy does not need to be called a prophecy, to be a prophecy.

A prophecy is still a prophecy, regardless if anyone ever recognizes it or not! The prophecies were hidden and the Jewish people did not recognize them.

They did not recognize the prophecy.

The Prophecies!

The prophecies are hidden.
The meanings are hidden.
The prophecies are riddles.
And the hiding of the prophecy, is part of the riddle.

We went searching for the prophecies…

And we found the Messiah!

It's just a game of Hide and Seek.
We need to learn how things are hidden.
It's just a game of Hide and Seek.

We need to learn… how to play!

ACT 2 VIGNETTE

Cue Jesus

So, WE NOW UNDERSTAND WHY THE JEWISH PEOPLE did not recognize the Messiah from the Old Testament Scriptures; it was because the Messiah had been hidden. But that was the Old Testament, surely the Jewish people would have recognized who Jesus is while He was performing so many incredible miracles among them. Surely then, they would have known Jesus is the Messiah.

When we think of Jesus and His ministry, we tend to think of Jesus widely and publicly proclaiming to everyone who He is, saying, "I am the Christ! I am the Messiah! I am... the Son of God!"

Yet, that couldn't be any farther from the truth. As we look at what He actually said and did, we see it is just the opposite. Jesus did not publicly proclaim His identity. The fact is, Jesus repeatedly told those He encountered, *not to tell anyone,* who He was!

Beginning with the Old Testament Scriptures, and carried forward to the arrival, ministry and subsequent death of Jesus, the identity of the Messiah will remain a mystery.

Nothing has changed!

The Messiah was concealed in the Old Testament. And now we are going to see the Messiah is also being concealed in the *New Testament.* We will see exactly why the Jewish people did not recognize who Jesus is. And again, we are going to see this responsibility does not fall to them.

Jesus kept His identity from them!

Welcome to Act 2 – Tell No One!

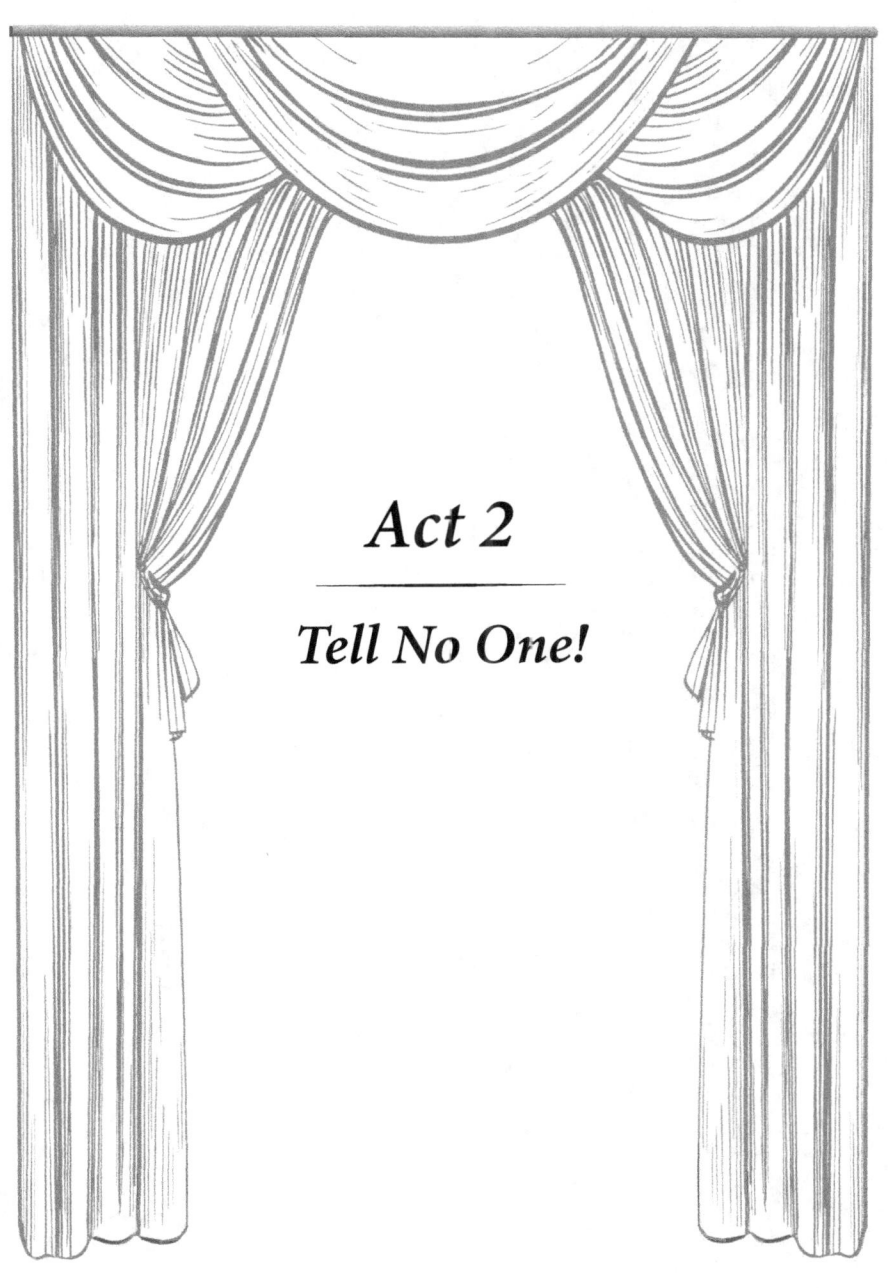

Act 2

Tell No One!

Enter Jesus

As just mentioned, we tend to think Jesus, as He went about ministering to people, would tell them who He was. We also would presume Jesus would instruct those He healed to go and tell everyone about their healing. It certainly would make for excellent advertising. That is in fact what we do today in our churches. Someone receives a healing, and we tell them to go tell all their friends about it.

But let's look at what Jesus actually said.

Healings – "Tell No One!"

We are going to see several examples of Jesus making a very deliberate effort to ensure His miracles are *not* to be made known. He specifically tells those He healed not to tell anyone about their healing.

Here is a story of a man with leprosy coming to Jesus and asking to be healed.

> *And behold, a leper came and worshiped Him, saying, "Lord, if You are willing, You can make me clean."*
>
> *Then Jesus put out His hand and touched him, saying, "I am willing; be cleansed."*
>
> *Immediately his leprosy was cleansed.*

Then Jesus said to the man,

> **"See that you tell no one**; but go your way, show yourself to the priest, and offer the gift that Moses commanded, as a testimony to them."*
>
> Matthew 8:2-4 NKJV e.a.

Jesus told the man to tell no one about his healing.

> *See that you tell no one!*

Here is another example; Jesus heals two blind men.

> *two blind men followed Him, crying out,*
> *"Have mercy on us, Son of David!"*
>
> *When He entered the house, the blind men came up to Him, and*
> *Jesus said to them,*
> *"Do you believe that I am able to do this?"*
>
> *They said to Him,*
> *"Yes, Lord."*
>
> *Then He touched their eyes, saying,*
> *"It shall be done to you according to your faith."*
>
> *And their eyes were opened.*

Then it says,

> *And Jesus sternly warned them:*
> ***"See that no one knows about this!"***
>
> *Matthew 9:27-30 NASB e.a.*

Matthew comments that Jesus *sternly warned them* they were to tell no one.

> *See that no one knows about this!*

Here is a third example; Jesus raises a little girl from the dead.

> *Then He took the child by the hand, and said to her,*
> *"Talitha, cumi,"*
>
> *which is translated, "Little girl, I say to you, arise."*
>
> *Immediately the girl arose and walked, for she was twelve years*
> *of age. And they were overcome with great amazement.*

And then it says,

> *But **He commanded them strictly that no one should know it***
>
> *Mark 5:41-43 NKJV e.a.*

Here again, it states Jesus *commanded them strictly* that no one was to know.

> *No one should know it!*

Jesus tells them again; this is a fourth example.

Here is a story of Jesus healing a man who was deaf.

> *Then they brought to Him one who was deaf and had an impediment in his speech, and they begged Him to put His hand on him.*
>
> **And He took him aside from the multitude**, *and put His fingers in his ears, and He spat and touched his tongue.*
>
> *Then, looking up to heaven, He sighed, and said to him, "Ephphatha," that is, "Be opened."*
>
> *Immediately his ears were opened, and the impediment of his tongue was loosed, and he spoke plainly.*

And then it says,

> **Then He commanded them that they should tell no one; but the more He commanded them, the more widely they proclaimed it.**
>
> *Mark 7:32-36 NKJV e.a.*

In this story, notice Jesus first takes the man away from the crowd to heal him privately. Then afterwards, Jesus *commanded* them to tell no one about it.

There is an intriguing comment added and it says,

> *but the more He commanded them, the more widely they proclaimed it.*
>
> *He commanded them not to tell anyone!*

Here we have a fifth example; He tells them yet again.

There is an account of Jesus healing a man who was blind.

> *Then He came to Bethsaida; and they brought a blind man to Him, and begged Him to touch him.*
>
> **So He took the blind man by the hand and led him out of the town.** *And when He had spit on his eyes and put His hands on him, He asked him if he saw anything.*
>
> *And he looked up and said,*
> *"I see men like trees, walking."*
>
> *Then He put His hands on his eyes again and made him look up. And he was restored and saw everyone clearly.*

And then it says,

> *Then He sent him away to his house, saying,*
> **"Neither go into the town, nor tell anyone in the town."**
>
> *Mark 8:22-26 NKJV e.a.*

Here again, Jesus first leads the man away to heal him privately. Then afterwards tells him not to tell anyone or even enter back into the village.

> *Neither go into the town, nor tell anyone in the town.*

Here is a sixth example; Jesus heals a young boy possessed by a demon.

> **When Jesus saw that a crowd was rapidly gathering,**
>
> *He rebuked the unclean spirit, saying to it,*
> *"You deaf and mute spirit, I command you, come out of him and do not enter him again."*
>
> *After crying out and throwing him into terrible convulsions, it came out;*
>
> *Mark 9:25-26 NASB e.a.*

In this story, it is noted that when Jesus saw a crowd rapidly gathering, He immediately commanded the spirit out of the boy. Here Jesus attempts to heal the boy, with the least number of witnesses present.

We have a seventh account recorded in the book of Matthew.

> *And great multitudes followed Him, **and He healed them all.
> Yet He warned them not to make Him known***

Matthew 12:15-16 NKJV e.a.

In all of these healings Jesus performed, He either gave strict orders that no one was to know about it, or attempted to heal the person privately with as few witnesses as possible. Jesus was literally *commanding people not to tell anyone* about their healings, or who He was!

There are other occasions however, where Jesus does publicly and openly heal the sick. Yet, we notice that in those circumstances, the healings were found to be offensive, or threatening, to the religious leadership.

For example, Jesus performed healings on the Sabbath when no work was to be done; this was offensive to the religious leaders. Jesus also performed miracles they themselves could not do, which threatened their positions of power. Jesus did, what they could not do!

In fact, these religious leaders felt so threatened by the miracles Jesus performed, they sought not only to kill Jesus, but appallingly, sought also to kill a man whom Jesus had raised from the dead!

Here is the story.

A Public Healing

Jesus was very close to the family of a man named Lazarus and his two sisters, Martha and Mary. Lazarus was Jesus' friend. It happened that Lazarus had died several days prior. When Jesus finally came to see the family, Martha met Him on the way.

In her sorrow, Martha said to Jesus,

> *"Lord, if You had been here, my brother would not have died.*

Jesus responded to her, saying,

> *"Your brother will rise again."*

Jesus then told Martha to remove the stone that sealed the tomb of Lazarus.

Martha said to Jesus,

> *"Lord, by this time there is a stench, for he has been dead four days."*
>
> *Jesus said to her,*
> *"Did I not say to you that if you would believe you would see the glory of God?"*
>
> *Then they took away the stone*

Then, with a loud voice for everyone to hear, Jesus called out to His friend,

> *"Lazarus, come forth!"*

And it says Lazarus walked out of the tomb, still bound in his grave clothes.

Jesus said to those standing nearby,

> *"Loose him, and let him go."*

The account goes on to say,

> *Then many of the Jews who had come to Mary, and had seen the things Jesus did, believed in Him.*

Then it says,

> *But some of them went away to the Pharisees and told them the things Jesus did.*
>
> *Then the chief priests and the Pharisees gathered a council and said, "What shall we do? For this Man works many signs. If we let Him alone like this, everyone will believe in Him, and the Romans will come and take away both our place and nation."*

And it says,

> *Then, from that day on, they plotted to put Him to death.*
>
> *But the chief priests plotted to put Lazarus to death also, because on account of him many of the Jews went away and believed in Jesus.*
>
> See John 11:21, 23, 39-41, 43-48, 53 and 12:10-11 NKJV

This was a very public healing and miracle. Jesus had raised a man from the dead in front of many witnesses. In response to this wonderful miracle, the religious leadership wanted to kill both Jesus and Lazarus.

So, this is one instance where Jesus did publicly perform a miracle, in this case raising a man from the dead. In all the other examples however, it is clearly evident Jesus did not want the healings to be made known. They were to remain secret. Jesus told them…

Tell no one!

Demons – "Be Quiet!"

Although we perhaps don't see as much of this today, there did seem to be quite a number of demons around in Jesus' day. I am convinced they are still present, and there is more going on around us than we are aware.

Let's look at the interactions Jesus had with these demons and His response to them.

Here is the story of Jesus encountering a man possessed by a demon and Jesus commanding the demon to be silent.

> *Now there was a man in their synagogue with an unclean spirit.*
>
> *And he cried out, saying,*
> *"Let us alone! What have we to do with You, Jesus of Nazareth? Did You come to destroy us? **I know who You are — the Holy One of God!**"*

And it says,

> *But Jesus rebuked him, saying,*
> **"Be quiet, and come out of him!"**
>
> Mark 1:23-25 NKJV e.a.

Here we see the demon saying, *"I know who You are — the Holy One of God!"* And Jesus rebuked the demon and commanded it, *"Be quiet, and come out of him!"*

The demon was attempting to reveal who Jesus was, but Jesus would not allow him to speak.

Here is another example; this is a story of a man living among the tombs who was possessed by demons. It says the demon recognized who Jesus was.

> *When he saw Jesus from afar, he ran and worshiped Him.*
>
> *And he cried out with a loud voice and said,*
> **"What have I to do with You, Jesus, Son of the Most High God?**
> *I implore You by God that You do not torment me."*
>
> *For He said to him,*
> **"Come out of the man, unclean spirit!"**
>
> Mark 5:6-8 NKJV e.a.

The demon knew who Jesus was. He identifies Jesus as the, *"Son of the Most High God."* And it says, Jesus commanded the demon to come out of the man.

Here is another account.

> *When the sun was setting, all those who had any that were sick with various diseases brought them to Him; and He laid His hands on every one of them and healed them.*
>
> *And demons also came out of many, crying out and saying, "You are the Christ, the Son of God!"*

And it says,

> **And He, rebuking them, did not allow them to speak, for they**
> **knew that He was the Christ.**
>
> *Luke 4:40-41 NKJV e.a.*

This same story is also related in the book of Mark.

> *Then He healed many who were sick with various diseases, and*
> *cast out many demons;* **and He did not allow the demons to**
> **speak, because they knew Him.**
>
> *Mark 1:34 NKJV e.a.*

Also in Mark is another account when Jesus does not let the demons identify Him.

> *And the unclean spirits, whenever they saw Him, fell down before*
> *Him and cried out, saying,*
> *"You are the Son of God."*
>
> **But He sternly warned them that they should not make Him**
> **known.**
>
> *Mark 3:11-12 NKJV e.a.*

Jesus was not allowing the demons to speak because they knew He was the Son of God. When they spoke, Jesus commanded them,

> *Be quiet and come out!*

There are two interesting points to take note of here.

The first is this:
The demons knew who Jesus was, even though the people did not.
The demons were able to see and recognize something about Jesus the people were not able to see. They recognized Him as the Son of God!

The second point is this:
The demons recognized Jesus did not want His identity as the Son of God to be made known. And because they knew this, the demons were trying to publicly expose His true identity.

> *I know who You are — the Holy One of God!*

Jesus would not allow the demons to reveal who He is.

Disciples – *"Tell No One!"*

Today, in our churches, we teach the new students to go evangelize and tell the world about Jesus. We would think Jesus would do the same with His students, the disciples. But Jesus didn't tell His disciples to proclaim who He was. Instead, we see Jesus told them, *not,* to tell anyone who He was!

Look at these examples.

Here is an account of Jesus asking His disciples, *"Who do you say that I am?"*

Jesus asked,

> *"Who do people say that the Son of Man is?"*
>
> *And they said,*
> *"Some say John the Baptist; and others, Elijah; but still others, Jeremiah, or one of the prophets."*
>
> *He said to them,*
> *"But who do you say that I am?"*
>
> *Simon Peter answered,*
> *"You are the Christ, the Son of the living God."*

And it says,

> **Then He warned the disciples that they should tell no one that He was the Christ.**
>
> *Matthew 16:13-16, 20 NASB e.a.*

Jesus told His disciples to tell no one who He is.

Here is a story of Jesus' appearance being physically changed before three of His disciples.

> *Now after six days Jesus took Peter, James, and John his brother, led them up on a high mountain by themselves; and He was*

> *transfigured before them. His face shone like the sun, and His clothes became as white as the light.*

Then,

> *behold, a bright cloud overshadowed them; and suddenly a voice came out of the cloud, saying,*
> *"This is My beloved Son, in whom I am well pleased. Hear Him!"*

And it says,

> *Now as they came down from the mountain, Jesus commanded them, saying,*
> ***"Tell the vision to no one*** *until the Son of Man is risen from the dead."*
>
> *Matthew 17:1-2, 5, 9 NKJV e.a.*

Jesus' identity was revealed to these three disciples through both the vision of Him being transformed and also through the word spoken from heaven.

"This is My beloved Son"

After this experience, Jesus gave very direct instructions to His disciples commanding them *they were not to tell anyone* about what they had just seen.

Tell the vision to no one!

Notice something else about this event.

Jesus told His disciples they were to tell *"no one"* about the vision. There were only three disciples on the mountain that day, Peter, James and John. These disciples were not to even tell the other nine disciples about the vision. So only *three of the disciples* knew of what had happened.

From these many passages it can unmistakably be seen that Jesus did not want His identity as the Son of God or as the Christ to be made known.

Jesus kept His identity hidden!

To further show Jesus' identity was certainly being kept hidden, here is another detail. Look again at the story of Jesus asking His disciples, *"Who do you say that I am?"*

> *He said to them,*
> *"But who do you say that I am?"*
>
> *Simon Peter answered,*
> *"You are the Christ, the Son of the living God."*
>
> *And Jesus said to him,*
> *"Blessed are you, Simon Barjona, because flesh and blood*
> *did not reveal this to you, but My Father who is in heaven.*
>
> *Matthew 16:15-17 NASB*

*"flesh and blood did not **reveal** this to you"*

The word translated as, *"reveal,"* is the Greek word, *'Apokalupto,'* which means *'to uncover or make known.'*[1] For something to be revealed, it must first be hidden!

Or, as Jesus said,

> *For there is nothing hidden which will not be revealed, nor has*
> *anything been kept secret but that it should come to light.*
>
> *Mark 4:22 NKJV*

Jesus' identity was hidden, and it was *revealed* to Peter through the Father.

No one knew this; "flesh and blood," did not know this. His identity was hidden from everyone, except the disciples who heard Peter say,

> *"You are the Christ, the Son of the living God."*

*The Father **revealed** who Jesus is to Peter!*

Why Did Jesus Keep His Identity Hidden?

Why did Jesus keep His identity hidden from His own people? As we saw from the first chapter, if the people had known who Jesus was, they never would have crucified Him. Again, this was God's plan and purpose from the very beginning. This is why the identity of the Messiah needed to remain hidden.

Look at these passages of Jesus confirming this very matter.

> *Now the Jews' Feast of Tabernacles was at hand.*
>
> *His brothers therefore said to Him,*
> *"Depart from here and go into Judea, that Your disciples also may see the works that You are doing. For no one does anything in secret while he himself seeks to be known openly. If You do these things, show Yourself to the world."*
>
> *For even His brothers did not believe in Him.*
>
> *Then Jesus said to them,*
> ***"My time has not yet come,*** *but your time is always ready.*
>
> *John 7:2-6 NKJV e.a.*

Jesus makes the point here that His time had not yet come. It was not time to publicly make Himself known. There was an appointed time when He was to be revealed and be made known.

When was Jesus to be revealed? Take a look again at the story of the transfiguration.

It says,

> *Now as they came down from the mountain, Jesus commanded them, saying,*
> *"Tell the vision to no one* ***until the Son of Man is risen from the dead.***"
>
> *Matthew 17:9 NKJV e.a.*

Jesus told His disciples to tell no one, *until,* He rose from the dead. No one was to know who He was, *until after,* He had been crucified!

After Jesus rose from the dead, He showed Himself to the disciples and to as many as 500 other people. You can reference this account from Paul in 1 Corinthians 15, verses 3-8.

Jesus would reveal His true identity only *after* He rose from the dead.

Tell No One!

We have just looked at multiple occasions and many different circum-stances where Jesus kept His identity hidden. Jesus could have used any of these occasions to make Himself known to the entire nation. Instead, He does the exact opposite. He tells people not to say who He is; He tells them to keep it a secret!

Jesus commanded those He healed to *tell no one* about their healing. Jesus commanded the demons to *be quiet* when they tried to say who He is.
Jesus commanded His disciples to *tell no one* He is the Christ.
Jesus declared His identity was *revealed* to Peter by the Father.

> *Jesus' identity was hidden.*
> *Jesus kept... His identity hidden!*
>
> *Tell no one!*

ACT 3 VIGNETTE

IF I GLORIFY MYSELF

W E HAVE JUST SEEN JESUS TELLING OTHERS not to say who He is. Jesus was keeping His identity as the Messiah hidden. In the next few chapters, we are going to see a continuation of this same theme.

Jesus Will Not Testify of Himself

Jesus said He would not testify or bear witness of Himself. He said those who speak of themselves seek their own glory.

Jesus said to the Jews,

> *He who speaks from himself seeks his own glory; but He who seeks the glory of the One who sent Him is true, and no unrighteousness is in Him.*
>
> *John 7:18 NKJV*

He also said,

> *"If I bear witness of Myself, My witness is not true. There is another who bears witness of Me, and I know that the witness which He witnesses of Me is true.*
>
> *John 5:31-32 NKJV*

And again, He said,

> *I do not seek My glory; there is One who seeks and judges.*
> *"Truly, truly, I say to you, if anyone keeps My word he will never see death."*
>
> *The Jews said to Him,*
> *"Now we know that You have a demon. Abraham died, and the prophets also; and You say, 'If anyone keeps My word, he will never taste of death.' "Surely You are not greater than our father Abraham, who died? The prophets died too;*

Then the Jews said to Jesus,

> **whom do You make Yourself out to be?"**

Jesus answered them saying,

> **"If I glorify Myself, My glory is nothing;**
> **it is My Father who glorifies Me**

John 8:50-54 NASB e.a.

Previously, we had seen Jesus kept His identity hidden by telling *others,* not to say who He is. Now we are seeing *Jesus Himself,* will not say who He is.

Jesus will not glorify Himself!

Welcome to Act 3 – Who Are You?

Act 3

Who Are You?

If You Are the Son of God, Prove It!

AFTER JESUS' WATER BAPTISM AND BAPTISM IN THE HOLY SPIRIT, the Holy Spirit led Jesus into the wilderness. It was there that a fallen angel (here and furthermore to remain unnamed) challenged Jesus to prove who He was.

This fallen angel said to Jesus,

> **"If You are the Son of God**, *command that these stones become bread."*

Rather than respond to the challenge, Jesus reproved him with Scripture. Jesus said,

> *"It is written, 'Man shall not live by bread alone, but by every word that proceeds from the mouth of God.'"*
>
> Matthew 4:3-4 NKJV e.a.

The fallen angel again challenged Jesus to prove who He was, this time using Scripture himself.

The fallen angel said to Jesus,

> **"If You are the Son of God**, *throw Yourself down.*
> *For it is written: 'He shall give His angels charge over you,'*
>
> Matthew 4:6 NKJV e.a.

Again, Jesus did not respond to the challenge, once more rebutting him with an overriding Scripture.
Jesus replied,

> *"It is written again, 'You shall not tempt the LORD your God.'"*
>
> Matthew 4:7 NKJV

The fallen angel was quoting Scripture in an attempt to get Jesus to testify of Himself. In effect, this fallen angel was saying,

> *If You are the Son of God, prove it!*

A special note needs to be made at this point. This was not a case of the fallen angel not knowing or trying to determine who Jesus is. We already saw in the previous chapter the demons knew exactly who Jesus is. They would say to Him, *"I know who You are — the Holy One of God!"* And Jesus would command them, *"Be quiet and come out!"*

This fallen angel knew who Jesus was; he attempted to provoke Jesus into disclosing His identity and make Himself known. In neither instance did Jesus respond to his challenges. Jesus did not try to defend or prove that He is the Son of God.

Here is another instance of, *some* of the people, saying this same thing to Jesus.

At the end of His life, while hanging upon the cross, some of those standing by called out to Jesus challenging Him to prove He is the Son of God.

The Jews said to Jesus,

> **If You are the Son of God**, *come down from the cross.*
> *let Him now come down from the cross, and we will believe Him.*
>
> Matthew 27:40, 42 NKJV e.a.

Come down from the cross and we will believe!

If You are the Son of God, prove it!

These taunts hurled at Jesus warrant a rebuke. A comment needs to be made regarding the reprehensible lack of compassion and hardness of the individuals who would say such a thing to a man who had been crucified, as he is hanging from a cross.

With nails in His hands, and nails in His feet, they say to Jesus,

> *"Come down from the cross now and we will believe."*

A man who did them no harm, but only good,

> *"Come down from the cross and we will believe."*

A man who healed their sick, and raised their loved ones from the dead,

> *"Come down from the cross and we will believe."*

> *If You are the Son of God, prove it!*

Jesus did not defend Himself, nor try to prove He is the Son of God. He easily could have come down from the cross. It is true, it was wholly for the cross that Jesus came, and that is the real reason *why* He did not bring Himself down.

Nevertheless, it must also be noted, Jesus certainly could have proved who He is by coming down from the cross, *but He did not.*

He chose to stay on the cross, rather than prove Himself the Son of God!

Whom Do You Make Yourself Out to Be?

The Jewish people on several occasions, directly asked Jesus who He was. In the opening vignette of this chapter, we saw one of our first examples of this.

They asked Him,

> *whom do You make Yourself out to be?*

And Jesus simply replied,

> *If I glorify Myself, My glory is nothing;*
> *it is My Father who glorifies Me*

> *John 8:53-54 NASB*

Notice, Jesus did not tell them who He is.
They asked, but He did not tell them!

If You Are the Christ, Tell Us!

During one of the feasts, Jesus was walking in the temple and the Jews had gathered around Him.

They said to Him,

> *"How long do You keep us in doubt?*
> *If You are the Christ, tell us plainly."*

Jesus responded and said to them,

> *"I told you, and you do not believe. The works that I do in*
> *My Father's name, they bear witness of Me.*
>
> *John 10:24-25 NKJV*

Here again, Jesus does not tell them who He is. Jesus has said He will not testify or bear witness of Himself. However, He *does say* the works He performs do testify of Him.

Jesus did not tell them who He is.

Who Are You?

The Jews again asked Jesus who He was.
They asked,

> *"Who are You?"*

Jesus responded, saying,

> *"What have I been saying to you from the beginning? "I have many*
> *things to speak and to judge concerning you, but He who sent Me*
> *is true; and the things which I heard from Him, these I speak to the*
> *world."*
>
> *John 8:25-26 NASB*

We have now seen three instances of Jesus being directly, clearly, and plainly asked who He was by the Jews.

They asked Him,

> *"Whom do You make Yourself out to be?"*
> *"If You are the Christ, tell us plainly."*

And a simple, direct,

> *"Who are You?"*

Yet, not once, did Jesus tell them who He is. He refused to testify of Himself.

> *"If I glorify Myself, My glory is nothing!"*

Friends and Enemies

Jesus did not attempt to answer the fallen angel or the Jews when they tried to get Him to prove He was the Son of God. And Jesus did not answer the Jews when they asked Him who He was.

But these were not His friends, these would be considered His enemies. What did Jesus say to those who were His friends?

John the Baptist

Let's look at John the Baptist, a man who was said to be a friend of Jesus.

John the Baptist is the one who declared Jesus to the people.

> *"Behold! The Lamb of God who takes away the sin of the world!"*
>
> John 1:29 NKJV

John the Baptist is the one who said of Jesus,

> *It is He who, coming after me, is preferred before me, whose sandal strap I am not worthy to loose.*

And,

> *This is He of whom I said,*
> *'After me comes a Man who is preferred before me, for He was*
> *before me.'*
>
> *John 1:27, 30 NKJV*

John is the one who said of Jesus,

> *He who has the bride is the bridegroom; but the friend of the*
> *bridegroom, who stands and hears him, rejoices greatly because of*
> *the bridegroom's voice. Therefore this joy of mine is fulfilled.*
>
> *John 3:29 NKJV*

John rejoiced because of his friend Jesus.
John said of Jesus,

> *He must increase, but I must decrease.*
>
> *John 3:30 NKJV*

John the Baptist, who, when Jesus came to be baptized by him, humbly said,

> *"I need to be baptized by You, and are You coming to me?"*
>
> *Matthew 3:14 NKJV*

John is the man of whom Jesus Himself testified,

> *I say to you, among those born of women there has not risen one*
> *greater than John the Baptist*
>
> *Matthew 11:11 NKJV*

By Jesus' own words, *no one was greater than John the Baptist.* John was a man who called Jesus his friend.

And yet…

While John was in prison, during a very dark hour of his life, when his hope was fading (John would shortly hereafter be executed), he sent his disciples to Jesus to ask Him one question, just one question!

Are You the Coming One?

John asked Jesus,

> *"Are You the Coming One, or do we look for another?"*

Jesus replied,

> *"Go and tell John the things which you hear and see: The blind see and the lame walk; the lepers are cleansed and the deaf hear; the dead are raised up and the poor have the gospel preached to them. And blessed is he who is not offended because of Me."*

> *Matthew 11:3-6 NKJV*

Jesus does not directly answer John's question. Instead, in the same manner in which He had previously answered the Jews, He also answers John.

To the Jews, who were His enemies, Jesus answered,

> *"What have I been saying to you?"*

Or, said another way,

> *"What have you heard me say?"*

To John, who was His friend, Jesus answered,

> *"Go and tell what you hear..."*

Jesus did not directly answer John's question and say, *"Yes, I am the Coming One."* Jesus did however, answer John *indirectly* by telling him to look at the works He was doing.

> *The blind see*
> *The lame walk*
> *The lepers are cleansed*
> *The deaf hear*
> *The dead are raised up*
> *And the poor have the gospel preached to them*

The works testify of who Jesus is.

> *"The works that I do in My Father's name, they bear witness of Me."*
> *"Go and tell John the things which you hear and see!"*

Jesus has been asked by the Jews who He is.
Jesus has been asked by John the Baptist who He is.

Now Jesus is going to ask some questions of His own.

The Christ, Whose Son Is He?

The Pharisees and Sadducees (the religious leaders of that day) had been questioning Jesus, testing Him. So Jesus also asked them a question in return.

Jesus, speaking of Himself, asked them this question,

> *"What do you think about the Christ? Whose Son is He?"*

The Jews said to Him,

> *"The Son of David."*

Then Jesus said,

> *"How then does David in the Spirit call Him 'Lord,'*

(For King David had written of the Christ),

> *'**The LORD said to my Lord**,*
> *"Sit at My right hand,*
> *Till I make Your enemies Your footstool"'?*

And Jesus said,

> *If David then calls Him 'Lord,' how is He his Son?"*

And the passage reads,

> *And no one was able to answer Him a word, nor from that day on did anyone dare question Him anymore.*

Matthew 22:42-46 NKJV e.a.

There was not a single person present that knew the answer to this question. Jesus asked the question, *knowing* they would not know the answer. And having asked the question, He does not give them the answer.

Jesus asked the Jews about the Christ, with no intention of giving them the answer. He did not tell them who the Christ was.

> *He did not tell them who He was!*

Who Do You Say That I Am?

Jesus also posed a question to His disciples. He asked them who they thought He was.

Jesus asked them,

> who do you say that I am?

Peter replied,

> "You are the Christ, the Son of the living God."

Jesus responded,

> "Blessed are you, Simon Barjona, because flesh and blood did not reveal this to you, but My Father who is in heaven.
>
> Matthew 16:15-17 NASB

Notice *who* told Peter that Jesus is the Christ, the Son of God.

It was not Jesus who told Peter.
It was the Father who told Peter.

> "Flesh and blood did not reveal this to you,
> but **My Father** who is in heaven."

Jesus did not tell His own disciples who He is; it was revealed to Peter by the Father.

Look closer at the very question itself.

Jesus asked His disciples,

> *"Who do you say that I am?"*

If Jesus had at any point told them who He is,
why would He then ask them who He is?

Think about that for a moment. Jesus is asking His disciples who they think He is. If Jesus had ever told them who He is, why then would He ask this question?

> *"Who do you say that I am?"*

Jesus did not tell His own disciples who He was!

Now, Jesus did "confirm" that He was the Son of God. But Jesus Himself did not tell or state this to Peter. He only confirmed what the Father had already told Peter.

> *"My Father revealed this to you."*

We have now seen several instances where Jesus had opportunities to reveal His identity, and yet, *He did not*!

> *Jesus did not testify of Himself!*

A Figure of Speech

John, one of the disciples, recognized how Jesus was talking and recorded several occurrences of this. He noticed when Jesus spoke, He did not speak plainly and clearly. John records that Jesus spoke using a figurative type of speech.

Here are a few examples.

Tell Us Plainly

This is a verse we had previously seen. Jesus was walking in the temple when the Jews gathered around Him.

They said to Him,

> "How long do You keep us in doubt?
> If You are the Christ, **tell us plainly**."
>
> *John 10:24 NKJV e.a.*

John mentions the Jews wanted Jesus to tell them *plainly* if He was the Christ.

Prior to this Jesus had been speaking to them and said,

> "Most assuredly, I say to you, he who does not enter the sheepfold
> by the door, but climbs up some other way, the same is a thief and
> a robber. But he who enters by the door is the shepherd of the sheep.
>
> *John 10:1-2 NKJV*

John commented on this and said,

> This **figure of speech** Jesus spoke to them, but they did not
> understand what those things were which He had been saying to
> them.
>
> *John 10:6 NASB e.a.*

John notes that Jesus was using a *figure of speech*, or a *type of speech*, and the Jews did not understand what He was saying.

I Will No Longer Speak in a Figurative Language

Here is another example. This time however, Jesus is not speaking publicly with the Jews. He is speaking privately with His own disciples and tells them He has been speaking to them in figurative language.

Jesus said to His disciples,

> "These things **I have spoken to you in figurative language**; but
> the time is coming when I will no longer speak to you in figurative
> language, but I will tell you plainly about the Father.
>
> *John 16:25 NKJV e.a.*

Notice, Jesus says He has not been speaking plainly to His disciples, but has been speaking to them in *figurative language.*

The word John used to say Jesus spoke using a *"figure of speech"* and the word Jesus used to say He spoke in *"figurative language"* is the same Greek word *'Paroimia.'* This word can also be translated as, *'Parable, Proverb or Dark saying.'*[2]

Jesus is telling His disciples that He has been speaking to them in parables and dark sayings!

Jesus said there was a time coming, *though as yet still future*, when He would no longer speak to the disciples in a *(Paroimia)* figurative language, but would speak to them *plainly.*

> *but the time is coming **when...***
> *I will no longer speak to you in figurative language,*
> **but I will tell you plainly**

The word Jesus used to say He would speak *"plainly"* to His disciples, and the word the Jews used when they asked Jesus to tell them *"plainly"* if He was the Christ, is the same Greek word *'Parrhesia'* which means to *'speak openly, without concealment or ambiguity.'*[3]

When Jesus had finished speaking, the disciples said to Him,

> *"See, now You are speaking **plainly**, and using no **figure of speech!***
>
> *John 16:29 NKJV e.a.*

The disciples said,

> *"Now You are speaking plainly ..."*

These verses unmistakably show that Jesus up until that point had not been speaking plainly and openly. Rather, they show Him speaking in figurative language, which can also be translated as, *parables.*

> *Jesus was speaking in parables!*

He Spoke the Same to All

In all these instances we have seen, Jesus had numerous opportunities to make Himself known and testify of Himself, but He would not. The way Jesus spoke with His disciples, was the same way He spoke to everyone.

Jesus did not speak plainly to the Jews.
Jesus did not speak plainly to His disciples.
Jesus did not tell the Jews who He was.
Jesus did not tell John the Baptist who He was.
And Jesus did not tell His own disciples who He was.

> *He spoke the same to all!*

When Jesus spoke,

> *He used figurative language!*

> *"How long do You keep us in doubt?*
> *If You are the Christ, tell us plainly."*

> *"I told you, and you do not believe!"*

ACT 4 VIGNETTE

If I Tell You Heavenly Things

J ESUS, SPEAKING TO THE JEWS AND PHARISEES, said,

> "Most assuredly, I say to you, he who does not enter the sheepfold
> by **the door**, but climbs up some other way, the same is a thief
> and a robber. But he who enters by **the door** is the shepherd of the
> sheep. To him the doorkeeper opens, and the sheep hear his voice;
> and he calls his own sheep by name and leads them out. And when
> he brings out his own sheep, he goes before them; and the sheep
> follow him, for they know his voice. Yet they will by no means
> follow a stranger, but will flee from him, for they do not know the
> voice of strangers."
>
> John 10:1-5 NKJV e.a.

John then wrote,

> This **figure of speech** Jesus spoke to them, **but they did not under-
> stand** what those things were which He had been saying to them.
>
> John 10:6 NASB e.a.

Jesus is using a figure of speech or type of speech, speaking of a door, but
the people do not understand what He is saying.

Now, Jesus tells them what He is doing.

There was a man of the Pharisees, a good man, named Nicodemus. He
came to speak privately with Jesus at night, as it were, in secret.

Nicodemus said to Jesus,

> "Rabbi, we know that You are a teacher come from God; for no one
> can do these signs that You do unless God is with him."

Jesus replied,

> "Most assuredly, I say to you, unless one is born again, he cannot
> see the kingdom of God."

And Nicodemus said,

> "**How can a man be born when he is old?** Can he enter a second
> time into his mother's womb and be born?"

Jesus said to him,

> *"Most assuredly, I say to you, unless one is born of water and the*
> *Spirit, he cannot enter the kingdom of God. That which is born of*
> *the flesh is flesh, and that which is born of the Spirit is spirit. Do*
> *not marvel that I said to you, 'You must be born again.' The wind*
> *blows where it wishes, and you hear the sound of it, but cannot tell*
> *where it comes from and where it goes. So is everyone who is born*
> *of the Spirit."*

And Nicodemus said again,

> **"How can these things be?"**

Jesus replied,

> *"Are you the teacher of Israel, and do not know these things? Most*
> *assuredly, I say to you, We speak what We know and testify what*
> *We have seen, and you do not receive Our witness.*

Then Jesus said,

> **If I have told you earthly things and you do not believe,**
> **how will you believe if I tell you heavenly things?**
>
> *John 3:2-12 NKJV e.a.*

Jesus had just said a person must be born again. He spoke a truth to
Nicodemus about the kingdom of heaven.

Jesus then said (paraphrased),

> *Flesh is flesh, spirit is spirit.*
> *If I told you about earthly things, that you know and are familiar*
> *with and yet you do not believe, how will you believe if I tell you*
> *about heavenly things, that you do not know and are not familiar*
> *with?*

When Jesus says we must be born again, He is speaking in terms of
earthly things, (flesh is flesh). Jesus is using the familiarity of natural
birth, to teach Nicodemus a truth about *heavenly things*, (spirit is spirit).

We all know what it means to be born of the flesh. In the same way, we all need to know what it means to be born of the Spirit.

Jesus was speaking of heavenly things.

> *You must be born again!*

But Nicodemus did not understand.

When Jesus was speaking to the Pharisees about "the door," He was speaking of heavenly things. Jesus was speaking to them in figurative language of something earthly, a door, to teach them a spiritual truth about heaven.

But they did not understand.

In the previous chapters, we have seen Jesus tell others not to say who He is. We have also seen, even when directly asked, *"Who are You?"* Jesus still would not say who He is. Instead, He spoke to them in figurative language.

> *"What have I been saying to you?"*

In this chapter, Jesus finally tells the people who He is.

Jesus tells them…

> *Heavenly things!*

Welcome to Act 4 – I Am

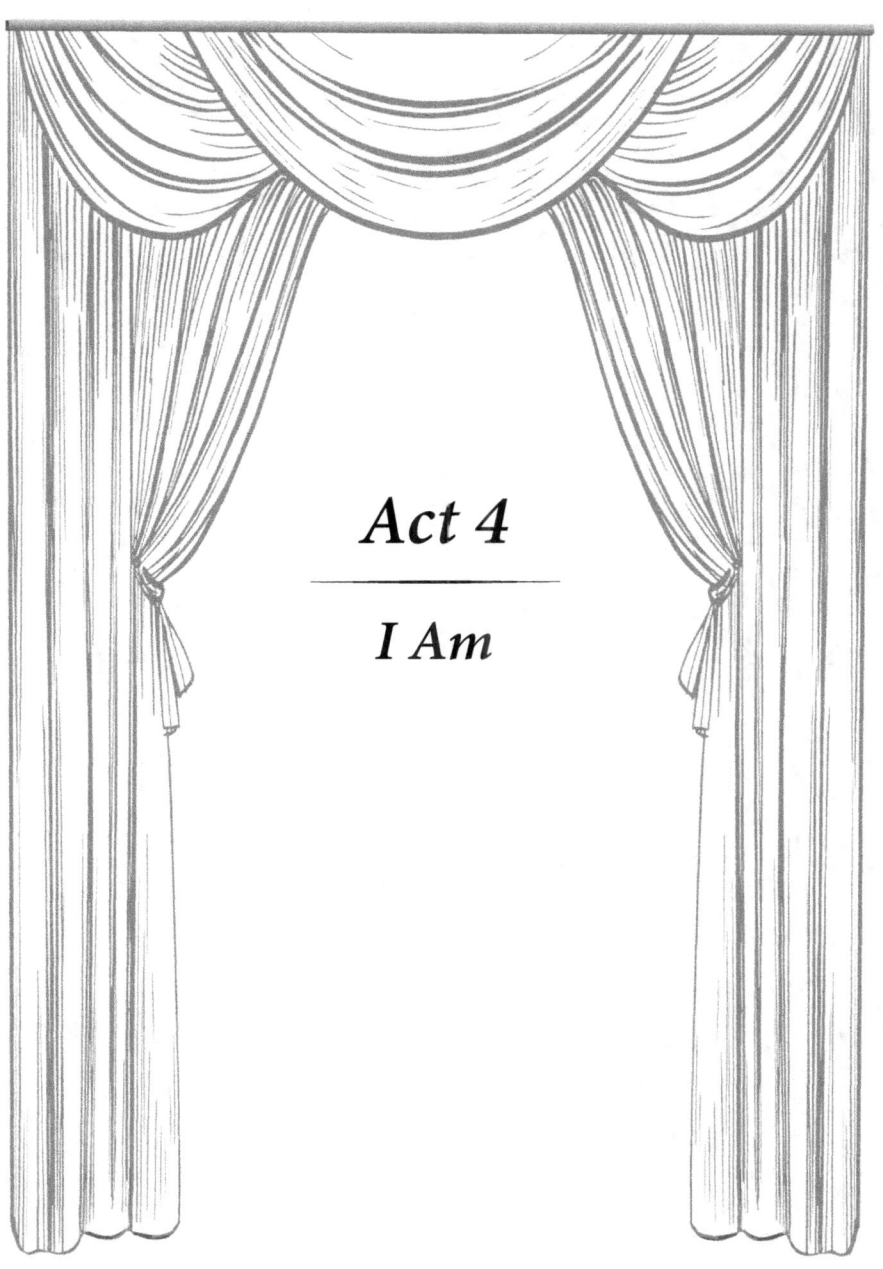

Act 4

I Am

I Am the Door

WHEN JESUS WAS SPEAKING TO THEM ABOUT THE DOOR, He said those who do not enter by the door are thieves and robbers.

He then went on to say,

> "Most assuredly, I say to you, **I am the door** of the sheep. All who ever came before Me are thieves and robbers, but the sheep did not hear them.
>
> **I am the door.** If anyone enters by Me, he will be saved, and will go in and out and find pasture. The thief does not come except to steal, and to kill, and to destroy. I have come that they may have life, and that they may have it more abundantly.
>
> *John 10:7-10 NKJV e.a.*

This statement Jesus made is the first of many, "*I am*" declarations He will make. He tells them,

> "*I am the Door!*"

Jesus tells the Pharisees He is the door of the sheep and anyone who enters through Him shall go in and out and find pasture. This is part of the same passage where it was noted they did not understand what He was saying to them.

Jesus is using a type of speech the people do not understand. He is using figurative speech.

Jesus is not speaking of an *earthly door*.
He is speaking of a *heavenly door*.

Jesus is speaking of heavenly things, using earthly terms, yet they still do not understand.

I Am the Good Shepherd

After Jesus said He is the door of the sheep, He then went on to tell them He is the shepherd of the sheep.

Jesus said,

> **"I am the good shepherd.** *The good shepherd gives His life for the sheep.*
>
> *But a hireling, he who is not the shepherd, one who does not own the sheep, sees the wolf coming and leaves the sheep and flees; and the wolf catches the sheep and scatters them. The hireling flees because he is a hireling and does not care about the sheep.*
>
> **I am the good shepherd**; *and I know My sheep, and am known by My own. As the Father knows Me, even so I know the Father; and I lay down My life for the sheep.*
>
> *And other sheep I have which are not of this fold; them also I must bring, and they will hear My voice; and there will be one flock and one shepherd.*
>
> John 10:11-16 NKJV e.a.

This is now the second, direct, *"I am"* declaration that Jesus makes of Himself.

"I am the Good Shepherd!"

Jesus tells the Pharisees He is the good shepherd and He lays His life down for His sheep. Here again, Jesus is describing heavenly things, using earthly terms.

Jesus is not speaking of being the shepherd of sheep; He is speaking of being the shepherd of women and men.

"The good shepherd gives His life for the sheep."

The Jews were not able to understand what Jesus was speaking about. They did not understand the *heavenly things*; it was nonsense to them.

After Jesus had finished speaking, it says,

> *Therefore there was a division again among the Jews because of these sayings.*
>
> *And many of them said,*
> *"He has a demon and is mad. Why do you listen to Him?"*
>
> *Others said,*
> *"These are not the words of one who has a demon. Can a demon open the eyes of the blind?"*
>
> *John 10:19-21 NKJV*

Jesus has just declared two things to them:

> *"I am the Door"*

And,

> *"I am the Good Shepherd"*

Again, Jesus is using language that the Jews or Pharisees do not understand. They were not able to comprehend what He was saying; they thought He was insane.

> *He is mad!*

I Am the Light of the World

There was another occasion when Jesus had been speaking to the Pharisees. Jesus said to them,

> **"I am the light of the world.** *He who follows Me shall not walk in darkness, but have the light of life."*
>
> *John 8:12 NKJV e.a.*

This is now the third instance we have seen of Jesus making a direct, "I am" declaration.

> *"I am the Light of the world!"*

The Jews wanted to know who Jesus was. They had been asking Him to tell them who He was. But now that He finally has, these men accuse Jesus of bearing witness of Himself.

Jesus, on a previous occasion, had said to them,

> *"If I bear witness of Myself, My witness is not true.*
>
> John 5:31 NKJV

Therefore, after Jesus said, *"I am the light of the world,"* the Pharisees said to Him,

> *"You bear witness of Yourself; Your witness is not true."*

Yet, Jesus replied,

> *"Even if I bear witness of Myself, My witness is true,*
>
> *It is also written in your law that the testimony of two men is true. I am One who bears witness of Myself, and the Father who sent Me bears witness of Me."*
>
> John 8:13-14, 17-18 NKJV

How can Jesus at one point say, *"If I bear witness of Myself, My witness is not true,"* then also say here, *"Even if I bear witness of Myself, My witness is true"*?

If Jesus was the *only one* to bear Him witness, His testimony would not be valid, or true. However, in this case, there is a second person who also bears Him witness, and that person is the Father. Therefore, His witness is true.

This would then resolve the apparent contradiction of these two statements. However, Jesus had clearly said He would not bear witness of Himself, or glorify Himself.

Jesus had said,

> *"If I glorify Myself, My glory is nothing;*
> *it is My Father who glorifies Me*
>
> John 8:54 NASB

With Jesus now saying, *"I am the light of the world,"* it certainly does sound as though He is glorifying Himself. It does appear He is testifying of Himself.

So here is the question:

Did Jesus really bear witness of Himself?

In one sense, it is true, Jesus did say who He is and therefore, He did bear witness of Himself. However, is a man really bearing witness of himself, if he speaks of things the people are not able to understand?

Jesus is speaking of heavenly things.

> *"If I have told you **earthly things** and you do not believe,*
> *how will you believe if I tell you **heavenly things**?"*

When Jesus said, *"I am the light of the world,"* He was using an earthly term, to speak a heavenly truth. He was speaking in terms of natural light that the people understood, to speak of the light from heaven that enlightens the hearts of women and men. He was speaking of *heavenly things*.

Here is the key:

If they do not believe when He speaks of earthly things, things they do know and do understand, how will they believe if He speaks of heavenly things, of which they know nothing?

If they do not understand when He speaks of earthly things, how will they understand when He speaks of heavenly things?

> *How can these things be?*

If the people did not know what *"the light of the world"* meant while Jesus was performing so many miracles among them, would they now know and understand, what that light was, simply because Jesus said, *"I am the light of the world"*?

If Jesus' identity *was not known,* and the "heavenly thing" of which He spoke also *was not known,* did Jesus then reveal His identity or testify of Himself when He in effect said,

"I am something you do not know"?

The true meaning of *"the light of the world"* was unknown, and because the *"heavenly thing"* was unknown, Jesus' identity remained unknown!

If you are unknown, and that which you speak of is also unknown, then you remain unknown. You will remain unknown, because they do not understand the things of which you speak.

So again, did Jesus bear witness of Himself? Yes, in a certain sense He did. And yet, in another very true sense, *to those who did not understand,* He did not.

"I am the light of the world!"

"You bear witness of Yourself; Your witness is not true."

I Am the Bread of Life

Jesus had just fed over five thousand people. The following day multitudes of people came looking for Him.

Jesus spoke to the Jews and said,

> *"Most assuredly, I say to you, you seek Me, not because you saw the signs, but because you ate of the loaves and were filled.*
>
> *"**I am the bread of life.** He who comes to Me shall never hunger, and he who believes in Me shall never thirst.*
>
> ***I am the bread of life.** Your fathers ate the manna in the wilderness, and are dead. This is the bread which comes down from heaven, that one may eat of it and not die.*

> ***I am the living bread*** *which came down from heaven. If anyone eats of this bread, he will live forever; and the bread that I shall give is My flesh, which I shall give for the life of the world."*
>
> John 6:26, 35, 48-51 NKJV e.a.

This is now the fourth, *"I am"* declaration Jesus has made.

> *"I am the Bread of Life!"*
> *"I am the Living Bread!"*

Notice however, how the people reacted.

> *The Jews then complained about Him, because He said,*
> *"I am the bread which came down from heaven."*
>
> *And they said,*
> *"Is not this Jesus, the son of Joseph, whose father and mother we know? How is it then that He says, 'I have come down from heaven'?"*

And,

> *The Jews therefore quarreled among themselves, saying,*
> *"How can this Man give us His flesh to eat?"*
>
> John 6:41-42, 52 NKJV

Notice they responded exactly as Nicodemus, who had said,

> *"How can these things be?"*

The people were not able to understand the things of which Jesus spoke. They were not able to comprehend who Jesus said He is.

> *"I am the Bread of Life!"*

So again, did Jesus actually say who He was? Yes, He did. But He used a type of speech, and spoke of things, they did not understand.

We have seen Jesus speaking to the Jews and Pharisees, who did not believe in Him. Now we will see Jesus speaking to those who did believe.

I Am the Resurrection and the Life

Here is the story again of the man named Lazarus. Lazarus had been sick, and his sisters, Martha and Mary, had sent word to Jesus so He might come heal their brother. But Jesus intentionally delayed coming to them. When He finally arrived, Lazarus had already been dead four days. Martha went to meet Jesus.

Martha said to Jesus,

> *"Lord, if You had been here, my brother would not have died. But even now I know that whatever You ask of God, God will give You."*

Jesus replied,

> *"Your brother will rise again."*

Martha then said,

> *"I know that he will rise again in the resurrection at the last day."*

And Jesus said,

> ***"I am the resurrection and the life.*** *He who believes in Me, though he may die, he shall live. And whoever lives and believes in Me shall never die.*
>
> *John 11:21-26 NKJV e.a.*

Here now is the fifth, direct, *"I am"* declaration Jesus has made.

> *"I am the Resurrection and the Life!"*

Notice that although this time Jesus is speaking to Martha, who believes in Him, Jesus is still using the same type of speech He used when speaking to the Jews and Pharisees. He is still using a figure of speech, speaking of heavenly things.

Again, Jesus speaks of heavenly things that are not understood by those to whom He is speaking. The only difference between this conversation with Martha, and the previous conversations Jesus had with the Jews and Pharisees, is the response of those to whom He spoke. He is now speaking to those who believe.

When Jesus was speaking to Nicodemus, He said,

> *"Most assuredly, I say to you, unless one is born again, he cannot see the kingdom of God."*
>
> *If I have told you earthly things **and you do not believe**, **how will you believe** if I tell you heavenly things?*
>
> *John 3:3, 12 NKJV e.a.*

And Nicodemus' response was,

> *"How can these things be?"*
>
> *John 3:9 NKJV*

Jesus said to Martha,

> *"I am the resurrection and the life. **He who believes in Me**, though he may die, he shall live. And whoever lives **and believes in Me** shall never die.*

Then Jesus asked her,

> ***Do you believe this?"***
>
> *John 11:25-26 NKJV e.a.*

Notice, Jesus did not ask Martha if she understood.
Jesus asked her *if she believed*.

> *"Do you believe?"*

And Martha's response was,

> *"Yes, Lord, **I believe** ..."*
>
> *John 11:27 NKJV e.a. par.*

There was no difference in what Jesus said to Martha or Nicodemus; the only difference was their response.

> *Martha believed!*

I Am the Way, the Truth, and the Life

The night Jesus was to be betrayed, the last night He would be with His disciples, we see Jesus still using this same figure of speech as He tells them He is going away.

Jesus said to His disciples,

> *"Let not your heart be troubled; you believe in God, believe also in Me. In My Father's house are many mansions; if it were not so, I would have told you. I go to prepare a place for you. And if I go and prepare a place for you, I will come again and receive you to Myself; that where I am, there you may be also.*
>
> *And where I go you know, and the way you know."*

Thomas, one of His disciples, said to Jesus,

> *"Lord, we do not know where You are going, and how can we know the way?"*

Then Jesus said,

> **"I am the way, the truth, and the life.** *No one comes to the Father except through Me.*
>
> *John 14:1-6 NKJV e.a.*

This is the sixth, direct, *"I am"* declaration Jesus has made.

> *"I am the Way, the Truth, and the Life!"*

Notice again, even though this time Jesus is speaking privately with His disciples, He is still using the same *"figure of speech"* as He did when He spoke to Martha. He is still using the same *"figure of speech"* as He did when He spoke to the Jews and Pharisees.

Jesus is still speaking of *"heavenly things"* and after all this time, the disciples still do not understand what He is saying.

When Thomas said to Jesus,

> *"Lord, we do not know where You are going, and how can we know the way?"*

Jesus replied,

> **"I am the way, the truth, and the life**. *No one comes to the Father
> except through Me. "If you had known Me, you would have known
> My Father also; and from now on you know Him and have seen
> Him."*

Another disciple, Philip, said to Him,

> *"Lord, show us the Father, and it is sufficient for us."*

Jesus then said,

> *"Have I been with you so long, and yet you have not known Me,
> Philip? He who has seen Me has seen the Father; so how can you
> say, 'Show us the Father'?* **Do you not believe** *that I am in the
> Father, and the Father in Me?*

> *John 14:5-10 NKJV e.a.*

Jesus is speaking in figurative language of heavenly things and the disciples still do not understand what He is saying. Yet, Jesus did not ask His disciples if they understood; He only asked if they believed.

> *"Do you not believe?"*

I Am the Vine

Jesus continued, saying,

> **"I am the true vine**, *and My Father is the vinedresser. Every branch
> in Me that does not bear fruit He takes away; and every branch that
> bears fruit He prunes, that it may bear more fruit. You are already
> clean because of the word which I have spoken to you. Abide in Me,
> and I in you. As the branch cannot bear fruit of itself, unless it abides
> in the vine, neither can you, unless you abide in Me.*

> **"I am the vine**, *you are the branches. He who abides in Me, and
> I in him, bears much fruit; for without Me you can do nothing.
> If anyone does not abide in Me, he is cast out as a branch and is*

withered; and they gather them and throw them into the fire, and they are burned.

If you abide in Me, and My words abide in you, you will ask what you desire, and it shall be done for you. By this My Father is glorified, that you bear much fruit; so you will be My disciples.

John 15:1-8 NKJV e.a.

This is now a seventh, direct, *"I am"* declaration Jesus makes.

"I am the Vine!"

Again, we see Jesus is speaking to His disciples using the same figure of speech while speaking of heavenly things. Jesus is using *earthly things* to describe *heavenly things*. Although the earthly description of a vine is understood, the heavenly side of how Jesus can be a vine, is not!

How can Jesus be a vine?
How can the disciples abide in Him?

How can these things be?

I Am in the Father

Here is one final, *"I am"* declaration Jesus makes that speaks of heavenly things.

Jesus spoke to His disciples and said,

*Do you not believe that **I am in the Father**, and the Father in Me? The words that I speak to you I do not speak on My own authority; but the Father who dwells in Me does the works.*

*Believe Me that **I am in the Father** and the Father in Me, or else believe Me for the sake of the works themselves.*

John 14:10-11 NKJV e.a.

This is now the eighth, *"I am"* declaration Jesus will make.

"I am in the Father."

This particular *"I am"* statement sounds more like He is telling them *what* or *where* He is, rather than *who* He is. However, this one *"I am"* statement, perhaps more than all the others, truly captures the essence and heavenly nature of who Jesus is.

Jesus is, *in the Father.*
This is, who Jesus is!

> *"He who has seen Me has seen the Father."*

Notice once again, Jesus did not tell His disciples to understand, He only told them to believe.

> *"**Believe Me** that I am in the Father...,*
> *or else **believe Me** for the sake of the works themselves."*

These are all spiritual things that simply cannot be understood by those who do not know what it means to be born of the Spirit. Earthly things are understood by those who are born of the flesh. In the same way, heavenly things are *only understood*, by those who are born of the Spirit.

You do not need to understand these things. You do not need to understand how Jesus can be a vine. You do not need to understand how Jesus can be the light of the world. You only need to believe what He said. You only need to believe, He is, who He said He is.

> *Jesus is the light of the world.*

> *You only need to believe... He is!*

Heavenly Things

In all these instances Jesus said who He is by speaking in figurative language of heavenly things.

> *"I am the Door"*
> *"I am the Good Shepherd"*
> *"I am the Light of the world"*
> *"I am the Bread of Life"*
> *"I am the Resurrection and the Life"*
> *"I am the Way, the Truth, and the Life"*
> *"I am the Vine"*

And finally,

> *"I am in the Father"*

Notice the list of all these, *"I am"* self-declarations Jesus made. Eight times Jesus declared, *"I am."* Eight times Jesus told them who He is!

Yet, even with all of these, *"I am"* declarations we see Jesus make, notice what is missing from the list; notice what Jesus did not say.

Not once, did Jesus declare and say, *"I am the Son of God!"*
Not once, did Jesus ever say, *"I am the Christ!"* or *"I am the Messiah!"*

Not one single time, is it recorded that Jesus ever made an "I am" statement declaring Himself to be the Son of God.

Instead, Jesus declared Himself using figurative language. And, in all of these "I am" statements Jesus did make, the people could not understand any of them. The people were not able to comprehend the heavenly things of which Jesus spoke. These statements were not understood, and because their meanings remained unknown, Jesus' identity also remained unknown.

He Spoke the Same to All

Regardless of who Jesus was speaking to...,
regardless of whether He was speaking to the Jewish people,
regardless of whether He was speaking to Martha,
or regardless of whether He was speaking privately with His own disciples,
regardless of who He was speaking to...,

> *Jesus spoke in the same manner to all!*

He spoke to them using figurative language.

They asked Him who He is, so He told them who He is.

> *"I am... the Light of the world!"*

ACT 5 VIGNETTE

Who Do You Say That I Am?

J ESUS ASKED HIS DISCIPLES,

> "Who do people say that the Son of Man is?"

> And they said,
> "Some say John the Baptist; and others, Elijah; but still others, Jeremiah, or one of the prophets."

Jesus asks His disciples, who *others*, say He is. He then asks the important question; He asks them, who *they*, say He is.

He asked them,

> "But who do **you** say that I am?"

Peter answered and said…

> "You are the Christ, the Son of the living God."
>
> *Matthew 16:13-16 NASB e.a.*

Welcome to Act 5 – You Say I Am!

Act 5

You Say I Am!

You Call Me Teacher and Lord

O N THE FINAL EVENING JESUS WOULD BE WITH HIS DISCIPLES, He clothed Himself with a towel, took water and washed His disciples' feet. He was teaching them they should serve one another, just as He had served them.

Jesus said to His disciples,

> **"You call Me Teacher and Lord; and you are right, for so I am.**
> *"If I then, the Lord and the Teacher, washed your feet, you also ought to wash one another's feet. "For I gave you an example that you also should do as I did to you.*
>
> John 13:13-15 NASB e.a.

Jesus says He is Teacher and Lord. This appears to be an instance of Jesus making yet another direct, "*I am*" statement. However, with all of the other "*I am*" declarations we have previously read, Jesus would first say, "*I am*," then, say who He is. For example:

> "**I am**... *the Light of the world.*"
> "**I am** *the Door.*"

However here, He said,

> "**You**... *call Me Teacher and Lord; and* **you**... *are right, for so* **I am**."

This is not a direct, "*I am*" statement. Take notice of exactly how He said this.

Jesus said,

> He is, *who the disciples said,* He is.
> I am, **who you say**, I am.

It was the disciples who called Jesus Teacher and Lord. Jesus only confirmed, *who the disciples said* He is.

> "*You call Me Teacher and Lord; and* **you are right** *for so I am.*"

This one instance is the closest occurrence we have seen so far of Jesus saying or confirming He is Lord. However, Jesus does not use the word Lord in the context of saying He is the Lord God. Rather, He uses it in the context of master and servant, teacher and student.

Jesus went on to say,

> *Most assuredly, I say to you, a servant is not greater than his master; nor is he who is sent greater than he who sent him.*
>
> *John 13:16 NKJV*

Jesus tells His disciples, He is, *who they say*, He is. Jesus speaking this way is intentional on His part. We will see Him using this same pattern of speech, repeated several more times.

> *I am, who **you say**, **I am**.*

Are You the King of the Jews?

Jesus was on trial before the Roman governor, Pontius Pilate, who asks Jesus if He is a king.

Pilate said to Jesus,

> *"Are You the King of the Jews?"*

Jesus replied,

> *"Are you speaking for yourself about this, or did others tell you this concerning Me?"*

Pilate responded,

> *"Am I a Jew? Your own nation and the chief priests have delivered You to me. What have You done?"*

Jesus said,

> *"My kingdom is not of this world. If My kingdom were of this world, My servants would fight, so that I should not be delivered to the Jews; but now My kingdom is not from here."*

And Pilate asked again,

> *"Are You a king then?"*

Then Jesus replied,

> *"**You say** rightly **that I am a king**. For this cause I was born, and for this cause I have come into the world, that I should bear witness to the truth. Everyone who is of the truth hears My voice."*
>
> *John 18:33-37 NKJV e.a.*

This appears to be another direct, *"I am"* statement. It is clear Jesus is a king, and not simply an earthly king, as He had just said,

> *"My kingdom is not of this world."*

Yet, even though it appears Jesus said, *"I am a king,"* that is not what He was saying. This in fact, is not an *"I am"* declaration at all. Notice *what* He said, and *how* He said it.

Jesus said,

> *"**You**... say rightly that I am a king."*

Jesus said it was Pilate, who said He was a king.
Jesus did not say it; Pilate said it!

From this text, it would appear Jesus did at least confirm He was a king. It is recorded He said,

> *"You say **rightly** that I am a king."*

However, we find some of the newer Bible translations have inserted the words 'rightly' or 'correctly' into the text. The original manuscripts do not contain this confirmation.

What these translations should actually, and accurately, say is,

> *"You say that I am a king."*

Although written in old style English, the King James version of the Bible has an accurate translation of what Jesus said.

> *Thou sayest that I am a king.*
>
> John 18:37 KJV

There are three other accounts of this interaction between Pilate and Jesus. In the books of Matthew, Mark and Luke, the newest translations also show Jesus as confirming what Pilate had asked, with Jesus saying, "*It is as... you say.*"

Matthew:	"~~It is as~~ *you say.*"	*Matthew 27:11 NKJV e.a.*
Mark:	"~~It is as~~ *you say.*"	*Mark 15:2 NKJV e.a.*
Luke:	"~~It is as~~ *you say.*"	*Luke 23:3 NKJV e.a.*

The text in the original Greek however, does not have the words, "It is as" for Jesus' response. He did not make a confirmative statement to Pilate. Jesus only said, "*You say*" or "*You said.*"

This would be similar to how we might speak today when we say, "You said it, not me."

> *Are You a king?*
> *You said it, not Me!*

The words, "It is as" are not part of the original text, and inserting these words into the sentence actually changes the meaning and intent of what Jesus said.

> *Are You a king?*
> *It is as you say.*

If Jesus had wanted to say, "*It is as you say,*" that's exactly what He would have said, but He did not.

This, is what He said.

> "*Are You a king?*"
> "*You say... that I am a king.*"

This is identical to the way Jesus spoke to His disciples, when He told them He is *"Teacher and Lord,"* with the exception of one important detail.

To the disciples, Jesus said,

> *"You call Me Teacher and Lord, and you are right, for so **I am**."*

Jesus did declare, *"I am."*

> ***I am**, who you say I am.*

With Pontius Pilate however, Jesus did not make any self-declaratory *"I am"* statement. Jesus never declared to Pilate, *"I am a king."* Jesus said Pilate is the one, who declared Him a king!

> *"Are You a king?"*
> *"You say I am."*

Tell Us if You Are the Christ, the Son of God

Jesus was taken before the high priest where He was interrogated and accused of many things, yet He remained silent. It was then that the high priest commanded Jesus to tell them if He was the Christ.

The high priest said to Jesus,

> *"I put You under oath by the living God:*
> *Tell us if You are the Christ, the Son of God!"*

Jesus replied,

> *"It is as **you said**. Nevertheless, I say to you, hereafter you will see the Son of Man sitting at the right hand of the Power, and coming on the clouds of heaven."*
>
> *Matthew 26:63-64 NKJV e.a.*

This version shows Jesus as confirming He is the Christ, saying, *"It is as... you say."* Again however, we find the words, "It is as" have been inserted into the text. The translation should only read, *"You say"* or *"You said."*

The books of Mark and Luke also record this interaction between the high priest and Jesus. Yet, there are discrepancies between the accounts as to exactly what Jesus said in response to the high priest's question. This time, the discrepancies lie not only in the translation, but also within the original manuscript text itself.

Here are the other two accounts.

"Tell us if You are the Christ, the Son of God!"

From the book of Mark, Jesus said,

> *"**I am**. And you will see the Son of Man sitting at the right hand of the Power, and coming with the clouds of heaven."*
>
> *Mark 14:62 NKJV e.a.*

From the book of Luke, Jesus said,

> *"**You** rightly **say that I am**."*
>
> *Luke 22:70 NKJV e.a.*

The word 'rightly' has again been added into the text in this version of the account in Luke, and it should be removed. It should only read, *"You say that I am."*

From these three separate accounts of this interaction between Jesus and the high priest we see the following:

Luke recorded:	*"You say that I am."*
Matthew recorded:	*"You say."*
Mark recorded:	*"I am."*

The Luke and Matthew accounts are similar as both record Jesus as saying, *"You say."*

Luke:	*"**You say** that I am."*
Matthew:	*"**You say**."*

The accounts in Luke and Mark are also similar as both record Jesus said, *"I am."*

Luke:	*"You say that **I am**."*
Mark:	*"**I am**."*

I believe, what is recorded in the book of Luke is the accurate recording of Jesus' statement. The account in Luke includes what was recorded in both the Matthew and Mark accounts, which also Matthew and Mark omitted from each other.

When the Matthew and Mark accounts are combined, it shows Jesus saying, *"You say I am,"* exactly as Luke wrote,

> *"You say that I am."*

There is no *"I am"* declaration being made here by Jesus!

The account in Mark, as written, shows Jesus making an emphatic, "I am" declaration, saying or confirming, "I am... the Christ." Mark is correct in that Jesus did say the words, *"I am."* But the account in Mark is incomplete, because those words as spoken by Jesus cannot stand alone. Those two words, "I am" were spoken as part of the sentence, *"You say I am."*

Taken by themselves, Jesus is declaring of Himself, *"I am... the Christ."* Taken as the full sentence, Jesus is saying it is the high priest who declared Jesus is the Christ, *"You say that I am."*

These two differing accounts are not mutually supportive or interchangeable.

We cannot have one verse in Mark, that shows Jesus declaring in the first-person of Himself, an *affirmative* of *"I am."* And also have another verse in Luke, that declares to a second person, to the high priest, a *non-confirmative,* *"You say I am."*

These are two different answers, with two entirely different meanings. The meaning of one self-confirms, "Yes, I am!" The meaning of the other has no confirmation at all. It neither confirms, nor denies, who Jesus is.

Jesus did not confirm who He is; He only said, *"You say that I am."*

Because of the omission in Mark's account of these two small words, "You say" the context and meaning of Mark chapter 14, verse 62 is wrong.

Jesus did not confirm or declare *"I am the Christ."* Jesus said the high priest is the one, who declared Him the Christ.

> *"Tell us if You are the Christ, the Son of God!"*

> *"You say I am."*

You Are the King of the Jews!

Looking back at Pilate's interaction with Jesus, the translation we looked at showed Pilate asking this question,

> *"Are You the King of the Jews?"*
>
> *John 18:33 NKJV*

When we look at the original Greek text however, it shows Pilate saying it in a derisive manner, as one leader mocking another. Pilate sarcastically, asked the question this way,

> *"You are the King of the Jews?"*

Notice Pilate's words. With disdain, he spoke the words, *"You are the King of the Jews."* In Pilate's sarcasm, he himself, declares Jesus a king!

> *"You are the King of the Jews!"*

You Are the Christ, the Son of God!

Now, look at the statement made by the high priest, we see the same type of declaration by the high priest himself.

The high priest said,

> *"I put You under oath by the living God:*
> *Tell us if You are the Christ, the Son of God!"*
>
> *Matthew 26:63 NKJV*

In the high priest's anger in commanding Jesus to tell them who He is, we see it is the high priest himself, who declares who Jesus is. In his anger, the high priest spoke the words declaring Jesus is the Christ, the Son of God.

"*Tell us if...* **You are the Christ, the Son of God!**"

Pilate, the highest Roman legal authority of the land, spoke these words to Jesus,

"*You are the King of the Jews!*"

The high priest, the highest Jewish religious authority of the land, spoke these words to Jesus,

"*You are the Christ, the Son of God!*"

And now we understand why, to both of these "supreme" rulers, Jesus only replied,

"**You say**... *that I am!*"

You Say, I Said, I Am

We are now going to see Jesus display His mastery of the law and language as He utterly confounds the Jews. Jesus will still be using this same pattern of speech in the form of, "*You say I am.*"

The Jews had just said to Jesus,

> *If You are the Christ, tell us plainly.*

Jesus replied,

> "*I told you, and you do not believe.*

As Jesus finished speaking, He said to them,

> *I and My Father are one.*"

It then says,

> *Then the Jews took up stones again to stone Him.*

Jesus said to the Jews,

> *"Many good works I have shown you from My Father. For which of those works do you stone Me?"*

The Jews answered and said,

> *"For a good work we do not stone You, but for blasphemy, and because You, being a Man, make Yourself God."*

Then Jesus said,

> *"Is it not written in your law, 'I said, "You are gods"'?*
> *If He called them gods, to whom the word of God came*
> *(and the Scripture cannot be broken),*
> *do you say of Him whom the Father sanctified and sent into the world,*
> *'You are blaspheming,' because I said, 'I am the Son of God'?*

John 10:24-25, 30-36 NKJV

This appears to be one instance where Jesus does say, *"I am the Son of God."*

In the preceding dialogue however, Jesus only said, *"I and My Father are one."* Prior to this we do not find anywhere that Jesus in fact said, *"I am the Son of God."* So, what is happening here?

This is fascinating, watch what Jesus is doing.

The Jews were getting ready to stone Jesus for blasphemy. Then Jesus, using their own Scriptures as a legal basis, gives them a question and riddle.

He said,

> *"Is it not written in your law, 'I said, "You are gods"'?"*

Jesus points out that in their own law they themselves are called gods. He then uses this for His own defense.

For Jesus' legal defense, He creates a direct comparison and contrast between the fact that in their law, they are called gods, and what they are accusing Him of, that is, breaking this same law by claiming He is the Son of God.

To paraphrase,

> *If you are called gods, am I blaspheming,*
> *because I said, 'I am the Son of God'?*

If God has called them gods, or if they themselves are all sons of God, He certainly cannot be blaspheming simply because He said He is the Son of God. This presented an impenetrable legal and logical defense which the Jews could not dispute.

Next, notice the similarity between the Scripture that Jesus quoted and the words He spoke that followed; both say, "*I said.*"

> "*Is it not written in your law, '**I said**, "You are gods"'?*"

And,

> "*because **I said**, 'I am the Son of God'?*"

This is a clue to what Jesus is doing and the, "*I said,*" is the key.

Jesus spoke the words, "*I said, you are gods.*" However, Jesus is not making this declaration Himself. We know Jesus is quoting a Scripture verse; He clearly said, "*Is it **not** written*… *'I said, "You are gods"'?*"

If we now apply this same understanding to the rest of what Jesus said, we will see He is saying exactly the same thing.

Jesus is not quoting what *He said*; Jesus is quoting what *they said*.

Since Jesus spoke the words, "*I said, 'I am the Son of God,'*" it does appear as though Jesus is making a declaration of Himself. However, Jesus was not making a declaration at all; He was asking a question.

Jesus was not telling them something; He was *asking* them something.

Jesus asked the Jews this question, "*Do you say…?*"

And every word that follows, is part of that one single question.

> "**Do you say…**
> *of Him whom the Father sanctified and sent into the world,*
> *'You are blaspheming,' because I said, 'I am the Son of God'?*"

Notice how Jesus structured this question. He said to them,

> *Do you say of* **Him** *(Him – speaking in the third-person of*
> *Himself) whom the Father sanctified and sent into the world,*
> *'* **You** *are blaspheming,' (You – speaking in the second-person of*
> *Himself)*
> *because* **I** *said, (I – speaking in the first-person of Himself)*
> *'I am the Son of God'?*

Jesus brilliantly asks them a question while speaking of Himself in the first, second, and third-persons of *I*, *You*, and *Him*.

> *Do you say of Him…?*

This extra text, this extra verbiage Jesus spoke, added no clarity to the question; to the contrary, it made the question complex. The references to *I*, *You*, and *Him*, contained within this question, had no other purpose except to confuse those looking to stone Jesus.

We can divide this question into several separate parts:

> **"Do you say…**
> *(of Him whom the Father sanctified and sent into the world,)*
> *('You are blaspheming,')*
> *(because I said, 'I am the Son of God')?"*

If we reduce the sentence to its primary parts, we clearly see the following:

> *"Do you say…, because I said, I am the Son of God?"*

The word "*because*" can also be translated as "*that*."

> *"Do you say…,* **that** *I said, I am the Son of God?"*

If we also remove "*that*" or "*because*" from the sentence we can now easily see what Jesus is truly saying.

> *"Do you say…, 'I said, I am the Son of God'?"*

Just as Jesus was quoting a Scripture verse when He said,

> *"Is it not written…, '* **I said**, *you are gods'?"*

Even so, Jesus is quoting the Jews when He said,

> *"Do you say..., 'I said, I am the Son of God'?"*

Jesus is only quoting what the Jews themselves were saying. It is the same as saying,

> *"You say, 'I said, I am'!"*

If you happen to think Jesus is playing semantics with words, you would be absolutely correct; that is *exactly* what He is doing!

This is the same pattern of speech we have seen Jesus use three other times.

To His disciples:	*"**You call Me** Teacher and Lord; and you are right, for so I am."*
To Pilate:	*"**You say** that I am a king."*
To the high priest:	*"**You say** that I am."*
And now to the Jews:	*"**You say**, 'I said, I am.'"*

Jesus did not declare, *"I am the Son of God."* This is not an *"I am"* declaration. Jesus only quoted to the Jews, what they were saying about Him.

> *"You say..., 'I said, I am the Son of God.'"*
> *"You say, 'I said, I am.'"*

Before Abraham Was, I Am

Here is a statement that is considered to be one of the greatest *"I am"* declarations Jesus ever made.

Jesus had just said to the Jews,

> *"Truly, truly, I say to you, if anyone keeps My word he will never see death."*

The Jews then said to Jesus,

> *"Now we know that You have a demon. Abraham died, and the prophets also; and You say, 'If anyone keeps My word, he will*

> *never taste of death.' "Surely You are not greater than our father Abraham, who died? The prophets died too;*

Then the whole interaction that follows is from this one question. The Jews asked Jesus,

> *whom do You make Yourself out to be?"*

Jesus said to them,

> *"If I glorify Myself, My glory is nothing; it is My Father who glorifies Me, of whom you say, 'He is our God'; and you have not come to know Him, but I know Him; and if I say that I do not know Him, I will be a liar like you, but I do know Him and keep His word.*

> *"Your father Abraham rejoiced to see My day, and he saw it and was glad."*

The Jews responded to Jesus and said to Him,

> *"You are not yet fifty years old, and have You seen Abraham?"*

And Jesus said,

> *"Truly, truly, I say to you, **before Abraham was born, I am**."*
>
> *John 8:51-58 NASB e.a.*

Another version says,

> *"Most assuredly, I say to you, **before Abraham was, I AM**."*
>
> *John 8:58 NKJV e.a.*

Here is quite an amazing "*I am*" statement!

In the Old Testament, Moses had asked God to tell him His name and God said to Moses,

> *"I AM WHO I AM."*

Then God said,

> *"Thus you shall say to the children of Israel, 'I AM has sent me to you.'"*
>
> *Exodus 3:14 NKJV*

The name of God is 'I AM' and now we see Jesus saying,

> *"Before Abraham was, I AM!"*

What do we say about a statement like this? Surely, Jesus is saying He is the "*I AM.*" Jesus is certainly declaring His divine nature as God, isn't He?

It is the common understanding that Jesus, by using the name of God, "*I AM*" in this manner, is referring to Himself as God. The Jews also believed this, for the next verse says they took up stones to stone Him.

> *Then they took up stones to throw at Him; but Jesus hid Himself and went out of the temple, going through the midst of them, and so passed by.*
>
> *John 8:59 NKJV*

Clearly, Jesus must be declaring He is the "*I AM.*" This is certainly how it appears. But things are not always as they seem. We need to remember what Jesus had just said to them,

> *"If I glorify Myself, My glory is nothing; it is My Father who glorifies Me"*

If Jesus was declaring He is the "*I AM,*" if Jesus was in fact declaring He is God, then He most certainly would have been glorifying Himself. Yet, this is something He has said He would not do.

So, what is Jesus doing? Something else must be happening here.

This "*I am*" term is understood to be a direct reference to God or to God's name, and correctly so. If this is to be taken as the name of God, "*I AM,*" then what did Jesus really say?

Jesus said, "*Before Abraham was, I AM.*"

If we substitute the word "*God*" for "*I AM*" (which is what the "*I AM*" refers to), then what Jesus actually said was, "*Before Abraham was, God.*"

That is a true statement!

"Before Abraham was, God."

We can also substitute other names of the Lord, such as *"Jehovah"* or *"YHWH."*

For example:

"Before Abraham was, Jehovah."

Or,

"Before Abraham was, YHWH."

All of these statements are completely accurate.
All of these statements are legally and technically correct.
All of these statements make perfect sense.
And all of these statements are exactly the same as,

"Before Abraham was, I AM."

Therefore, we see Jesus did not say He is the *"I AM"* and Jesus did not glorify Himself. He only said, *"Before Abraham was, I AM,"* which translated means,

Before Abraham was, God!

Anyone, legally and technically, can make this same statement.
Anyone can say,

Before Abraham was, I AM!

This statement by Jesus, is unquestionably a play on words. Even our current understanding of this verse recognizes it as such, with Jesus using the name of God, *"I AM."*

So, consequently, when Jesus is asked, *"Whom do you make yourself out to be?"* He does not give them a clear answer. Though it does appear He did state who He is, nevertheless, legally and technically, He did not. He only said,

"Before Abraham was born, 'God'!"

I Told You That I Am

Here is one instance when Jesus did in fact say who He is. Jesus was in the garden at night with His disciples when the Roman soldiers and Pharisees came to arrest Him.

Jesus asked them,

> *"Whom do you seek?"*
>
> *They answered Him,*
> *"Jesus the Nazarene."*
>
> *He said to them,*
> ***"I am** He."*
>
> *And Judas also, who was betraying Him, was standing with them. So when He said to them, "I am He," they drew back and fell to the ground.*
>
> *Therefore He again asked them,*
> *"Whom do you seek?"*
>
> *And they said,*
> *"Jesus the Nazarene."*
>
> *Jesus answered,*
> ***"I told you that I am** He;*
>
> *John 18:4-8 NASB e.a.*

Jesus has finally declared who He is!
Jesus has identified Himself as... Jesus; *"Jesus the Nazarene."*

> *"I told you that I am!"*

There is no *"He"* in the original manuscripts. Jesus actually only said, *"I am"* or *"I told you that I am."*

Jesus' use of *"I am"* here is also thought to be another reference to the name of God. In fact, when Jesus said, *"I am,"* everyone, including the soldiers, fell backwards to the ground. Something powerful had just happened; Jesus said, *"I AM!"*

Therefore, it is possible Jesus intended for this "*I am*" to have a dual meaning. However, He does not directly use it here as such. They are looking for Jesus and He simply says, "*I am.*"

So here is one "*I am*" statement where Jesus did say who He is.

> "*Whom do you seek?*"
> "*Jesus the Nazarene.*"
>
> "*I told you that I am.*"

Jesus has said He is Jesus!

Yet even with this, Jesus still did not directly say, "*I am Jesus.*" He only told them,

> "*I am.*"

I Know That Messiah Is Coming

Here in our final example, we find a single instance, just one instance, when Jesus truly does identify Himself as the Messiah of Israel.

Jesus was alone, without His disciples, resting near a well. A woman came to the well to draw water when Jesus began speaking with her.

> *Jesus said to her,*
> *"Give Me a drink."*
>
> *For His disciples had gone away into the city to buy food.*
>
> *Then the woman of Samaria said to Him,*
> *"How is it that You, being a Jew, ask a drink from me, a Samaritan woman?" For Jews have no dealings with Samaritans.*
>
> *Jesus answered and said to her,*
> *"If you knew the gift of God, and who it is who says to you, 'Give Me a drink,' you would have asked Him, and He would have given you living water."*

The woman said to Him,
"Sir, You have nothing to draw with, and the well is deep. Where then do You get that living water? Are You greater than our father Jacob, who gave us the well, and drank from it himself, as well as his sons and his livestock?"

Jesus answered and said to her,
"Whoever drinks of this water will thirst again, but whoever drinks of the water that I shall give him will never thirst. But the water that I shall give him will become in him a fountain of water springing up into everlasting life."

The woman said to Him,
"Sir, give me this water, that I may not thirst, nor come here to draw."

Jesus said to her,
"Go, call your husband, and come here."

The woman answered and said,
"I have no husband."

Jesus said to her,
"You have well said, 'I have no husband,' for you have had five husbands, and the one whom you now have is not your husband; in that you spoke truly."

The woman said to Him,
"Sir, I perceive that You are a prophet. Our fathers worshiped on this mountain, and you Jews say that in Jerusalem is the place where one ought to worship."

The woman recognizes she is speaking with a prophet of God and seizes upon her opportunity. There is one question she has deep in her heart.

She asks Jesus,

Where is God? Where can I worship God?

Jesus had said,

> *For where your treasure is, there your heart will be also.*
>
> Matthew 6:21 NKJV

The first words out of her mouth, out of the depth of her heart, came the *only thing* she wanted to know,

> *Where can I find God?*

Jesus saw her desire and said to her,

> *"Woman, believe Me, the hour is coming when you will neither on this mountain, nor in Jerusalem, worship the Father. You worship what you do not know; we know what we worship, for salvation is of the Jews.*
>
> *But the hour is coming, and now is, when the true worshipers will worship the Father in spirit and truth; for the Father is seeking such to worship Him. God is Spirit, and those who worship Him must worship in spirit and truth."*
>
> *The woman said to Him,*
> *"I know that Messiah is coming" (who is called Christ).*
> *"When He comes, He will tell us all things."*

And Jesus said to her,

> *"I who speak to you am He."*
>
> See John 4:7-26 NKJV

This one verse, this one self-declarative *"I am"* statement, is the only instance we find of Jesus clearly and freely saying who He truly is. Here, Jesus says He is the Messiah, the Christ!

Pay attention though, as to *how* He actually said this.

Jesus did not say, *"I am the Messiah."*
Jesus did not say, *"I am the Christ."*

What He said was,

> *"I who speak to you am He."*

Again, there is no "He" in the actual manuscript text. Jesus' actual words were,

> *"I who speak to you am."*

To paraphrase,

> *I who speak to you am, (who **you spoke of**)*

Or,

> *I who speak to you am, (who **you said**)*

This is the same pattern of speech we have seen Jesus use repeatedly.

> *I am who **you say**!*

Notice also, *to whom* Jesus made this statement declaring Himself to be the Messiah, the Christ. There was only a single person present who heard Jesus say these words. Jesus did not say this publicly. Jesus' disciples were not even there, it says in the beginning of the text,

> *His disciples had gone away into the city to buy food.*

Afterwards, when the disciples returned, it says,

> *they marveled that He talked with a woman*
>
> John 4:27 NKJV

Jesus identified Himself to a woman, not to a man, as their culture would have demanded. Furthermore, she was not even Jewish; she was a Samaritan.

> *"How is it that You, being a Jew, ask a drink from me,*
> ***a Samaritan woman?"***

If there were any doubts about the validity of Jesus concealing His identity from the Jewish people, intentionally keeping it hidden from them, this one insight, this one revelation of a prophecy Jesus made, will conclusively prove this fact once and for all.

No Prophet Is Accepted in His Own Country

At one point, Jesus had been speaking to the Jews in their synagogue and said to them,

> *"Assuredly, I say to you, no prophet is accepted in his own country.*
>
> *But I tell you truly, many widows were in Israel in the days of Elijah, when the heaven was shut up three years and six months, and there was a great famine throughout all the land; but to none of them was Elijah sent except to Zarephath, in the region of Sidon,* **to a woman who was a widow.**
>
> Luke 4:24-26 NKJV e.a.

No prophet is accepted in his own country and unto none of them in Israel was the prophet sent, except,

> *"to Zarephath, in the region of Sidon,* **to a woman who was a widow."**

Jesus said to the woman at the well,

> *"Go, call your husband, and come here."*
>
> *The woman answered and said,*
> *"I have no husband."*
>
> *Jesus said to her,*
> *"You have well said, 'I have no husband,' for you have had five husbands, and the one whom you now have is not your husband; in that you spoke truly."*

And the woman said to Jesus,

> *"Sir, I perceive that* **You are a prophet.**
>
> John 4:16-19 NKJV e.a.

No prophet is accepted in his own country and unto none of them in Israel was the prophet sent.

Except that is…

> *to a Samaritan woman,* **who was a widow!**

Jesus Declared Himself to No One in Israel

In all of Jesus' teachings throughout all of Israel, in all of His teachings to His disciples, to all of the Jews and to the many multitudes that Jesus spoke, His only declaration that He is the Christ, the Messiah of Israel, was given privately to a Samaritan woman, who was a widow.

"I know that Messiah is coming" (who is called Christ).
"When He comes, He will tell us all things."

"I who speak to you am He!"

ACT 6 VIGNETTE

No One Knows the Son!

J ESUS CHRIST, SON OF THE FATHER, THE SON OF GOD. We know Jesus is the Son of God. Every Christian born again knows this truth. We know this now, but there was a time when no one knew it. The Jewish people did not know Jesus as the Son of God.

In all the interactions Jesus had with the people, He never told them, "I am the Son" or, "I am the Son of God." We will see when Jesus speaks of the Son, He talks only figuratively. He speaks of the Son using only third-person references, as though He is speaking of someone else.

Speaking to the crowds, Jesus said,

> All things have been delivered to Me by My Father, and **no one knows the Son** except the Father. Nor does anyone know the Father except the Son, and the one to whom the Son wills to reveal Him.
>
> Matthew 11:27 NKJV e.a.

Jesus tells the people about the Son, but does not tell them who the Son is. Instead, He tells them…

"No one knows the Son!"

Welcome to Act 6 – The Son

Act 6

The Son

No One Knows

LOOKING MORE CLOSELY AT THIS PASSAGE, notice that Jesus initially speaks of Himself specifically in the first-person and speaks of the Father, calling Him, "*My Father.*"

> "*All things have been delivered to **Me** by **My Father***"

However, Jesus then makes a shift and begins speaking in the third-person of, "*the Son.*"

> "*and no one knows **the Son** except the Father.*
> *Nor does anyone know the Father except **the Son**,*
> *and the one to whom **the Son** wills to reveal Him.*"

Jesus, by inference, identified Himself as the Son when He said the Father is *His* Father. Yet, this is as close as He gets to speaking of Himself as the Son. All other references to the Son are now in the third-person, as though He is now speaking of someone else

> "*And **no one knows the Son** except the Father.*"

Jesus is the Son. Jesus could have given this message speaking entirely of Himself in the first-person and said,

> "*And no one knows (**Me**) except the Father.*
> *Nor does anyone know the Father except (**Me**),*
> *and the one to whom (**I**) will to reveal Him.*"

Here are three other examples of Jesus speaking in this same manner.

Of That Day and Hour No One Knows

Jesus was speaking to His disciples about end time events and said,

> "*Now learn the parable from the fig tree: when its branch has already become tender and puts forth its leaves, you know that*

159

> *summer is near; so, you too, when you see all these things, recognize that He is near, right at the door.*
>
> *"Truly I say to you, this generation will not pass away until all these things take place. "Heaven and earth will pass away, but My words will not pass away.*

And then He said,

> *"But of that day and hour no one knows, not even the angels of heaven, nor **the Son**, but the Father alone.*
>
> *Matthew 24:32-36 NASB e.a.*

Here, Jesus speaks in the third-person of *"the Son,"* yet, He is actually speaking of Himself. Jesus could have spoken in the first-person and said,

> *"But of that day and hour no one knows, not even the angels of heaven, nor **(I)**, but the Father alone."*

The Son Shall Make You Free

This is a very well-known passage. Jesus speaking to the Jews said,

> *"Truly, truly, I say to you, everyone who commits sin is the slave of sin. "And the slave does not remain in the house forever; **the son** does remain forever.*
>
> *"If therefore **the Son** shall make you free, you shall be free indeed.*
>
> *John 8:34-36 NASB e.a.*

Jesus is the Son, yet, He does not directly speak of Himself. He could have given this message speaking in the first-person. This is the true meaning of His message; Jesus could have said,

> *"And the slave does not remain in the house forever;*
> ***(I)** do remain forever.*
> *If therefore **(I)** shall make you free, you shall be free indeed."*

For God So Loved the World

Here is one of the most familiar and beloved passages in the entire Bible. It is certainly, by far, the greatest evangelistic message that has ever been written or spoken.

Jesus said to Nicodemus,

> "For God so loved the world, that He gave His only begotten **Son**, that whoever believes in **Him** shall not perish, but have eternal life. "For God did not send **the Son** into the world to judge the world, but that the world might be saved through **Him**.

John 3:16-17 NASB e.a.

Jesus delivers a truly wonderful message of God's love: *"For God so loved the world...."* Notice however, how the message was delivered. Jesus goes on to say, *"that He gave His only begotten **Son**."* Jesus speaks using only third-person references to the *"Son"*; He does not mention or speak directly of Himself.

*"that whoever believes in **Him** shall not perish, but have eternal life."*

We know, and take for granted, that Jesus is the Son. We may even take for granted Jesus speaking this way in the third-person. However, we need to remember the people during this time did not know Jesus is the Son. Nobody, except the disciples, knew this.

Not once, did Jesus ever plainly or directly say He is the Son or declare, *"I am the Son."* Now, add to this, what Jesus is doing here...

This message *about* the Son, was spoken *by* the Son. This message, *as spoken by Jesus*, is exactly how someone else, someone *other than the Son*, would say it.

Imagine for a moment if you will, Jesus, while speaking these words to Nicodemus, gesturing with His hand, pointing towards someone standing off in the distance.

Pointing towards that person, Jesus says,

> *"For God so loved the world, that He gave His only begotten* **Son,** *that whoever believes in* **Him***...* (Him..., that person over there) *shall not perish, but have eternal life. "For God did not send* (Him), **the Son** (that person), *into the world to judge the world, but that the world might be saved through* **Him.** (that person... over there!)

This message, as spoken by Jesus about the Son, is exactly how someone *who is not the Son* would say it. This is how *we* would say it; this is in fact, exactly how we do say it! We quote Jesus verbatim when telling others about God's love.

We say to them,

> *"For God so loved the world, that He gave His only begotten Son, that whoever believes in Him shall not perish, but have eternal life!"*

That is how we say it today, because we are speaking of *Him!* We are speaking of Jesus, the Son. Jesus said it exactly the same way we say it. He was speaking of Himself, yet, spoke only of *"Him."*

When Jesus speaks of the Son in the third-person, He is directing the attention of the people away from Himself and pointing them towards the Son. He is concealing His identity. He speaks as though telling them, *"I am not the Son!"*

This is important and needs to be understood. This is one of the reasons the Jewish people did not recognize Jesus as their Messiah.

Jesus is intentionally directing the attention of the people away from Himself. Those hearing Jesus speak this way would come away with the natural and expected impression that Jesus was speaking of someone else, that Jesus is not this person, "the Son," of whom He is speaking.

It would literally have the same effect as if Jesus had actually said to them, "I am not the Son; that person over there, *He… is the Son.*"

> *"Whoever believes in **Him** (that person), shall not perish, but have eternal life."*

When Jesus gave this message however, He was indeed speaking of Himself. This is the true meaning of His message; this is what He could… have said,

> *"For God so loved the world, that He gave (**Me**), His only begotten Son, that whoever believes in (**Me**) shall not perish, but have eternal life.*

That is the wonderful truth of His message. Notice the difference, notice the clarity of how that sounds, compared to how He actually said it.

> *"whoever believes in (**Me**) shall not perish, but have eternal life."*

Versus,

> *"whoever believes in (**Him**)…*

Whether speaking in the first-person, or third-person, the meaning is the same. But the first-person message is clear, the other is not.

It would have been much easier for Jesus to give the message in the first-person, rather than speak in the third-person of the Son as He did. If Jesus had delivered the message this way, it would have been absolutely clear; the message would have been plain and simple. Everyone would have easily understood who Jesus is, if… He had spoken this way.

But He did not!

Jesus intentionally spoke in the third-person of the Son, rather than speak of Himself.

Today, many things in the Bible are so well known and familiar to us that we have a tendency to take them for granted. We take for granted that Jesus is the Son. It is so clearly obvious to us that Jesus is speaking of Himself when He speaks of the Son, that we do not for even a moment consider what He is doing; we never give it a second thought.

However, we need to be mindful of the fact that Jesus said,

> *"No one knows the Son."*
> *No one!*

Connections to the Son

In Act 1, we found details within prophecies that could be used as references to other prophecies. The meaning of the prophecies, when taken individually, remained a riddle. However, when those prophecies were added together, we gained additional insight into their meanings.

Now watch what Jesus does here…

Jesus said,

> *"For God did not send the Son into the world to judge the world,*
> *but that the world might be saved through Him.*
>
> *John 3:17 NASB*

Jesus spoke only of the Son here, He did not mention Himself. On another occasion however, Jesus said of Himself,

> *I did not come to judge the world but to save the world.*
>
> *John 12:47 NKJV*

Notice the similarity between these two statements, except for the subject of whom the statements are speaking, they are nearly identical. In the first, Jesus speaks of the Son; in the second, Jesus speaks of Himself.

The Son	*(was not sent)* **to judge the world, but that the world might be saved**
I	*did not come* **to judge the world, but to save the world**

We can actually exchange the subjects in these two sentences and it would not change their meanings at all. They both would still say exactly the same thing.

I	*(was not sent)* **to judge the world, but that the world might be saved**
The Son	*did not come* **to judge the world, but to save the world**

When Jesus said of Himself,

> *"I did not come to judge the world but to save the world."*

He was making a connection, or giving us a reference back to the similar statement He had also made about the Son.

By making these two similar statements, Jesus is identifying Himself as the Son. In one statement He speaks of the Son, in another He speaks of Himself, and both statements point towards one another.

> *The latter statement points to the first, and the first to the last.*

The Son Was Sent

Jesus, speaking of the Son, said,

> *"For God so loved the world, that He gave His only begotten Son, that whoever believes in Him shall not perish, but have eternal life. "For God did not **send the Son** into the world to judge the world, but that the world might be saved through Him. "He who believes in Him is not judged;*
>
> *John 3:16-18 NASB e.a.*

Here Jesus says the Son was sent.

> *"For God did not **send the Son**..."*

Later, Jesus speaking of Himself said,

> *"Truly, truly, I say to you, he who hears My word, and believes Him who **sent Me**, has eternal life, and does not come into judgment, but has passed out of death into life.*
>
> *John 5:24 NASB e.a.*

Here Jesus says He was sent.

*"he who hears My word, and believes Him who **sent Me**..."*

There are key words being used here, *send* or *sent, eternal life,* and *judgment.* Jesus used each of these in both statements.

He who believes in **(the Son who was sent)**,	has **eternal life** and is not **judged**.
He who believes Him who **(sent Me)**,	has **eternal life**, and does not come into **judgment**.

Jesus, by speaking of Himself being sent, is directing us to what He had also said about the Son being sent. He is joining the two statements and making the connection of Himself to the Son.

Here is one final, wonderful example.

This Is Eternal Life

Jesus, on the last night He would be with His disciples, lifted His eyes towards heaven and prayed,

> *"Father, the hour has come. Glorify Your Son, that Your Son also may glorify You, as You have given Him authority over all flesh, that He should give eternal life to as many as You have given Him.*

And then He said,

> **And this is eternal life, that they may know** *You, the only true* *God, and* **Jesus Christ whom You have sent.**

> *John 17:1-3 NKJV e.a.*

This is eternal life, that they may know Jesus Christ, whom You sent.

He who believes in **(the Son who was sent)**,	has **eternal life**
He who believes Him who **sent Me**,	has **eternal life**
This is **eternal life**,	that they may know **Jesus Christ, whom You sent.**

Teaching us about eternal life, Jesus spoke of Himself in three different ways.

> *The Son was sent.*
> *He was sent.*

And,

> *Jesus Christ was sent.*

> **"This is eternal life,** ...
> *that they may know Me, Jesus Christ, the Son, whom You sent!"*

This is eternal life, that we may know Jesus Christ, the Son, who was sent.

Father, Glorify Your Son

Jesus asked His Father to glorify the Son, so the Son may give us eternal life.

> *"Father, the hour has come.* **Glorify Your Son** ...
> **that He should give eternal life** *to as many as You have given Him."*

Jesus made this request to glorify the Son on our behalf, so we might have eternal life.

Father, Glorify Me

Jesus then made a request of His own. Speaking of Himself, for Himself, Jesus said to His Father,

> *I have glorified You on the earth. I have finished the work which You have given Me to do. And now, O* **Father,** **glorify Me** *together with Yourself, with the glory which I had with You before the world was.*
>
> *John 17:4-5 NKJV e.a.*

Jesus had said He would not glorify Himself; He said His Father would glorify Him. Now, being at the end of His life, Jesus asks His Father to glorify Him.

> *"Father, glorify Me…*
> *with the glory which I had with You before the world was."*

This request Jesus made for Himself.

Even in this prayer to His Father, Jesus did not say, *"Father, I am your Son."* Jesus spoke of the Son in the third-person, and made a request specifically for *"the Son."* Then, Jesus made a separate, personal request specifically for Himself.

But what He said of Himself, He also said of the Son!

Jesus did in fact say He is the Son, it was just in *the way* He said it.

> *"Father, glorify your Son, glorify Me."*

Speaking of Himself, He Spoke of the Son

When Jesus gave us this wonderful message and said,

> *"For God so loved the world, that He gave His only begotten Son,*
> *that whoever believes in Him shall not perish, but have eternal life."*

though He spoke only of the Son, we know He was actually speaking of Himself.

And when Jesus said,

> *"He who hears My word, and believes Him who sent Me, has*
> *eternal life"*

though He spoke only of Himself, we know He was actually speaking of the Son.

He was pointing us to the Son!

> *Jesus, **speaking only of the Son**, spoke of Himself.*
> *Jesus, **speaking only of Himself**, spoke of the Son.*

These similar statements Jesus made, point towards one another, so they might tell us, so we might see, that Jesus is the Son. We may take it for granted today, but the Jewish people never recognized what Jesus had said to them!

Jesus did in fact say He is the Son.

It was just in the way He said it.

"*For God so loved the world, that He gave* **Me***, His only begotten* **Son***, that whoever believes in* **Me** *shall not perish, but have eternal life. For God did not send* **Me** *into the world to judge the world, but that the world might be saved through...* **Me**."

Jesus Christ, the Son

ACT 7 VIGNETTE

The Son of Man

THE TERM, "SON OF MAN," IS ANOTHER NAME OR TITLE JESUS frequently used. It simply means, *"of man"* or *"born of man"*; it speaks of one's humanity.

Every person living today could be referred to as *"a son, or daughter, of man."* The term *"son of man,"* because it is so general in nature, is almost insignificant in its use. When Jesus uses it, it is at times taken for granted. Nevertheless, there is something very special about the title, *"Son of Man,"* as Jesus uses it.

Here we will see Jesus refers to *"the Son of Man"* only in the third-person, while never directly referring to Himself as the Son of Man.

When Jesus was before the high priest, the high priest said to Him,

> *Tell us if You are the Christ,* **the Son of God!**

As previously seen, Jesus replied,

> **"You say...** *that I am."*

He then went on to say,

> *Nevertheless, I say to you, hereafter you will see* **the Son of Man**
> *sitting at the right hand of the Power, and coming on the clouds of*
> *heaven.*
>
> See Luke 22:70 and Matthew 26:63-64 NKJV e.a. par.

Notice the two different names being used here: The high priest asks Jesus if He is *"the Son of God,"* yet, Jesus responds by saying,

> *"hereafter you will see* **the Son of Man**...*"*

Jesus could have replied,

> *"you will see* **the Son of God**...*"*

Or even perhaps,

> *"you will see* **Me**...*"*

But that is not what Jesus said!

Welcome to Act 7 – He Said, "the Son of Man"

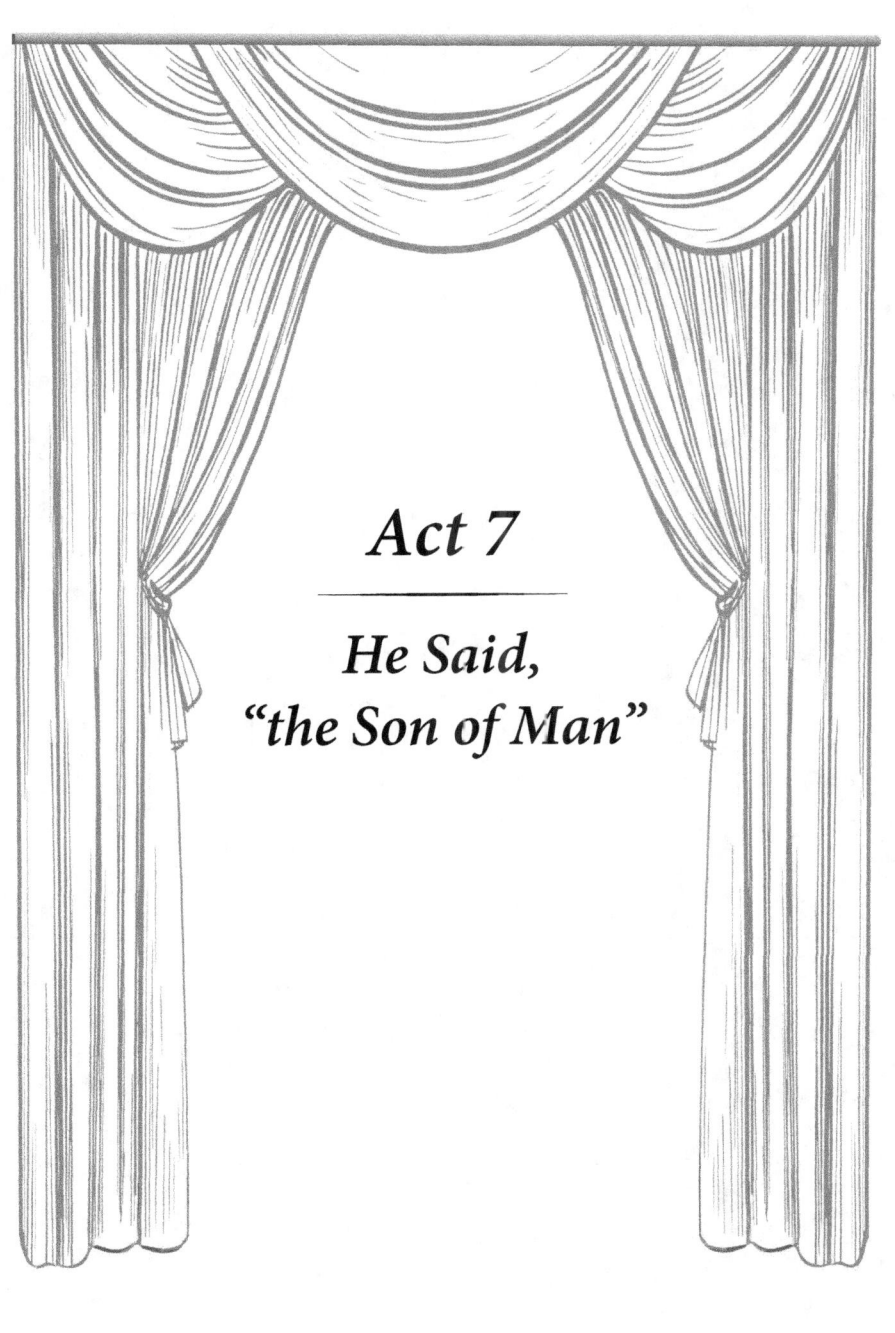

Act 7

He Said, "the Son of Man"

THE SON OF GOD, HE IS THE SON OF MAN

JESUS, SPEAKING TO THE JEWS, SAID,

> *Most assuredly, I say to you, the hour is coming, and now is, when the dead will hear the voice of **the Son of God**; and those who hear will live.*
>
> *For as the Father has life in Himself, so He has granted the Son to have life in Himself, and has given Him authority to execute judgment also, because **He is the Son of Man**.*

John 5:25-27 NKJV e.a.

Jesus identifies the Son of God as the Son of Man, yet, notice *how* He said it. Jesus did not say, *"The Son of God is the Son of Man."* He instead spoke of the Son of God indirectly by saying, *"**He**... is the Son of Man."*

Notice also how He speaks of the two names. Jesus mentions the Son of God at the beginning of His message, and the Son of Man at the end. This separation of the two names within His message is intentional.

There are many details clearly stated in this message. But there is one detail, more important than all the others, that is not so clearly stated. It is told in two different parts, with other details inserted between.

> *Most assuredly, I say to you, the hour is coming, and now is, when the dead will hear the voice of **the Son of God**;*

> *and those who hear will live. For as the Father has life in Himself, so He has granted the Son to have life in Himself, and has given Him authority to execute judgment also,*

> *because **He is the Son of Man**.*

Jesus does not clearly or plainly say, "the Son of God is the Son of Man." Yet, that is the primary message presented here. This simple message is found within the entirety of the message. It is in fact, a message within a message.

This one passage, even with all of the extra detail, contains one of the clearest, most direct statements Jesus makes showing the identity of someone as the Son of Man.

> *"The Son of God, He is the Son of Man."*

Jesus told the Jews and His disciples a parable about the kingdom of heaven.

Jesus said,

> *"The kingdom of heaven is like a man who sowed good seed in his field; but while men slept, his enemy came and sowed tares among the wheat and went his way.*

Jesus' disciples came to Him afterwards and said,

> *"Explain to us the parable of the tares of the field."*

Jesus answered and said to them,

> *"He who sows the good seed is **the Son of Man**. The field is the world, the good seeds are the sons of the kingdom, but the tares are the sons of the wicked one.*
>
> *Matthew 13:24-25, 36-38 NKJV e.a.*

Jesus has just identified someone else as the Son of Man.

> *"**He who sows the good seed** is the Son of Man."*

At this point we have two people identified as the Son of Man:

> *"The Son of God, He **is the Son of Man**."*

And,

> *"He who sows the good seed **is the Son of Man**."*

But exactly who this *"Son of Man"* is, has not yet been revealed.

As they were on their way to Jerusalem Jesus took His disciples aside to speak with them. Jesus said,

> *"Behold, we are going up to Jerusalem, and **the Son of Man** will be betrayed to the chief priests and to the scribes; and they will condemn Him to death and deliver Him to the Gentiles; and they will mock Him, and scourge Him, and spit on Him, and kill Him. And the third day He will rise again."*
>
> Mark 10:33-34 NKJV e.a.

Today we know Jesus was speaking of Himself when He said this. It was Jesus who would be condemned, mocked, spit on, scourged and crucified. It was Jesus who would three days later, *"rise again."* There is no question who this is referring to. Jesus is the Son of Man.

Nevertheless, notice *how* Jesus spoke. He did not speak directly of Himself. He only mentioned *"the Son of Man"* and spoke only of *"Him"* in the third-person.

> *"**The Son of Man** will be betrayed to the chief priests."*
> *"They will kill **Him**. And the third day **He** will rise again."*

Jesus called His disciples and a crowd of people to gather around Him. Jesus said to them,

> *For whoever is ashamed of **Me** and My words in this adulterous and sinful generation, of him **the Son of Man** also will be ashamed when He comes in the glory of His Father with the holy angels.*
>
> Mark 8:38 NKJV e.a.

Notice what Jesus is doing, He first speaks of *Himself*, then speaks of someone He calls, *"the Son of Man."* Jesus spoke, *as though*, He was speaking of someone else. This would give the impression the Son of Man is someone other than Jesus.

> *"Whoever is ashamed of **Me**, **the Son of Man** will be ashamed of him."*

We know Jesus is speaking of Himself. He could have spoken in the first-person and said,

> *"For whoever is ashamed of Me and My words in this adulterous and sinful generation, of him (**I**) also will be ashamed when (**I**) come in the glory of (**My**) Father with the holy angels."*

> *He speaks as though, He is speaking of someone else.*

Jesus said to those who had gathered around Him,

> *I say to you, whoever confesses **Me** before men, him **the Son of Man** also will confess before the angels of God. But he who denies Me before men will be denied before the angels of God.*
>
> Luke 12:8-9 NKJV e.a.

Again, Jesus speaks of Himself first, then speaks of someone else He calls, "*the Son of Man*." Jesus was speaking of Himself here. He could have said it this way,

> *"I say to you, whoever confesses Me before men,*
> *(**I**) also will confess him before the angels of God."*

In these last two passages, Jesus deliberately mentions Himself alongside of, or contrasted with, the Son of Man.

> *"Whoever is ashamed of Me, the Son of Man will be ashamed of him."*
> *"Whoever confesses Me, the Son of Man will confess him."*

> *He spoke as though, He spoke of someone else.*

Jesus said to His disciples,

> *"Assuredly I say to you, that in the regeneration, when **the Son of Man** sits on the throne of His glory, you who have followed **Me** will also sit on twelve thrones, judging the twelve tribes of Israel.*
>
> Matthew 19:28 NKJV e.a.

Here again Jesus speaks of *the Son of Man*, then speaks of *Himself*.

Notice, Jesus did not say *"I"* will sit on *"the throne of My glory."*
Jesus specifically said, *"the Son of Man"* will sit on *"the throne of His glory."*

Here we have seen three instances that would give the impression that Jesus *is not* the Son of Man. Jesus very deliberately speaks of Himself, then contrasts this by speaking separately of the Son of Man.

Jesus speaks as though He is speaking of two separate and distinct persons:

Himself, and someone else named, *the Son of Man.*

Here are several other examples showing Jesus speaking only of the Son of Man.

> *And as Moses lifted up the serpent in the wilderness,*
> *even so must **the Son of Man** be lifted up,*
> *that whoever believes in Him should not perish but have*
> *eternal life.*
>
> John 3:14-15 NKJV e.a.

> *What then if you should see **the Son of Man** ascend where He was*
> *before?*
>
> John 6:62 NKJV e.a.

> *No one has ascended to heaven but He who came down from*
> *heaven, that is, **the Son of Man***
>
> John 3:13 NKJV e.a.

> ***the Son of Man** did not come to be served, but to serve, and to*
> *give His life a ransom for many.*
>
> Matthew 20:28 NKJV e.a.

Jesus speaks to His disciples about faith and says,

> *when **the Son of Man** comes, will He find faith on the earth?*
>
> Luke 18:8 NASB e.a.

Notice, Jesus did not say,

> *"when **(I)** come, will **(I)** find faith on the earth?"*

He specifically said,

> *"when **the Son of Man** comes, will **He** find faith on the earth?"*

As a last example, Jesus speaking privately to His disciples said,

> *"Now **the Son of Man** is glorified, and God is glorified in Him. If God is glorified in Him, God will also glorify Him in Himself, and glorify Him immediately.*

John 13:31-32 NKJV e.a.

Jesus specifically speaks of the Son of Man being glorified. He does not directly speak of Himself.

We have now seen numerous instances, where Jesus intentionally does not identify Himself as the Son of Man. In three of these instances, Jesus speaks of Himself, then separately mentions the Son of Man. In eight of the passages, Jesus makes no mention of Himself at all, but speaks specifically, *and only*, of the Son of Man.

Jesus Glorifies the Son of Man

In all of these passages we have read, Jesus could have spoken directly of Himself, yet He did not. As previously seen, Jesus said He would not glorify Himself. He intentionally avoided testifying of and bringing glory to Himself.

However...

Jesus *will* testify of the Son of Man.

To the high priest, Jesus said,

> *Nevertheless, I say to you, hereafter you will see **the Son of Man sitting at the right hand of the Power, and coming on the clouds of heaven.***

Matthew 26:64 NKJV e.a.

Jesus is testifying to the greatness of the Son of Man; He is glorifying the Son of Man.

He did not say,

> "you will see (**Me**) sitting at the right hand of the Power."

If Jesus had said this, He would have been testifying of, and glorifying Himself. Instead, He testifies of and glorifies the Son of Man.

Here are some examples showing Jesus speaking of the glory of the Son of Man.

> "When **the Son of Man** comes in **His glory**, and all the holy angels with Him, then He will sit on **the throne of His glory**.
>
> Matthew 25:31 NKJV e.a.

> Then they will see **the Son of Man** coming in the clouds with **great power and glory**.
>
> Mark 13:26 NKJV e.a.

> For whoever is ashamed of Me and My words, of him **the Son of Man** will be ashamed when He comes in **His own glory**, and in His Father's, and of the holy angels.
>
> Luke 9:26 NKJV e.a.

> For **the Son of Man** will come in **the glory** of **His** Father with **His** angels
>
> Matthew 16:27 NKJV e.a.

In these passages Jesus speaks of the Son of Man coming in the clouds with great power and glory. He speaks of the Son of Man sitting on His glorious throne. He speaks of the Son of Man coming in the glory of the Father with His angels.

Jesus speaks of the glory of the Son of Man, yet, He does not glorify Himself.

They Took the Son of Man for Granted

Jesus at times spoke as though He was not the Son of Man. However, Jesus used the term, "the Son of Man," so frequently, that many times the disciples simply took it for granted He was speaking of Himself.

Here are some examples.

In the books of Mark and Luke there are nearly identical accounts of Jesus telling His disciples the Son of Man was to suffer and be killed.

In the book of Mark, it says,

> *And He began to teach them that **the Son of Man** must suffer many things and be rejected by the elders and the chief priests and the scribes, and be killed, and after three days rise again.*
>
> Mark 8:31 NASB e.a.

In the book of Luke, it also says,

> *"**The Son of Man** must suffer many things, and be rejected by the elders and chief priests and scribes, …*
>
> Luke 9:22 NKJV e.a. par.

Both of these accounts record Jesus as saying,

> *"**The Son of Man** must suffer many things"*

If we look at the same account in the book of Matthew however, we see something slightly different.

Matthew wrote,

> *From that time Jesus began to show to His disciples that **He** must go to Jerusalem, and suffer many things from the elders and chief priests and scribes, and be killed, and be raised the third day.*
>
> Matthew 16:21 NKJV e.a.

Both Mark and Luke record Jesus as saying "*the Son of Man*" would suffer and be killed. However, Matthew comments that Jesus began to show His disciples that "*He*," Jesus Himself, would suffer and be killed.

Jesus did not say, "*He*" would suffer and be killed.
Jesus said, "*the Son of Man*" would suffer and be killed.

The point is this: To the disciples, the term, "*the Son of Man*," was so synonymous with Jesus Himself, that when He said, "*the Son of Man*," they heard Him speak as though He was speaking of *Himself*.

Notice, this is a <u>reversal</u> from how Jesus actually spoke. When Jesus spoke of the Son of Man,

> *He spoke as though He was speaking of someone else.*

Look at Peter's response after Jesus told His disciples *"the Son of Man"* was to suffer and be killed. Both Matthew and Mark point out that Peter then took Jesus aside and rebuked Him.

Peter said to Jesus,

> *"Far be it from You, Lord; this shall not happen to You!"*
>
> *Matthew 16:22 NKJV*

Notice, Peter says, *"This shall not happen to **You**."*

This is what is being shown: Even though Jesus said *"the Son of Man"* was going to suffer and be killed, the disciples understood it to mean (*and took it for granted to mean*) that Jesus was simply speaking of Himself.

Mark, one of the two writers who correctly recognized that Jesus did say, *"the Son of Man,"* also then went on to say He was stating the matter plainly.

> *And He began to teach them that **the Son of Man** must suffer many things and be rejected by the elders and the chief priests and the scribes, and be killed, and after three days rise again.*
>
> ***And He was stating the matter plainly.***
>
> *Mark 8:31-32 NASB e.a.*

Although He spoke only in third-person reference of *"the Son of Man,"* Mark says Jesus was *"stating the matter plainly."*

Let's take a closer look.

Mark writes,

> *Then He took the twelve aside again and began to tell them the things that would happen to **Him**:*

> *"Behold, we are going up to Jerusalem, and* **the Son of Man** *will be betrayed to the chief priests and to the scribes; and they will condemn Him to death and deliver Him to the Gentiles*
>
> Mark 10:32-33 NKJV e.a.

Mark says Jesus began to tell the disciples, *things that would happen to* **Him**.

However, this is not entirely accurate. Jesus did not tell the disciples "*He*" would be delivered to the chief priests. Jesus *specifically* said this would happen to, "*the Son of Man.*" But Mark says Jesus was speaking of *Himself*.

When Jesus came down from the mountain after His transfiguration, He spoke to the disciples about the Son of Man.

Mark wrote the following,

> *And as they were coming down from the mountain, He gave them orders not to relate to anyone what they had seen, until* **the Son of Man** *should rise from the dead.*
>
> *And they seized upon that statement, discussing with one another* **what rising from the dead might mean.**
>
> Mark 9:9-10 NASB e.a.

Jesus told the disciples they were not to tell anyone what they had seen,

> *"until the Son of Man should rise from the dead."*

Mark records the disciples then began discussing with each other,

> *"what rising from the dead might mean."*

Notice, there is no mention at all of what, "*the Son of Man*" might mean. There is only a discussion of what, "*rising from the dead*" might mean.

The disciples do not question the term, "*the Son of Man*" or Jesus' use of it. It does not seem strange or odd to them that Jesus, though speaking of Himself, is speaking in third-person references of the Son of Man. The disciples do not question this at all.

They thought He was stating the matter plainly!

> *They heard Him speak of the Son of Man, as though He spoke of Himself.*

It is so clearly evident Jesus is speaking of Himself when He speaks of the Son of Man, that we might wonder, "Why spend so much time on something that seems so plainly obvious?"

Because, that is exactly the point;

> *It is too obvious!*

Jesus used the term, *"the Son of Man"* so frequently, the disciples did not even question who He was referring to. There was never any discussion among the disciples as to who the Son of Man might be.

We take it for granted that Jesus is the Son of Man.
The disciples also took it for granted.

The point is this: If it is so obvious to the disciples that *Jesus is the Son of Man*, and, if it is so clearly understood by them that *Jesus is the Son of Man*, then, why doesn't Jesus simply speak of Himself in the first-person, at least to His disciples?

Because something has been hidden, and something is being made known.

> *Something is being highlighted!*

This is one of those simple things even a child could see. The intentional use is so unconcealed, its meaning so transparent, we do not pay any attention to it; we just walk on by.

> *"Jesus is the Son of Man. Nothing to see here, move along!"*

Here is another example where the disciples take for granted that Jesus is speaking of the Son of Man.

Jesus asked His disciples,

> *"Who do people say that the Son of Man is?"*

> *And they said,*
> *"Some say John the Baptist; and others, Elijah;*
> *but still others, Jeremiah, or one of the prophets."*

Then Jesus asked them,

> *"But who do you say that I am?"*

And Peter answered,

> *"You are the Christ, the Son of the living God."*
>
> *Matthew 16:13-16 NASB*

This conversation was also recorded in the books of Mark and Luke. Look at what they wrote.

In the book of Mark, it says,

> *"Who do people say that I am?"*
>
> *Mark 8:27 NASB*

In the book of Luke, it likewise says,

> *"Who do the people say that I am?"*
>
> *Luke 9:18 NASB*

Notice these two versions quote Jesus as saying, *"Who do people say that **I am**?"* and not as Matthew wrote, *"Who do people say that **the Son of Man is**?"*

Matthew records that Jesus said, *"the Son of Man."*
Mark and Luke both say He said, *"I."*

There is also one other translation of the book of Matthew that reads as follows,

> *"Who do men say that I, the Son of Man, am?"*
>
> *Matthew 16:13 NKJV*

There is however, a very definite problem with this particular manuscript version and translation.

If…, Jesus had said, *"Who do men say that **I, (the Son of Man), am**?"* Jesus would have been directly identifying Himself as the Son of Man.

This would be the same as saying, "*I am the Son of Man.*"

"*I, the Son of Man, am.*"

It is recorded over 80 times in the Gospel accounts of Jesus speaking of the Son of Man. And there are absolutely no other instances, not one, of Jesus ever directly identifying Himself as the Son of Man, and Jesus did not do so here either.

When we recognize the incredible lengths to which Jesus goes *to avoid* directly saying He is the Son of Man, we will see that this version clearly is in error.

A more direct statement cannot be made than, "I, the Son of Man, am," except to say, "I am the Son of Man!" This is the only instance stating Jesus did so, and this one solitary case, is disputed by all the other manuscript accounts.

This leaves only two other possibilities of what Jesus said:

"*Who do people say that the Son of Man is?*"

Or,

"*Who do people say that I am?*"

From here, both of these statements are viable, so we will expand on both. Regardless of which account accurately recorded what Jesus said, the conclusion as we shall see, will be the same.

In the normal course of conversation, it would be natural to ask these two questions together:

"*Who do people say that I am?*"

followed by,

"*But who do you say that I am?*"

Both of these ask the question, "*who (do you and others) say that I am?*" This is natural and makes more sense, than saying,

"*Who do people say that the Son of Man is?*"

followed by,

"*But who do you say that I am?*"

One asks, "*Who the Son of Man is*"; the other asks, "*Who I am.*"

With this questioning, Jesus would be asking for the identity of *two different people*. It does not seem to make logical sense to ask the questions this way.

And yet, I believe this is exactly what Jesus said.

This fits precisely with the pattern of speech Jesus frequently used. Jesus often spoke of Himself, then, spoke of the Son of Man separately.

For now though, this is the important point to be seen. As mentioned earlier, regardless of which way we go with this, the outcome will be the same.

If Jesus said,

> "*Who do people say that the Son of Man is?*"

then the two accounts of Mark and Luke are in error. They missed the fact that Jesus said, "*the Son of Man.*" When Jesus said, "*the Son of Man,*" they heard it as though He spoke of Himself and said, "*I.*"

However, if Jesus said,

> "*Who do people say that I am?*"

then the account in Matthew is in error. When Jesus spoke of Himself, Matthew heard it as though He said, "*the Son of Man.*"

The point is this: One or more of the authors misquoted Jesus, as speaking of *the Son of Man*, when He actually spoke of *Himself*, or, as speaking of *Himself*, when He actually spoke of *the Son of Man*.

It is clear that to the disciples, Jesus' use of the term "the Son of Man" is simply synonymous with Jesus speaking of Himself. The disciples took the term "the Son of Man" for granted and missed what Jesus said.

> *They took "the Son of Man" for granted.*

The Jewish People Do Not Know Who the Son of Man Is

Although the disciples understood Jesus is the Son of Man, we will see from the following text the Jewish people did not. We will also see another instance of the disciples hearing Jesus as speaking of Himself, when He actually said, *"the Son of Man."*

This is probably among the best known of all the quotes of Jesus Christ. *As it is recorded by John*, Jesus said to the Jewish people,

> *And I, if **I** am lifted up from the earth, will draw all peoples to Myself.*

There is a problem with this verse however. Look at the response of the Jewish people to what Jesus said.

They asked Him,

> *"We have heard from the law that the Christ remains forever; and how can You say, '**The Son of Man must be lifted up**'?*
>
> **Who is this Son of Man?"**

> *John 12:32, 34 NKJV e.a.*

John records Jesus as saying,

> *"if **(I)** am lifted up"*

Yet, the Jewish people responded by asking,

> *"How can You say, '**The Son of Man must be lifted up**'?"*

This does not make sense. *According to this account*, Jesus did not mention the Son of Man at all.

However, if Jesus said, *"if (the Son of Man) is lifted up,"* and the people responded by asking about the Son of Man, this then makes perfect sense.

Jesus spoke about *the Son of Man*, and the Jews asked about *the Son of Man*.

Is it possible however, this question by the people is referring to a previous statement Jesus made?

Jesus elsewhere did say,

> And as Moses lifted up the serpent in the wilderness,
> even so must the Son of Man be lifted up
>
> *John 3:14 NKJV*

Is their response a reference to this statement Jesus previously made?

If the Jewish people had recognized Jesus spoke about Himself being lifted up, and remembered Jesus had also spoken of the Son of Man being lifted up, they would have then made the association between these two different statements. They would have known Jesus was referring to Himself as the Son of Man.

But they did not!

For the next question they asked Him was,

> *"Who is this Son of Man?"*

Therefore, this was not a reference to any previous statement Jesus made. This was a direct response to what Jesus said here, *about the Son of Man.*

The Jewish people did not understand that Jesus is the Son of Man. It was not obvious, and they did not take for granted Jesus was speaking of Himself, when He spoke of the Son of Man. They did not know who this Son of Man was.

As a result, when Jesus said, "the Son of Man," they heard, "*the Son of Man.*"

The Jewish people correctly heard what Jesus actually said.

> *"And I, if (**the Son of Man**) is lifted up from the earth, will draw all peoples to Myself."*

> *"How can You say, '**The Son of Man** must be lifted up'?"*
> *"Who is this Son of Man?"*

John on the other hand…

John knew who the Son of Man was. He knew Jesus was speaking of Himself. This is yet *another* example where John, one of the disciples, took for granted that Jesus was speaking of Himself, when He actually said, "the Son of Man."

Jesus is using the same figure of speech He has used many times before. He is speaking of Himself, then separately speaking of the Son of Man.

> *"And **I**, if **(the Son of Man)** is lifted up from the earth, will draw all peoples to Myself."*

> *I will draw all peoples to myself, if **the Son of Man** is lifted up.*

Jesus did not say, "*if I am lifted up.*"

> *He said, "the Son of Man"!*

Who Is This Son of Man?

Here is one final point to consider regarding this particular event. Notice how Jesus responded when they asked Him who the Son of Man is.

The people asked Him,

> *Who is this Son of Man?*

Jesus said to them,

> *"A little while longer the light is with you. Walk while you have the light, lest darkness overtake you; he who walks in darkness does not know where he is going. While you have the light, believe in the light, that you may become sons of light."*
>
> *John 12:34-36 NKJV*

This is a direct, clear request by the Jewish people asking Jesus to tell them who this Son of Man is. Yet, Jesus did not tell them. He answered them using figurative language.

The people earlier had also directly asked Jesus who He was.

They asked Him,

> *"Who are You?"*

And Jesus responded by saying,

> *"What have I been saying to you from the beginning? "I have many things to speak and to judge concerning you, but He who sent Me is true; and the things which I heard from Him, these I speak to the world."*

John 8:25-26 NASB

These two questions, *"Who are You?"* and *"Who is this Son of Man?"* are two sides of the same coin. The questions are literally asking for the identity of the same person. The answer would be the same for both.

Each time Jesus is asked, His response is the same. He answers them using only obscure figurative language. This is not a coincidence. It shows clear intent.

He does not tell them who He is.
He does not tell them who the Son of Man is.

> *"Who is this Son of Man?"*

> *"A little while longer the light is with you.*
> *Walk while you have the light, lest darkness overtake you; …"*

The Son of Man Is Hidden

In the previous verse Jesus was asked who the Son of Man is and He did not tell them. Now we are going to see several verses showing the identity of the Son of Man was actually being hidden.

Look at this next verse. And notice again the same pattern of speech Jesus continues to use; He speaks of the Son of Man, then speaks of Himself.

Jesus said to the Jews,

> *"When you lift up **the Son of Man**, then you will know that **I** am He*

John 8:28 NKJV e.a.

At first glance this verse *appears* to show Jesus saying He is the Son of Man. Nevertheless, it warrants a closer look. To begin, it should be noted there is no "*He*" in the actual text. Therefore, the text should only read,

"then you will know that I am."

Now, let's look again at what He said.

Jesus first said, "*When… you lift up the Son of Man*,"
Next He said, "*then… you will know that I am.*"

Jesus tells them, *after* the Son of Man has been lifted up, *then, and only then*, will they know He is the Son of Man.

Therefore, even though Jesus made this statement that in effect said who He is, His identity as the Son of Man would remain hidden, until *after* He had been crucified. The Jewish people still did not know *who this Son of Man is*, who was to be lifted up.

*"When you lift up the Son of Man, **then you will know** that I am."*

Here is another example.

> *And as it was in the days of Noah, so it will be also in the days of the Son of Man: They ate, they drank, they married wives, they were given in marriage, until the day that Noah entered the ark, and the flood came and destroyed them all.*
>
> *Likewise as it was also in the days of Lot: They ate, they drank, they bought, they sold, they planted, they built; but on the day that Lot went out of Sodom it rained fire and brimstone from heaven and destroyed them all.*

Then Jesus said,

> *Even so will it be in the day when **the Son of Man is revealed**.*
>
> *Luke 17:26-30 NKJV e.a.*

When Jesus says, *"in the day when the Son of Man is revealed,"* He is speaking of a day that is, even to this day, *still yet in the future.* The Son of Man will be revealed in the future.

The Son of Man has not yet been revealed.

Jesus spoke to His disciples about the return of the Son of Man. Jesus said to them,

> *"Immediately after the tribulation of those days the sun will be darkened, and the moon will not give its light; the stars will fall from heaven, and the powers of the heavens will be shaken.* **Then the sign of the Son of Man will appear in heaven**, *and then all the tribes of the earth will mourn, and* **they will see the Son of Man** *coming on the clouds of heaven with power and great glory.*
>
>

Matthew 24:29-30 NKJV e.a.

Then the sign of the Son of Man will appear in heaven.
Then…, they will see the Son of Man.

Then…, the Son of Man will no longer be hidden!

Jesus told the people no sign would be given to them.
Jesus said to the crowds,

> *"An evil and adulterous generation seeks after a sign, and* **no sign will be given** *to it except the sign of the prophet Jonah. For as Jonah was three days and three nights in the belly of the great fish, so will the Son of Man be three days and three nights in the heart of the earth.*
>
>

Matthew 12:39-40 NKJV e.a.

Jesus said, *"no sign will be given"* to the people except, *"the sign of Jonah."* Jonah was *no sign at all* to the Ninevites, *until after*, he had been three days and three nights in the belly of the great fish. Likewise, the Son of Man would be *no sign at all* to the people, *until after*, He had risen from the dead.

> *For as Jonah was three days and three nights in the belly of the great fish, so will the Son of Man be three days and three nights in the heart of the earth.*

Therefore, while Jesus (the Son of Man) was still alive, *prior to His crucifixion*, there would be *"no sign given"* to the people.

"No sign will be given"

The Son of Man was still hidden!

We do however, have one instance where Jesus actually says the Son of Man has in fact been seen.

Jesus said to His disciples,

> *Assuredly, I say to you, there are some standing here who shall not taste death **till they see the Son of Man** coming in His kingdom.*
>
> *Matthew 16:28 NKJV e.a.*

Mark and Luke also record this conversation, but they do not mention the Son of Man.

In the book of Mark, it reads,

> *"Assuredly, I say to you that there are some standing here who will not taste death till they see the kingdom of God present with power."*
>
> *Mark 9:1 NKJV*

In the book of Luke, it reads,

> *But I tell you truly, there are some standing here who shall not taste death till they see the kingdom of God.*
>
> *Luke 9:27 NKJV*

Notice from the three accounts, they quote nearly verbatim with each other (which is what we should expect) until they reach a certain point, then the three accounts diverge.

Each of the three accounts say,

> *"Assuredly, I say to you, there are some standing here who shall not taste death till they see ..."*

It is after the point of "*till they see …*" that the accounts differ. What exactly were they going to see?

Matthew records:	"*the Son of Man coming in His kingdom.*"
Mark records:	"*kingdom of God present with power.*"
And Luke records simply:	"*the kingdom of God.*"

What we have are two accounts that do not mention the Son of Man and only one account that does. There is however, one other piece of information contained within *all three* of the accounts that indicates Jesus did in fact say "*the Son of Man*" as only Matthew wrote. This detail will be explained later in the chapter.

Therefore, if we use Matthew's account stating the Son of Man, and compile it with the other two accounts, we would have Jesus saying something similar to the following:

> "*Assuredly, I say to you, there are some standing here who shall not taste death till they see …,*
>
> **the Son of Man coming in the kingdom of God with power.**"

Six days after Jesus said this, He took three of His disciples, Peter, James and John, up to a high mountain. Then it says of Jesus,

> *and He was transfigured before them. His face shone like the sun, and His clothes became as white as the light.*
>
> *Matthew 17:2 NKJV*

The disciples saw Jesus changed before their very eyes, and saw what Jesus earlier described as,

> *the Son of Man coming in the kingdom of God with power.*
>
> *The Son of Man has now been revealed!*

Jesus had said to His disciples,

> *for assuredly, I say to you that many prophets and righteous men desired to see what you see, and did not see it, and to hear what you hear, and did not hear it.*
>
> *Matthew 13:17 NKJV*

Many men in the past had desired to see Jesus and now the Son of Man is finally being revealed in all His glory. However, He was only revealed to Peter, James and John.

>   *The Son of Man was revealed to only three!*

To all of the other disciples,
and,
to all of the Jewish people,

>   *The Son of Man was still hidden!*

How Is It Written of the Son of Man?

When Jesus was coming down from the mountain with Peter, James and John, He told them not to tell anyone what they had seen *"until after"* the Son of Man rose from the dead.

The disciples then asked Jesus,

>   *"Why is it that the scribes say that Elijah must come first?"*

And Jesus said to them,

>   *"Elijah does first come and restore all things. And yet **how is it written of the Son of Man** that He will suffer many things and be treated with contempt?*
>
>   *Mark 9:11-12 NASB e.a.*

Notice the question Jesus asks.

>   *"How is it written of the Son of Man that He will suffer?"*

Jesus is not making a statement here. He is asking a question; *"**How** is it written?"* Jesus is giving the disciples a clue to look and see *"How"* it had been written the Son of Man would suffer.

Jesus also said this,

> *"Behold, we are going up to Jerusalem, and **all things which are written** through the prophets **about the Son of Man will be accomplished**.*
>
> *Luke 18:31 NASB e.a.*

Here Jesus says,

> *"**All things which are written** about the Son of Man will be accomplished."*

Jesus spoke of *"the sign"* of the Son of Man, and here He says, *"all things"* were written about the Son of Man. Therefore, it should be written in the Old Testament Scriptures that the Son of Man would be a sign.

And we find that in fact, it is!

The Son of Man Will Be a Sign

The Lord spoke to the prophet Ezekiel and said,

> *son of man, … I have made you a sign to the house of Israel.*
>
> *See Ezekiel 12:3, 6 NKJV par.*

The Lord said again to Ezekiel,

> *"Son of man, … Say, 'I am a sign to you.*
>
> *See Ezekiel 12:9, 11 NKJV par.*

In both of these passages, the Lord calls Ezekiel *"son of man"* and says that he will be a sign.

The Lord said again to Ezekiel,

> *"Son of man, …*
> *'Speak to the house of Israel, "Thus says the Lord GOD, …*
> *Ezekiel will be a sign to you;*
>
> *See Ezekiel 24:16, 21, 24 NASB par.*

The Lord called Ezekiel "*son of man.*"

The Lord also said Ezekiel will be "*a sign*" to the house of Israel.

Therefore, the Lord did in fact say in the Old Testament Scriptures, the Son of Man will be a sign to the house of Israel.

Jesus said to the people,

> "*For just as Jonah became a sign to the Ninevites, so will the Son of Man be to this generation.*
>
> Luke 11:30 NASB

When He said this, He was speaking of, and referring to these prophetic passages in the book of Ezekiel that say,

> *The Son of Man will be a sign.*

However, there is no actual direct statement from the Lord saying, "*the son of man will be a sign.*" It is always an indirect association.

The Lord did not say,

> "*The Son of Man will be a sign to you.*"

The Lord said,

> "*Son of man, …*
> '*Speak to the house of Israel, "Thus says the Lord GOD, …*
> *Ezekiel will be a sign to you;*
>
> "*Ezekiel, (son of man), will be a sign to you.*"

Notice the layering, or the indirect association:
The Lord refers to Ezekiel as "*son of man.*"
The Lord instructs Ezekiel to speak to the House of Israel.
Then, the Lord tells Ezekiel to say, "*Ezekiel will be a sign to you.*"

Furthermore, when we view the entire passage as shown on the next page, we see each part of this message is separated by several other sentences. Here is the entire section as it is written in the book of Ezekiel. Notice the separation between the outlined text.

And the word of the LORD came to me saying,
"Son of man, behold, I am about to take from you the desire of
your eyes with a blow; but you shall not mourn and you shall not
weep, and your tears shall not come. "Groan silently; make no
mourning for the dead. Bind on your turban and put your shoes on
your feet, and do not cover your mustache and do not eat the bread
of men." So I spoke to the people in the morning, and in the evening
my wife died. And in the morning I did as I was commanded. The
people said to me, "Will you not tell us what these things that you
are doing mean for us?" Then I said to them, "The word of the
LORD came to me saying, "Speak to the house of Israel, "Thus
says the Lord GOD, 'Behold, I am about to profane My sanctuary,
the pride of your power, the desire of your eyes and the delight of
your soul; and your sons and your daughters whom you have left
behind will fall by the sword. 'You will do as I have done; you will
not cover your mustache and you will not eat the bread of men.
'Your turbans will be on your heads and your shoes on your feet.
You will not mourn and you will not weep, but you will rot away
in your iniquities and you will groan to one another. 'Thus Ezekiel
will be a sign to you; according to all that he has done you will
do; when it comes, then you will know that I am the Lord GOD.'"

Ezekiel 24:15-24 NASB e.a.

The Lord has intentionally put a large separation in His message between
addressing Ezekiel as "son of man" and His mentioning "Ezekiel will be
a sign." Even with this separation however, this is exactly what it says,

> *"Son of man, …*
> *'Speak to the house of Israel, "Thus says the Lord GOD, …*
> *Ezekiel will be a sign to you.*

All of this extra text, while certainly pertinent to the message, is also
intentionally being used as a covering to obscure the view of this short
prophetic message.

> *"The Son of Man will be a sign to you!"*

When this text is not being highlighted, it is scarcely noticeable this prophetic message even exists. This short, simple message, is being hidden within this long, detailed message in the Old Testament.

The Prophecy Was Hidden

The message, "*Ezekiel will be a sign to you*" is a prophetic word from the Lord to Israel. It is a prophecy.

The message, "*The Son of Man will be a sign to you*," is also a prophetic word from the Lord, that speaks of the Messiah of Israel. It too is a prophecy, but it was hidden within this text.

It is a prophecy, hidden within, a prophecy!

This is another prophecy regarding the Messiah of Israel that had been hidden. It was hidden by an indirect association.

The prophecy, "*The son of man will be a sign to you*,"
was hidden within,
The prophecy, "*Ezekiel will be a sign to you*."

The prophecy was hidden!

The Lord hid this prophecy about the Messiah, within His prophecy about Ezekiel. If we now go back and look again at what Jesus said about Jonah, we will see He is doing this very same thing.

The Sign of Jonah

Jesus said to the crowds,

> "*This generation is a wicked generation; it seeks for a sign, and yet no sign will be given to it but **the sign of Jonah**. "**For just as Jonah became a sign** to the Ninevites, **so will the Son of Man be** to this generation.*
>
> *Luke 11:29-30 NASB e.a.*

And also,

> *"An evil and adulterous generation seeks after a sign, and no sign will be given to it except **the sign of the prophet Jonah**. **For as Jonah was** three days and three nights in the belly of the great fish, **so will the Son of Man be** three days and three nights in the heart of the earth.*
>
> *Matthew 12:39-40 NKJV e.a.*

Jesus speaks about Jonah and the Son of Man. What Jesus says about Jonah, He associates to the Son of Man. Here, Jesus is pointing to the Son of Man being three days and three nights in the heart of the earth. He is telling the people His death and subsequent resurrection *will be a sign* to them.

This clearly is the sign Jesus is speaking of.

> *"so will the Son of Man be three days and three nights in the heart of the earth."*

Yet, there is also another message hidden within the text of these messages.

Two Different Signs

There are actually two different things being said of the Son of Man here. Look at these two sentences:

So will the Son of Man be... | *three days and three nights in the heart of the earth*
So will the Son of Man be... | *a sign*

Those two sentences declare what *"the Son of Man"* will be. Now look at those same two sentences when we outline what *"the sign"* will be.

So will the Son of Man be... | *three days and three nights in the heart of the earth*
So will | *the Son of Man* | *be... a sign*

In the first sentence, the *"three days and nights in the heart of the earth,"* is the sign. In the second sentence, *"the Son of Man,"* is the sign.

The *"three days and nights in the heart of the earth,"* is one sign.
The *"Son of Man,"* is a second, different sign.

A Hidden Association

Jesus is saying the Son of Man will be a sign to this generation. Yet, notice this subtle detail.

Jesus first said, *"For just as Jonah became* **a sign** *to the Ninevites,"*
Then, He said, *"so will the Son of Man be* [____] *to this generation."*

Notice what is missing from the second statement. Jesus did not say,

> *"so will the Son of Man be* **a sign** *... to this generation"*

He intentionally omitted the words, "a sign" and said only,

> *"so will the Son of Man be* [____] *to this generation"*

Jesus did not say the words, *the Son of Man will be a sign*, but that is exactly what the message is.

> *The Son of Man will be a sign!*

Jesus Spoke to the People as the Lord Spoke to Ezekiel

Jesus spoke to the people precisely in the same manner as the Lord spoke to Ezekiel, using indirect associations.

The Lord called Ezekiel "Son of Man."
Then the Lord said, "Ezekiel will be a sign to you."

> *Ezekiel,* Son of Man *will be a sign to you.*

Next, we see Jesus refers to Jonah as "a sign."
Then Jesus said the Son of Man will be as Jonah was.

> *"so will the Son of Man be* a sign."

Furthermore, notice the separation in Jesus' words that say, "*The Son of Man will be a sign.*" This is the same structuring as seen written in Ezekiel's prophecy.

> "*An evil and adulterous generation seeks after a sign, and no sign will be given to it except* **the sign of the prophet Jonah.** **For as Jonah was** *three days and three nights in the belly of the great fish,* **so will the Son of Man be** *three days and three nights in the heart of the earth.*
>
> Matthew 12:39-40 NKJV e.a.

Within the message as a whole, we see the individual statements that compose another message. It is a prophecy of the Messiah.

"The Son of Man will be a sign!"

The prophecy, "*The Son of Man will be a sign,*"
was hidden within,

the prophecy, "*the sign of the prophet Jonah. For as Jonah was three days and three nights in the belly of the great fish, so will the Son of Man be*"

His message, was hidden within, His message.

The prophecy was hidden!

In the Old Testament, the Lord never said the words, "the Son of Man will be a sign to you." Yet, that is exactly what His message was.

"Ezekiel, (Son of Man), will be a sign to you."

In the New Testament, Jesus never said the words, "the Son of Man will be a sign." Yet, that is exactly what His message was.

"For just as Jonah became a sign
so will the Son of Man be… (a sign)."

Jesus spoke to the people just as the Lord had spoken to Ezekiel!

A Diversion

Jesus pointed the people towards one sign, while hiding another.

Jesus spoke of Jonah as being a sign.
However, prior to Jesus saying this, Jonah was not known as a sign.

Jesus also spoke of the Son of Man as being a sign.
However, He did not mention Ezekiel, who was known as both, *"son of man"* and, *"a sign."*

> *What Jesus spoke of, (Jonah), was not known to be a sign.*

And,

> *What was known to be a sign, (Ezekiel), Jesus did not speak of.*

Jesus spoke of Jonah; He did not speak of Ezekiel.

> *Jesus said the Son of Man will be a sign*
> *Just as Ezekiel had said*
> *But Jesus did not point them to Ezekiel*
> *He pointed them to Jonah instead!*

> *"The Son of Man will be a sign. Look at Jonah!"*

The reference to Jonah was a diversion away from Ezekiel. When Jesus spoke of the Son of Man being a sign, He spoke of Jonah; He did not speak of Ezekiel.

He did not say,

> *The Son of Man will be a sign, just as the prophet Ezekiel was.*

He said,

> *The Son of Man will be…, just as the prophet Jonah was.*

> *It was… a diversion!*

Jesus did not say, *"I am the Son of Man and I will be a sign to you."*
He did not even say, *"The Son of Man will be a sign to you."*

Jesus spoke only indirectly by referring to *"the sign of the prophet Jonah,"* who was *"three days and three nights in the belly of the great fish."*

Jesus gives clues He is speaking prophetically to the people, yet, He did not say it plainly for them to understand.

Remember what the people said to Jesus,

> *If You are the Christ,* **tell us plainly**.
>
> *John 10:24 NKJV e.a.*

The Lord spoke again to Ezekiel,

> *'And you,* **son of man** ...
> *Thus* **you will be a sign to them***, and they shall know that I am the LORD.'*
>
> *Ezekiel 24:25, 27 NKJV e.a. par.*

"Son of Man" Is a Prophetic Title

The Lord refers to the prophet Ezekiel as *"son of man"* more than 90 times in the Old Testament. During some of these times Ezekiel is told to tell Israel the same things Jesus also spoke to Israel. The term *"Son of Man"* is a prophetic title the Jewish people should have recognized. They should have recognized Jesus was speaking of these Scriptures. The only remaining question is whether Jesus actually did identify Himself as the Son of Man to Israel and, if so, how?

Did Jesus Say He Is the Son of Man?

Jesus said to the Jews,

> *"Most assuredly, I say to you, unless you eat the flesh of the Son of Man and drink His blood, you have no life in you.*
>
> *Whoever eats My flesh and drinks My blood has eternal life, and I will raise him up at the last day.*
>
> *John 6:53-54 NKJV*

Afterwards, Jesus explained privately to His disciples that He was speaking of the Spirit, *not* His flesh.

He said to His disciples,

> *It is the Spirit who gives life; the flesh profits nothing.*
> *The words that I speak to you are spirit, and they are life.*
>
> John 6:63 NKJV

Jesus was speaking of *the Spirit,* when He said, *"eat My flesh."*

Jesus makes two separate statements here:
First, He says they must eat the flesh and drink the blood of *"the Son of Man."*
Then, He says they must eat *"My flesh"* and drink *"My blood."*

Jesus is making an association between,

   "the flesh of the Son of Man"
and,
   "My flesh."

Although this is an *indirect* association, it is very clear; He speaks of both in the same context.

From this statement it is possible to identify,

   the flesh and blood of the Son of Man
is,
   the flesh and blood of Jesus.

Therefore, it is possible to identify Jesus is the Son of Man here.

However…

First, notice again, as was His pattern of speech, Jesus spoke of the Son of Man, then spoke of Himself separately.

Next, notice Jesus covers what is being said here by saying they must eat His flesh and drink His blood, which is egregiously offensive to the Jews.

The Jewish people had very strict dietary laws given to them by the Lord Himself, stating which *animals* they were to eat, and which animals they were not to eat. And now Jesus (*according to their perspective and understanding*) is speaking to them of cannibalism.

> *"eat My flesh and drink My blood…"*

The text goes on to say,

> *Therefore many of His disciples, when they heard this, said, "This is a hard saying; who can understand it?"*
>
> *From that time many of His disciples went back and walked with Him no more.*
>
> John 6:60, 66 NKJV

The people were not able to hear what Jesus said.

Therefore, even though Jesus made a statement that could have identified Him as the Son of Man, He spoke this in such a repulsive way that the people were not able to listen to it. It was a stumbling block to them.

Jesus said to His disciples,

> ***"Does this offend you?*** *What then if you should see the Son of Man ascend where He was before? It is the Spirit who gives life; the flesh profits nothing. The words that I speak to you are spirit, and they are life.*
>
> John 6:61-63 NKJV e.a.

When John the Baptist sent men to Jesus to ask if He was the expected "*Coming One,*" Jesus said to them,

> *"Go and tell John the things which you hear and see: The blind see and the lame walk; the lepers are cleansed and the deaf hear; the dead are raised up and the poor have the gospel preached to them.* ***And blessed is he who is not offended because of Me.***"
>
> Matthew 11:4-6 NKJV e.a.

"Blessed is he who is not offended because of Me!"

The people were offended by what Jesus said and were not able to listen to it. They did not hear what He said!

Jesus' actual message was, *He is the Son of Man.* Yet, saying they must eat His flesh and drink His blood was such an offensive and difficult statement that this became the only thing they heard. If we ourselves were to hear someone say this today, it would be exactly the same for us. We would be repulsed by it.

They did not hear Jesus saying, *"I am the Son of Man."*
They only heard Him say, *"eat My flesh and drink My blood."*

This became the focus of what Jesus said and it diverted their attention *away from* Jesus identifying Himself as the Son of Man.

It was a distraction and diversion.

> *"Who can listen to it?"*

There is a story of a paralyzed man who was brought to Jesus so he might be healed.

Jesus said to the man who was paralyzed,

> *"Son, your sins are forgiven."*

Then it says,

> *But some of the scribes were sitting there and reasoning in their hearts, "Why does this man speak that way? He is blaspheming; who can forgive sins but God alone?"*

Jesus therefore said to the Jews,

> *"Why are you reasoning about these things in your hearts? "Which is easier, to say to the paralytic, 'Your sins are forgiven'; or to say, 'Get up, and pick up your pallet and walk'? "But so that you may know that the Son of Man has authority on earth to forgive sins" —* He said to the paralytic,

> *"I say to you, get up, pick up your pallet and go home."*

And the man stood up!

> *And he got up and immediately picked up the pallet and went out in the sight of everyone, so that they were all amazed and were glorifying God, saying, "We have never seen anything like this."*
>
> *Mark 2:5-12 NASB*

There are several details in this story that Jesus uses to indicate He is the Son of Man.

The first, is the two similar statements referring to *"forgiving sins"* which in one of them Jesus forgave the man's sins. In the other, He said *the Son of Man* had the authority to forgive sins. Jesus is making a connection to Himself as the Son of Man.

The second and most obvious detail here is the demonstration of the healing itself. This too should have been an indication to the Jews, that Jesus was *"the Son of Man"* who had *"the authority to forgive sins."* However, there is not a clear association between forgiving sins and healing the sick. Which is why Jesus said,

> *"Which is easier to say, 'Your sins are forgiven'; or, 'Get up, and walk'?"*

The third detail is this: The account of this healing is also recorded in the books of Luke and Matthew. The three accounts are similar and quote nearly verbatim with each other.

In the book of Luke, it says,

> *"But, so that you may know that the Son of Man has authority on earth to forgive sins," — He said to the paralytic —*
> *"**I say to you**, get up, and pick up your stretcher and go home."*
>
> *Luke 5:24 NASB e.a.*

However, look at what Matthew wrote.
In the book of Matthew, it says,

> *"But so that you may know that the Son of Man has authority on earth to forgive sins" — then He said to the paralytic,*
> *"Get up, pick up your bed and go home."*
>
> *Matthew 9:6 NASB*

Notice what is missing in Mathew's account.

Both Mark and Luke record Jesus as saying,

> **"I say to you…**, get up, pick up your pallet and go home."

Matthew records only,

> "Get up, pick up your bed and go home"

Matthew did not record Jesus as saying, "*I say to you.*" Matthew missed a critical detail.

Jesus said,

> "so that you may know the Son of Man has authority …,
> **I say to you…**"

This is a significant omission. This carried the very essence of what Jesus was saying. When Jesus uses the phrase, "*I say to you,*" it is authoritative. It carries with it a meaning of authority. It is spoken with authority.

> "*I say to you!*"

When Jesus said, "*I say to you,*" He was identifying Himself as "*the one who had authority.*" He was identifying Himself as "*the Son of Man.*"

When Jesus taught the people in their synagogues, they said of Him that He taught with authority.

> the people were astonished at His teaching, **for He taught them as one having authority**, and not as the scribes.
> *Matthew 7:28-29 NKJV e.a.*

> And they were astonished at His teaching, **for His word was with authority.**
> *Luke 4:32 NKJV e.a.*

In a passage we saw earlier, Jesus also spoke of the Son of Man having authority.

Jesus said to the Jews,

> *Most assuredly, **I say to you**, the hour is coming, and now is, when the dead will hear the voice of the Son of God; and those who hear will live.*
>
> *For as the Father has life in Himself, so He has granted the Son to have life in Himself, and **has given Him authority** to execute judgment also, **because He is the Son of Man**.*
>
> John 5:25-27 NKJV e.a.

When Jesus said, "*I say to you*," everything He said afterwards is included with that statement.

Jesus said,

> "*I say to you ..., the Father has given Him authority ..., because He is the Son of Man.*"

This passage and the passage of the healing of the paralyzed man, are two separate instances quoting Jesus as saying the Son of Man has authority. In both of these statements, Jesus also says, "*I say to you.*"

From these two passages we begin to see another "*pattern of speech*" emerging.

With the above passage, He said,

> "***I say to you** ..., the Father has given Him authority, because He is the Son of Man.*"

And from the passage of the healing of the paralyzed man,

> "*So that you may know the Son of Man has authority..., **I say to you**"*

Notice what Jesus is doing here. He is making an indirect association between Himself and the Son of Man.

Jesus did not say He had authority; Jesus said *the Son of Man* had authority. Yet, Jesus said the Son of Man had authority, *with authority!*

> *so that you may know that the Son of Man has authority …,*
> *I say to you, (**with authority**), get up, pick up your pallet and go*
> *home.*
>
> *Mark 2:10-11 NASB e.a. par.*

> *And they were astonished at His teaching, **for His word was with***
> ***authority.***
>
> *Luke 4:32 NKJV e.a.*

When Jesus said to the man, "*your sins are forgiven*," it created a significant controversy and distraction. Jesus saying the man's sins were forgiven became the focal point; it became what the people focused on. It was a diversion.

For then they said,

> "*Why does this man speak that way? He is blaspheming; who can forgive sins but God alone?*"

Then, Jesus gives them His real message… He is the Son of Man.

> "*But so that you may know that the Son of Man has authority on earth to forgive sins, I say to you, (with authority), get up, pick up your pallet and go home.*"

Their attention and focus were on Jesus saying the man's sins were forgiven. Then, the man's healing became the primary focus of their attention.

For it says,

> *And he got up and immediately picked up the pallet and went out in the sight of everyone, so that **they were all amazed** and were glorifying God, saying, "**We have never seen anything like this.**"*
>
> *Mark 2:12 NASB e.a.*

Jesus was telling them He is the Son of Man. Jesus in effect said to them, "*I am the Son of Man!*" Yet, their focus was not on who the Son of Man is; their focus was on forgiving sins and the man's healing.

An analogy to this would be the use of sleight of hand. The illusionist creates a distraction having the spectators focus on his left hand so they will not see what his right hand is doing.

Jesus made mention of this very thing when He told the people,

> *do not let your left hand know what your right hand is doing, so that your giving* **will be in secret**
>
> *Matthew 6:3-4 NASB e.a.*

Jesus is doing the same here. Jesus is having them watch (and listen) to what His left hand is doing, so they will not see (or hear) what His right hand is doing.

On the left He says, "*Your sins are forgiven.*"
While on the right He says, "*I am the Son of Man.*"

Jesus was keeping a secret. Jesus intentionally said, "*Your sins are forgiven*" to create the distraction needed, so they would not hear Him say He is the Son of Man.

> *It was a diversion!*

Even with the wonderful demonstration of His power to heal the paralyzed man, afterwards, they still did not know who the Son of Man is.

They saw what He did:

> "*We have never seen anything like this.*"

But they did not hear what He was saying:

> "*So that you may know the Son of Man has authority,*
> *I say to you, (with authority), get up, take up your pallet and go home.*"

> "*I am the Son of Man!*"

I Say to You

There are over 130 instances recorded in the Gospels of Jesus using the phrase *"I say to you."* Just as it was common for Jesus to use the term, *"the Son of Man,"* it was even more common for Jesus to use the phrase, *"I say to you."*

Look at the following verses.

Jesus spoke to His disciples and told them the Son of Man will judge the nations of the earth when He returns.

Jesus said,

> *"When* **the Son of Man** *comes in His glory, and all the holy angels with Him, then He will sit on the throne of His glory. All the nations will be gathered before Him, and He will separate them one from another, as a shepherd divides his sheep from the goats. And He will set the sheep on His right hand, but the goats on the left.*
>
> *Then* **the King will say** *to those on His right hand, 'Come, you blessed of My Father, inherit the kingdom prepared for you from the foundation of the world: for I was hungry and you gave Me food; I was thirsty and you gave Me drink; I was a stranger and you took Me in; I was naked and you clothed Me; I was sick and you visited Me; I was in prison and you came to Me.' "Then the righteous will answer Him, saying, 'Lord, when did we see You hungry and feed You, or thirsty and give You drink? When did we see You a stranger and take You in, or naked and clothe You? Or when did we see You sick, or in prison, and come to You?'*

Notice what the King says,

> *And the* **King will answer and say** *to them, 'Assuredly,* **I say to you,** *inasmuch as you did it to one of the least of these My brethren, you did it to Me.'*

> *"Then He will also say to those on the left hand, 'Depart from Me, you cursed, into the everlasting fire prepared for the [fallen angel] and his angels: for I was hungry and you gave Me no food; I was thirsty and you gave Me no drink; I was a stranger and you did not take Me in, naked and you did not clothe Me, sick and in prison and you did not visit Me.' "Then they also will answer Him, saying, 'Lord, when did we see You hungry or thirsty or a stranger or naked or sick or in prison, and did not minister to You?'*

Notice again what the King says,

> *Then He will answer them, saying, 'Assuredly,* **I say to you,** *inasmuch as you did not do it to one of the least of these, you did not do it to Me.' And these will go away into everlasting punishment, but the righteous into eternal life."*
>
> Matthew 25:31-46 NKJV e.a. par.

Jesus says, "**the King** will say, '**I say to you.**'"
Who is the King? The King is the Son of Man.

> *"When* **the Son of Man** *comes in His glory, and all the holy angels with Him, then He will sit on the throne of His glory. ...,*
> *Then* **the King will say** *..., I say to you"*

Jesus tells them in this story the Son of Man will say, "*I say to you.*"

Notice however, Jesus never actually said, "*The Son of Man will say, 'I say to you.'*" Jesus only said, "*the King will say, 'I say to you.'*"

There is an *indirect association* being made between the Son of Man and the King. The Son of Man is the King yet, it is the King who says, "*I say to you.*"

There is also an *indirect association* being made between Jesus and the Son of Man, but it is hidden several layers deep.

In the first layer, Jesus is known to frequently say, "*I say to you.*"
In the second layer, in the story "*the Son of Man*" is identified as "*the King.*"

> "*When the Son of Man comes ...,*
> *He will sit on the throne of His glory ...,*
> *Then the King ...,*"

At the third layer, it is "*the King*" who says, "*I say to you.*"

> "*And the King will answer and say to them, 'Assuredly, I say to you,*'"

At the fourth layer, we see it is "*the Son of Man*" who will say, "*I say to you.*"

At the fifth and final layer, is the association of Jesus and the Son of Man who both say, "*I say to you.*"

1. Jesus will often say, "*I say to you.*"
2. "*The Son of Man*" is "*the King.*"
3. "*The King will say, 'I say to you.'*"
4. "*The Son of Man, (the King), will say 'I say to you.'*"
5. Both Jesus and the Son of Man will say, "*I say to you.*"

What Is Jesus Saying?

Jesus told them He is the Son of Man, yet, it was hidden deep within His story. Hidden within His message of the judgment and separation of the sheep from the goats, was another message. Hidden within His message, was the real message.

I am the Son of Man!

His message, was hidden within, His message.

"I Say to You" and "the Son of Man"

Here we will see examples highlighting Jesus' use of yet another pattern of speech saying, "*I say to you*" while also speaking of "*the Son of Man.*"

> "Most assuredly, **I say to you**, hereafter you shall see heaven open, and the angels of God ascending and descending upon **the Son of Man**."
>
> *John 1:51 NKJV e.a.*

> "Take heed that you do not despise one of these little ones, for **I say to you** that in heaven their angels always see the face of My Father who is in heaven. For **the Son of Man** has come to save that which was lost.
>
> *Matthew 18:10-11 NKJV e.a.*

> When they persecute you in this city, flee to another. For assuredly, **I say to you**, you will not have gone through the cities of Israel before **the Son of Man** comes.
>
> *Matthew 10:23 NKJV e.a.*

Earlier, we saw a verse in Matthew showing Jesus using this same pattern of speech saying, "*I say to you …*" while also speaking of "*the Son of Man.*"

Jesus said to His disciples,

> Assuredly, **I say to you**, there are some standing here who shall not taste death till they see **the Son of Man** coming in His kingdom.
>
> *Matthew 16:28 NKJV e.a.*

Remember, there are two other books that also recorded this conversation, but they do not mention the Son of Man. However, all three of the accounts do record Jesus as saying, "*I say to you.*"

Jesus had a pattern of speech saying, "*I say to you*" while also speaking of "*the Son of Man.*" It is because of this, I believe Jesus did say, "*until they see the Son of Man,*" as only Matthew recorded.

> "Assuredly, **I say to you**, there are some standing here who shall not taste death till they see …,
>
> **the Son of Man** coming in the kingdom of God with power."

Now let's look at some final verses, where Jesus gives the clearest indications yet, that He is the Son of Man.

Jesus will again be using the pattern of speech, speaking of *Himself*, then also speaking of, *"the Son of Man."* This time however, Jesus will be making the associations quite clear.

The Betrayal

When Jesus was eating His last meal with His disciples, He spoke to them and foretold that one of them would betray Him.

Jesus said,

> *"Assuredly, I say to you, one of you who eats with Me will* **betray Me."**
>
> *And they began to be sorrowful, and to say to Him one by one, "Is it I?" And another said, "Is it I?"*

And Jesus said to them,

> *"It is one of the twelve, who dips with Me in the dish. The Son of Man indeed goes just as it is written of Him, but woe to that man by whom* **the Son of Man is betrayed!** *It would have been good for that man if he had never been born."*
>
> *Mark 14:18-21 NKJV e.a.*

Observe two things about the above passage.
Jesus says,

> *"one of you will* **betray Me"**

Then He says,

> *"but woe to that man by whom* **the Son of Man is betrayed."**

Jesus deliberately states two different people will be betrayed. He identifies the person by two different names or titles; *He* will be betrayed, and *the Son of Man* will be betrayed. Jesus is speaking of Himself and the Son of Man in the same context.

With this pattern of speech, Jesus speaks the same of both, *so it can be understood*, He is speaking of Himself as the Son of Man.

Remember though, Jesus is speaking only to His disciples here.

Although the disciples already knew or understood Jesus is the Son of Man, they took it for granted. By speaking of His betrayal in this manner, Jesus is highlighting the use of the term *"the Son of Man."* Jesus wanted His disciples, *and us*, to notice His use of it. He wanted us to know there is something special about the title, *"the Son of Man."*

Look at this next verse. Jesus was in the Garden of Gethsemane, just before He was to be arrested.

Jesus said to His disciples,

> *Behold, the hour is at hand and* **the Son of Man is being betrayed** *into the hands of sinners.* *"Get up, let us be going; behold, the one who* **betrays Me** *is at hand!"*
>
> Matthew 26:45-46 NASB e.a.

Jesus is speaking of being betrayed, and again states it two different ways.

Jesus states *the Son of Man* is being betrayed.
Then states *He* is being betrayed.

As a final example, take a look at this verse which also speaks of Jesus' betrayal. Judas, one of Jesus' disciples, led the soldiers and officers to Jesus to have Him arrested. Judas came up to kiss Jesus to identify Him to the officers.

Jesus said to Judas,

> *"Judas, are you betraying the Son of Man with a kiss?"*
>
> Luke 22:48 NKJV

Who did Judas betray with a kiss? *Jesus.*
Who did Jesus say that Judas was betraying with a kiss? *"the Son of Man."*

Jesus identifies Himself as the Son of Man. This would also clearly highlight Jesus' use of the term, *"the Son of Man."*

It would be normal to say, *"are you betraying Me?"*

Yet, Jesus said, *"are you betraying the Son of Man?"*

It was His pattern of speech.

> *It was a figure of speech!*

These three passages of Jesus' betrayal are the clearest statements seen so far of Jesus saying or indicating He is in fact the Son of Man.

Nevertheless...

There is one more!

Do You Believe in the Son of Man?

Here is a story of a man who had been born blind whom Jesus healed. The man was afterwards cast out of the synagogue for testifying it was Jesus who had healed him. I have included background of the passage narrative to show the importance of exactly what the man did, as a way to set the scene to show exactly what Jesus did.

This man had already testified once to the Pharisees that he had been born blind and Jesus was the one who had healed him, yet, they did not believe him. The Pharisees then brought in the adult man's parents who also testified that he had indeed been born blind, but they did not know how he could now see.

Therefore, the Pharisees brought the man in a second time and began to question him again. And here is where we pick up our story.

The Pharisees said to the man,

> *"Give God the glory! We know that this Man (Jesus) is a sinner."*
>
> *He answered and said,*
> *"Whether He is a sinner or not I do not know. One thing I know: that though I was blind, now I see."*

> *Then they said to him again,*
> *"What did He do to you? How did He open your eyes?"*
>
> *He answered them,*
> *"I told you already, and you did not listen. Why do you want to hear it again? Do you also want to become His disciples?"*
>
> *Then they reviled him and said,*
> *"You are His disciple, but we are Moses' disciples. We know that God spoke to Moses; as for this fellow, we do not know where He is from."*

Notice how the man responds.

> *The man answered and said to them,*
> *"Why, this is a marvelous thing, that you do not know where He is from; yet He has opened my eyes! Now we know that God does not hear sinners; but if anyone is a worshiper of God and does His will, He hears him. Since the world began it has been unheard of that anyone opened the eyes of one who was born blind. If this Man were not from God, He could do nothing."*
>
> *They answered and said to him,*
> *"You were completely born in sins, and are you teaching us?"*
>
> *And they cast him out.*
>
> *John 9:24-34 NKJV par.*

Notice the heart and courage of this man. This man has been blind his entire life, but when the Pharisees revile him, he does not fear them; now he can see! He does not hesitate to say exactly what he thinks of them, the religious leaders, *the Pharisees* of that day!

> *"Why, this is a marvelous thing, that you do not know where He is from; yet He has opened my eyes!"*

And the text says the man was *"cast out"* of the synagogue for saying this.

And now for the main passage. It says that Jesus afterwards heard that the man had been cast out of the synagogue.

Jesus found the man and said to him,

> *"Do you believe in the Son of Man?"*
>
> *He answered,*
> *"Who is He, Lord, that I may believe in Him?"*

Then Jesus replied,

> *"You have both seen Him, and He is the one who is talking with you."*

And the man said,

> *"Lord, I believe."*
>
> *And he worshiped Him.*
>
> John 9:35-38 NASB

Jesus has finally identified Himself as the Son of Man! Yet, notice once more, how He said it.

First, Jesus said, *"Do you believe in the Son of Man?"*
Then, He said, *"You have both seen Him, and He is the one who is talking with you."*

Jesus is using another indirect association to identify Himself as the Son of Man, albeit this time, the association is quite clear!

Jesus, *while talking* to the man, says,

> *"He is the one **who is talking** with you."*

Who is talking to the man? *Jesus.*
Who did Jesus say is talking to the man? *"the Son of Man."*

Of all the *"Son of Man"* statements Jesus has made, this one passage is the clearest declaration that Jesus is the Son of Man.

Yet, take note in all of these passages, Jesus never once said, *"I am the Son of Man."* Jesus always veiled that He is the Son of Man within His words, by *the way* He spoke.

> *It was **how** He spoke!*

Jesus has finally declared He is... the Son of Man.

And now we see *how* He declared it.

> *He (the Son of Man) is the one who is talking with you*
> *I am (the Son of Man) who is talking with you.*

There is a discrepancy however, with the previous passage as to whether Jesus said,

> *"Do you believe in the Son of Man?"* or, *"the Son of God?"*

Other versions say,

> *"Do you believe in the Son of God?"*
>
> *John 9:35 NKJV*

This is not a minor discrepancy. There is a significant difference between the meanings of these two titles. The titles, *"Son of God"* and *"Son of Man"* are not synonymous with each other; they are used for two different purposes.

One is born of God; one is born of man.

Although in this particular instance they do happen to be referring to the same person of Jesus Christ, they are still *two different titles*, used for *two different purposes*.

If Jesus had said, *"Do you believe in the Son of God?"* and then said, *"You have both seen Him, and He is the one who is talking with you,"* this would have been the only instance of Jesus declaring He is the Son of God.

As we have already seen, nowhere else did Jesus ever directly declare He is the Son of God. If Jesus had said, *"the Son of God"* He would have been testifying of Himself and in effect saying,

> *"I am the Son of God!"*

The fact that this is the only instance that records Jesus declaring He is the Son of God, and the fact this *one and only instance is in dispute* (other versions say, *"the Son of Man"*), strengthens the position that Jesus did not say, *"the Son of God."*

There is other evidence within the text itself that also supports this view.

Remember the response of the Jews when Jesus said,

> *I and My Father are one.*
>
> *John 10:30 NKJV*

The Jews took up stones to stone Him.
And when Jesus said,

> *before Abraham was born, I am.*
>
> *John 8:58 NASB*

The Jews again took up stones to stone Him.

Whenever the Jews felt Jesus was claiming to be God or the Son of God, they tried to stone Him for blasphemy. The problem with the "*Son of God*" version is the text says Pharisees were present who heard Jesus say these things.

According to this version of John 9:35, Jesus identifies Himself as the Son of God, yet, there is absolutely no reaction from the Jews or Pharisees when He said this. Look at the rest of the story and we will see the Pharisees finally do react to something Jesus says, but it was not to Jesus saying He is the Son of God.

Jesus said,

> "*For judgment I have come into this world, that those who do not see may see, and that those who see may be made blind.*"

And then it says,

> *Then **some of the Pharisees who were with Him** heard these words, and said to Him,*
> "*Are we blind also?*"
>
> *John 9:39-40 NKJV e.a.*

The Pharisees reacted to Jesus saying, "*that those who do not see may see*" and said,

> "*Are we blind also?*"

The Pharisees did not react at all to Jesus, *as recorded*, saying,

> *"Do you believe in the Son of God?"*
> *"He is the one who is talking with you."*

When Jesus said this,

> *The Pharisees said nothing!*

The Pharisees were present when Jesus said these things. If Jesus had in fact said *"the Son of God"* they would have taken up stones to stone Him!

But they did not!

There was absolutely no reaction at all from the Pharisees when He said, *"You have both seen Him, and He is the one who is talking with you."* There was no reaction because…, Jesus did not say, *"Do you believe in the Son of God?"*

> *He said, "the Son of Man"!*

To Those Who Were Rejected

Notice to whom it was that Jesus identified Himself as the Son of Man.

Jesus said it to a man who had been cast out of the synagogue and rejected by the Jewish leadership. He said it to a man who had been rejected by his people. It was to this man only, that Jesus identified Himself as the Son of Man.

> *"Do you believe in the Son of Man?"*
> *"Who is He, Lord, that I might believe?"*
> *"You have both seen Him, and He is the one who is talking with you."*

Also remember this, the only person to whom Jesus identified Himself as the Messiah, the Christ, was not to one of His own people, the Jews; it was to a Samaritan woman. It was to a person who also had been rejected by the Jewish people.

> "I know that Messiah is coming" (who is called Christ).
>
> "I who speak to you am He."

John 4:25, 26 NKJV

To this man, a blind beggar, rejected by the Jewish leadership, and to this woman, a Samaritan, rejected by the Jewish people, did Jesus identify Himself.

To these two people only, did Jesus clearly and plainly declare who He is!

> "He is the one who is **talking with you**."
> "I who **speak to you** am He."

If you want to know who this Jesus is,

> "He is the one who is speaking to you!"

The Son of God, He Is the Son of Man

Earlier, we saw Jesus say this about the Son of God.

> "The Son of God, He is the Son of Man."

Jesus has identified two people as the Son of Man.

> The Son of God, is the Son of Man.

And,

> Jesus, is the Son of Man.

Jesus, the Son of Man, is the Son of God!

In Jesus' own words, using *only indirect associations* and *indirect identifications*, comes this declaration,

> I am the Son of God!

Jesus did say He is the Son of God.

> It was just in the way He said it!

Known by Many Names

Jesus was known by many names or titles: Jesus the Nazarene, Jesus of Nazareth, the son of Joseph, the son of Mary, the son of David, Lord, Rabbi, Master, Teacher.

Nathanael said to Jesus,

> *"Rabbi, You are the Son of God! You are the King of Israel!"*
>
> *John 1:49 NKJV*

Peter said to Jesus,

> *"You are the Christ, the Son of the Living God."*
>
> *Matthew 16:16 NASB*

Jesus was known by many names, yet, no one ever referred to Jesus, or called Him by the name, *"Son of Man."*

Jesus was never known by the people to be *"the Son of Man"* and the disciples took that name for granted. Not once did anyone, be they the Jewish people or His own disciples, ever refer to Him or call Him by *that name.*

We take it for granted that Jesus is the Son of Man. Yet, we need to realize Jesus was the only person to ever use, or even speak those words, with the exception of this one instance when the people asked Him,

> *Who is this Son of Man?*

Remember How He Spoke

After Jesus had been buried and the Sabbath had passed, women came to Jesus' tomb early in the morning. The women found the stone used to seal the tomb rolled away, and the tomb empty. Then they saw two men or angels in dazzling clothing, described in Matthew as having an appearance like lightning.

Here is the story.

> *Now on the first day of the week, very early in the morning, they, and certain other women with them, came to the tomb bringing the spices which they had prepared. But they found the stone rolled away from the tomb. Then they went in and did not find the body of the Lord Jesus. And it happened, as they were greatly perplexed about this, that behold, two men stood by them in shining garments. Then, as they were afraid and bowed their faces to the earth,*

The angels said to them,

> *"Why do you seek the living among the dead? He is not here, but is risen!* **Remember how He spoke** *to you when He was still in Galilee,* **saying,** *'**The Son of Man** must be delivered into the hands of sinful men, and be crucified, and the third day rise again.'"*

And it says,

> *And they remembered His words.*
>
> Luke 24:1-8 NKJV e.a.

The angels told the women to remember *how* He spoke.

He said, "the Son of Man"!

In Closing

The angels said to the women,

> *"Why do you seek the living among the dead?*
> *He is not here, but is risen!*
>
> *Luke 24:5-6 NKJV*

Jesus had said to the Jews,

> *You search the Scriptures, for in them you think you have eternal*
> *life; and these are they which testify of Me.*
>
> *John 5:39 NKJV*

Why do you seek the living among the dead?

~ *Intermission* ~

OPENING VIGNETTE

HE WILL OPEN HIS MOUTH IN PARABLES

IN THE PRECEDING PAGES, IT HAS BEEN THE IDENTITY OF JESUS, the Messiah of Israel, that had been hidden. Now, we are going to see something new, something else that also has been hidden.

Something else has been hidden!

Jesus spoke many things to the people in parables. He used the following parables to speak about the kingdom of heaven.

> *"To what shall I liken the kingdom of God? It is like leaven, which a woman took and **hid** in three measures of meal till it was all leavened."*
>
>

Luke 13:20-21 NKJV e.a.

> *"The kingdom of heaven is like a treasure **hidden** in the field, which a man **found** and **hid** again; and from joy over it he goes and sells all that he has and buys that field.*
>
> Matthew 13:44 NASB e.a.

> *"Again, the kingdom of heaven is like a merchant **seeking** fine pearls, and upon **finding** one pearl of great value, he went and sold all that he had and bought it.*
>
> Matthew 13:45-46 NASB e.a.

Jesus used many parables when speaking to the people. Matthew writes that Jesus fulfilled the following prophecy.

> *"I will open My mouth in parables;*
> *I will utter things hidden since the foundation of the world."*
>
> Matthew 13:35 <u>NASB</u>

He will open His mouth in parables.

Welcome to Act 8 – The Parables

Act 8

The Parables

SOMETHING HAS BEEN HIDDEN

IN THE THREE PARABLES WE JUST READ, there is a common theme: *Something has been hidden.* The parables refer to something hidden, or speak of something being sought and something having been found.

- In the first parable, leaven is "*hid*" in three measures of meal.
- In the second parable, a treasure is "*hidden*" in a field, which when "*found*," is then "*hid*" again.
- In the third parable, a merchant is "*seeking*" or searching for fine pearls and "*finds*" one of great value.

These parables all refer to something hidden, but do not say what that something is. Jesus did not say what was hidden, but He did say it was "*like the kingdom of heaven.*"

> *The kingdom of heaven is like… a treasure hidden*
> *The kingdom of heaven is like… something hidden*

The prophecy Matthew referenced to Jesus, states He will open His mouth in parables and,

> "*will utter **things hidden** since the foundation of the world.*"

The prophecy speaks of "*things*" that are hidden: "*hidden things.*" What these "*things*" are is not yet known. But what it is declaring is that the things that will be uttered or spoken of, are in fact hidden. And they have been hidden from the very foundation of the world.

> "*I will utter things **hidden since the foundation of the world**.*"

This prophetic statement shows before the world came into being, a mystery was set in motion. Before the very foundation of the world, something, or "*some things,*" were hidden.

> *Something has been hidden!*

These hidden things, how will they be spoken of?
Through the use of parables.

> *"I will open My mouth in parables;*
> *I will utter things hidden since the foundation of the world."*

Through the use of parables, the hidden things will be spoken of.
In the parables, the hidden things will be mentioned.

From this verse we see that the parable is the method or instrument which
has been chosen to speak of, or tell about these hidden things.

> *Hidden things will be spoken of in parables.*

If we ask, why were these things hidden, for what purpose? We find we
may not be able to fully answer this question. But Jesus Himself has
provided at least a partial answer.

Jesus was questioned by His disciples as to why He spoke to the people
in parables.

The disciples asked Him,

> *"Why do You speak to them in parables?"*
>
> *Jesus answered them,*
> *"To you it has been granted to know the mysteries of the kingdom*
> *of heaven, but to them it has not been granted.*
>
> *Matthew 13:10-11 NASB*

Jesus also said,

> *those who are outside get everything in parables*
>
> *Mark 4:11 NASB*

Jesus in speaking and referring to His disciples said,

> *"To you it has been granted to know the mysteries of the kingdom*
> *of heaven"*

Then regarding the others, He said,

> *"but to them it has not been granted."*

Why did He speak to the others in parables?

Because, it had not been granted for them to know...

> *"the mysteries of the kingdom of heaven"*

The word translated here as *"granted"* is the Greek word *'Didomi'* which can also be translated as *'to give, to allow or to permit.'*[4]

In the most basic terms Jesus was saying,

> *"It is not allowed for them to know."*
> *"It is not permitted for them to know."*

And... in another very real sense it can also be said, Jesus Himself was not allowed to tell them.

> *Jesus was not permitted to tell them!*

Why had it not been granted for them to know?

Jesus continued,

> *"Therefore I speak to them in parables; **because while seeing they do not see, and while hearing they do not hear, nor do they understand**. "In their case the prophecy of Isaiah is being fulfilled, which says,*
>
> > *'**You will keep on hearing, but will not understand;**
> > **You will keep on seeing, but will not perceive;**
> > For the heart of this people has become dull,
> > With their ears they scarcely hear,
> > And they have closed their eyes,
> > Otherwise they should see with their eyes,
> > Hear with their ears,
> > And understand with their heart and return,
> > And I would heal them.'*
>
> *Matthew 13:13-15 NASB e.a.*

Jesus states, because the Jewish people have been witnesses to the things He has done, and still do not see, and have heard the things He has taught, and still do not hear, they have in fact closed their eyes and closed their ears.

Therefore, they will continue to see and yet not see and continue to hear and yet not hear.

Because they have closed their eyes,

> *It has been hidden from them!*

Jesus said to the Jews,

> *though you do not believe Me, **believe the works**, so that you may know and understand that the Father is in Me, and I in the Father.*
>
> *John 10:38 NASB e.a.*

> *"Woe to you, Chorazin! Woe to you, Bethsaida! For **if the mighty works which were done in you had been done in Tyre and Sidon, they would have repented long ago** in sackcloth and ashes.*
>
> *Matthew 11:21 NKJV e.a.*

> *"O Jerusalem, Jerusalem, the one who kills the prophets and stones those who are sent to her! How often I wanted to gather your children together, as a hen gathers her chicks under her wings, **but you were not willing!***
>
> *Matthew 23:37 NKJV e.a.*

As Jesus approached the city of Jerusalem, He wept over it and said,

> *"If you had known in this day, even you, the things which make for peace! **But now they have been hidden from your eyes.***
>
> *because **you did not recognize** the time of your visitation."*
>
> *Luke 19:42, 44 NASB e.a.*

Because they did not recognize the time of their visitation, now these things have been hidden from their eyes.

Now these things were hidden from them.

> *To them it has not been granted to know...*
> *the mysteries of the kingdom of heaven*
>
> *To them it has been hidden!*

Oh, what a terrible state for the people to be in, that the kingdom of heaven should be hidden from them.

Jesus had told the people,

> *"A little while longer the light is with you. Walk while you have the light, lest darkness overtake you; he who walks in darkness does not know where he is going. While you have the light, believe in the light, that you may become sons of light."*

> *John 12:35-36 NKJV*

Because the people refused to believe in Jesus,
because they refused to believe His words,
because they refused to believe His miracles,
the light that had been made available to them has now been taken away!

> *"Why do You speak to them in parables?"*
>
> *"To you it has been granted to know the mysteries of the kingdom of heaven, but to them it has not been granted. "For whoever has, to him more shall be given, and he will have an abundance;*

And then Jesus said,

> *but whoever does not have, even* **what he has shall be taken away from him.**

> *Matthew 13:10-12 NASB e.a.*

> *Because they refused to believe, their light had been taken away!*

Dark Sayings

We find versions of the following passage recorded in both the Old and New Testaments.

In the book of Matthew, it says,

> *"I will open My mouth in parables;*
> *I will utter things hidden since the foundation of the world."*

> *Matthew 13:35 NASB*

In the book of Psalms, we read,

> *I will open my mouth in a parable;*
> *I will utter dark sayings of old*

Psalm 78:2 NKJV

> *I will utter **dark sayings** of old*

The author of this verse prophesied that through the use of parables, He will utter dark sayings. The word translated as "*dark sayings*" is the Hebrew word '*Chiydah*' which can be interpreted as '*a riddle or difficult, perplexing or hard question.*'[5]

In the book of Ezekiel the Lord says to the prophet,

> "*Son of man, pose a **riddle**, and speak a **parable** to the house of Israel*

Ezekiel 17:2 NKJV e.a.

First, notice again, this is another prophecy being addressed to Ezekiel as "*son of man*" which we now know speaks prophetically of Jesus Christ.

Jesus, the Son of Man,

> *will pose a **riddle**, and speak a **parable** to the house of Israel.*

The Lord tells Ezekiel to give *a riddle* to the house of Israel *by… speaking to them a parable.*

The word used here for "*riddle*" is '*Chiydah*,' the same word used above for "*dark sayings*." The clearest illustration we have of the use of this word is by the Lord Himself when He speaks about Moses.

The Lord said,

> *I speak with him (Moses) face to face,*
> *Even plainly, and not in (Chiydah) **dark sayings**;*

Numbers 12:8 NKJV e.a. par.

In this verse there is a contrast being made between speaking openly and plainly as opposed to speaking in dark sayings with hidden meanings.

With the "*dark sayings*" it is a hidden type of speech one must contemplate or ponder. However, with Moses the Lord speaks "*face to face.*" The Lord speaks plainly; Moses understands. The dark and hidden sayings are contrasted against plain and clear speech.

> "*I will open My mouth in parables;*
> *I will utter things hidden since the foundation of the world.*"
>
> Matthew 13:35 <u>NASB</u>

Or, if paraphrased,

> *I will open My mouth in **riddles and dark sayings**,*
> *and I will utter hidden things*
>
> "*Why do You speak to them in parables?*"
>
> *Because to them it has not been granted to know the mysteries of the kingdom of heaven!*
>
> "*Therefore I speak to them in parables*
>
> See Matthew 13:35, 10-11, 13 <u>NASB</u> par.

The Purpose of the Parables

What is the purpose of the parables?

Parables are normally seen as teaching aids, used to help convey a truth or a lesson. Parables use similitudes and comparative speech to give understanding. They are used to help bring a level of clarity to a topic that may otherwise be difficult to understand.

Parables can and normally would be used to teach, but is this the only purpose for which a parable can be used? Are they used only to teach, and only to give understanding?

If this is true, why then are they given to the people, *if it is not permitted* for them to know?

There are many teachings and commentaries on the subject of whether the parables are used to teach and reveal or whether they are used to hide. There are in fact some parables that are meant to teach and reveal. Nevertheless...

Some parables are meant to hide!

Some of the parables Jesus used *were not* teaching aids, or hearing aids to help the people hear and understand. Rather, some of them were in fact, *'not-hearing'* aids. They were used for those who did not hear, so they would not hear, and for those who did not see, so they would not see.

The parables in this case, as used by Jesus, are not being used to teach and explain as they normally would be used. But rather,

They are being used to hide.

There are some parables Jesus spoke that were able to be understood. These parables were intended to be understood and were used to teach and to reveal.

Here is an example of a parable the Pharisees understood.

Jesus said,

> *"Hear another parable: There was a certain landowner who planted a vineyard and set a hedge around it, dug a winepress in it and built a tower. And he leased it to vinedressers and went into a far country. Now when vintage-time drew near, he sent his servants to the vinedressers, that they might receive its fruit. And the vinedressers took his servants, beat one, killed one, and stoned another. Again he sent other servants, more than the first, and they did likewise to them.*
>
> *Then last of all he sent his son to them, saying, 'They will respect my son.'*
>
> *But when the vinedressers saw the son, they said among themselves, 'This is the heir. Come, let us kill him and seize his inheritance.'*

> *So they took him and cast him out of the vineyard and killed him.*

Then Jesus said to them,

> *"Therefore, when the owner of the vineyard comes, what will he do to those vinedressers?"*

The Pharisees replied,

> *"He will destroy those wicked men miserably, and lease his vineyard to other vinedressers who will render to him the fruits in their seasons."*
>
> *Jesus said to them,*
> *"Have you never read in the Scriptures:*
>> *'The stone which the builders rejected*
>> *Has become the chief cornerstone.*
>> *This was the LORD's doing,*
>> *And it is marvelous in our eyes'?*
>
> *"Therefore I say to you, the kingdom of God will be taken from you and given to a nation bearing the fruits of it. And whoever falls on this stone will be broken; but on whomever it falls, it will grind him to powder."*

And Matthew wrote,

> *Now when the chief priests and Pharisees heard His parables, **they perceived (or understood) that He was speaking of them**.*
>
> Matthew 21:33-45 NKJV e.a. par.

The parables that can be understood *are meant to be understood*. They are meant to teach and to reveal.

And yet, notice this, although it says the Pharisees understood, *Jesus was speaking about them...*

They still did not understand, *the parable was speaking about Jesus.*
They still did not understand, *Jesus is the Son of the owner of the vineyard.*

They understood only part of the parable, *that He was speaking about them*. They understood what could be understood; the remainder of the parable remained hidden.

Today, we understand this parable because we know how Jesus died.

There are some parables that cannot easily be understood. There are some parables that need to be pondered and thought upon. Some parables speak about things that are hidden.

Here is an example of a parable that is not yet fully understood.

> *"To what shall I liken the kingdom of God? It is like leaven, which a woman took and **hid** in three measures of meal till it was all leavened."*
>
> *Luke 13:20-21 NKJV e.a.*

The kingdom of God is like leaven? Leaven is used to represent sin or hypocrisy. Hidden in three measures of meal? Until it was all leavened?

To this day, *there have been, and continue to be*, numerous commentaries written on the meaning of this parable. If the meaning of the parable were clear and could be understood, there would be no need for all of these commentaries.

> *The parables that cannot be understood,*
> *are not intended to be understood.*

What Is Being Hidden?

What is being hidden? What are the *hidden things* the parables are speaking of? What are they hiding?

Jesus said *they are mysteries*.

> *"To you it has been granted to know **the mysteries** of the kingdom of heaven, but to them it has not been granted.*
>
> *Matthew 13:11 NASB e.a.*

To them it has not been granted to know "*the mysteries*" of the kingdom of heaven. The parables are used to keep the mysteries of the kingdom of heaven hidden.

Jesus spoke to them in parables or, *riddles and dark sayings*, to speak to them of "*mysteries.*"

"*Mysteries*" are being spoken of in parables.

Or, if said another way,

"*Mysteries*" are being spoken of in "*riddles.*"

The *mystery being spoken of* is hidden within, *a riddle*.
Notice the dual mysteries.

The mystery of: *The kingdom of heaven.*
And,
The mystery of: *The meaning of the parable or riddle.*

> *I will open My mouth in riddles and dark sayings*
> *about mysteries that have been hidden from the foundation of the*
> *world.*

Do the Parables Reveal the Mystery?

If Jesus speaks in a parable, *of a mystery*, does the parable He spoke then reveal the mystery?

> "*I will open My mouth in parables;*
> *I will **utter** things hidden since the foundation of the world.*"
>
> Matthew 13:35 <u>NASB</u> e.a.

He will *utter* hidden things.
He will *mention* hidden things.
He will *talk of* hidden things.
He will *speak of* hidden things.
He will *speak of things* that have been hidden from the foundation of the world.

Of these things He will speak.

If we say something is hidden, have we revealed the thing which is hidden?
If we say something is hidden, has it then been found?
If we say there is a mystery, have we then revealed the mystery?

To know *of a mystery* is not to know *the secret* of the mystery. On the contrary, to know *of a mystery* is part of the mystery itself. For it must first be known there is in fact a mystery, for there to even be a mystery.

If we do not know there is a mystery,

> *then there is no mystery at all!*

If we speak in riddles of a mystery, have we revealed the mystery?
If we speak in dark sayings of a mystery, have we revealed the mystery?
If we speak in parables with unknown meanings, have we revealed the mystery?

In speaking all these parables, the mystery has not been revealed. To the contrary, the mystery grows ever more, a mystery.

> *The parables do not reveal the mystery.*
> *The parables help create the mystery.*

A special note needs to be made here: The parables do not actually hide the things that have been hidden (*they were hidden from the foundation of the world*). The parables speak of hidden things while still keeping them concealed. The parables create the mystery of the things that are hidden.

> *I will open my mouth in a parable;*
> *I will utter dark sayings of old*
>
> > Psalm 78:2 NKJV

Notice this and see,

> *The parables speak of a mystery.*
> *The parables create the mystery.*

Who Are the Parables for?

Jesus mentions two separate and distinct groups of people.

> "**To you** it has been granted to know
> the mysteries of the kingdom of heaven,
> **but to them** it has not been granted.
> "Therefore I speak **to them** in parables

Matthew 13:11, 13 NASB e.a.

Two groups of people are identified.
Two groups of people are mentioned.
There is one group to whom it has been granted.
There is a second group to whom it has not been granted.

Notice also, when Jesus identifies the two groups, He also identifies what each group has been given or granted.

To you,
It has been granted
to know the mysteries of the kingdom of heaven

To them,
It has not been granted
I speak to them **in parables**

There are two groups of people.
Each group is given something.
Each group is given something different.
Each group is given a gift.
Each group is given a different gift.

One gift is: "*to know the mysteries of the kingdom of heaven.*"
The other gift is: "*the parables.*"

There are two gifts.
Each gift is different.
Each gift is for a specific group.
Each gift is given *to only one group.*
Each gift *is only for the group to which it was given.*

There are two groups and two gifts.

There are two different groups.

There are two different gifts.

Just as it is clearly shown with the first gift:

To one group it was given that they should know, but to the other group it was not.

> **"To you it has been granted to know**
> *the mysteries of the kingdom of heaven,*
>
> **but to them it has not**
>
> Matthew 13:11 NASB e.a.

Even so, it is in the same manner with the second gift:

To one group it was given the parables, but to the other group it was not.

> *"Therefore **I speak to them** in parables*
>
> Matthew 13:13 NASB e.a.
>
> **I speak to them**, *not to you!*

Here is a mystery. The parables are not for those to whom it has been granted to know. Rather, the parables are for those to whom, *"it has not been granted to know."*

The parables *are not* for those who see.

The parables are for those who do not see.

> *because while seeing they do not see,*

The parables *are not* for those who hear.

The parables are for those who do not hear.

> *and while hearing they do not hear,*

The parables *are not* for those who understand.

The parables are for those who do not understand.

> *nor do they understand.*
>
> *Therefore I speak to them in parables*
>
> See Matthew 13:13 NASB

The parables, as stated by Jesus, *are for*:
those who do not see,
those who do not hear,
and,
those who do not understand.

Those who see and hear, are given the knowledge of the kingdom of heaven.
Those who do not see or hear, are given the parables.

John wrote,

> *But although He had done so many signs before them, they did not believe in Him,*
>
> *Therefore they could not believe, because Isaiah said again:*
> *"He has blinded their eyes and hardened their hearts,*
> *Lest they should see with their eyes,*
> *Lest they should understand with their hearts and turn,*
> *So that I should heal them."*
>
> *John 12:37, 39-40 NKJV*

Matthew writes,

> *All these things Jesus spoke to the crowds in parables,*
> *and He did not speak to them without a parable.*
>
> *Matthew 13:34 NASB*

The parables *are not* for those who believe.
The parables are for those who do not believe!

This is an extremely important point; it must be fully understood.

When Jesus spoke in parables, the parables were not spoken for His disciples and those who did believe; the parables were spoken for the multitudes who did not believe.

Jesus explained some of the parables to His disciples. *The explanation* of the parable was for the disciples, because it was granted to them to know. However, the unexplained parable itself was for the multitude, because it was not granted for them to know.

The parables are not for those who believe.
The parables are for those who do not.
The parables are not for us who believe.
The parables are for those who do not.

Because the parables are not for us, the parables are not for us *to use* to understand the kingdom of heaven. This is a very important point hidden within His teaching. It is a mystery that will become even more evident later.

Teachings on the Parables

Regarding teachings that the parables do not hide, but are used only to teach and help the people understand, we can make the following observations.

Teachers and commentators that believe the parables are only used to bring understanding and are not used to hide, continue to hold this view even while they themselves would readily admit they do not understand all of the parables.

Also, if these parables were in fact used by Jesus to speak to those, *who did not believe* to help *them* understand, why is it then, even to this day when reading the parables that *we who do believe* still do not understand?

Finally, with the exception of the parables that were explained, with over 2,000 years of Christian knowledge, study, and education, there is still no clear or certain understanding for some parables.

> *"To what shall we liken the kingdom of God? Or with what* **parable** *shall we picture it?*
>
> *It is like a mustard seed which, when it is sown on the ground, is smaller than all the seeds on earth; but when it is sown, it grows up and becomes greater than all herbs, and shoots out large branches, so that the birds of the air may nest under its shade."*
>
> *Mark 4:30-32 NKJV e.a.*

This is another example of a parable of the kingdom of God that no one fully understands and no one has been able to explain. Commentary after commentary has been written trying to explain the details in this parable.

So why is it then, we who say we believe, still do not understand these parables? Well, one reason would be,

because they were not given to us.

But, if the parables were given to the people *who did not believe*, why then did they not understand the parables?

because it had not been granted for them to know!

Here is one other point to see regarding the subtleties of the mystery of the parables.

The parables that were explained privately to the disciples, so that *only the disciples would know*, were actually given and explained, so that *all would know.*

Jesus intended that the explanations to those parables would be for everyone to hear, because He knew they would be written down. Now, because those explanations have been written down, everyone can understand the meaning of those parables, not just the disciples.

The Purpose of a Parable

What is the purpose of a parable?

If the purpose of a parable is to bring about understanding,
and yet,
the parable itself requires an explanation for its meaning to be understood,
then,
the parable is not a self-sufficient educator.

Thus, the parable is incomplete because it is without an explanation.

If the parable was created for the purpose of bringing about understanding, and yet,

it is unable to bring about that understanding without the use of further explanation,

then,

the parable has failed the very purpose for which it was created.

The parable has failed its purpose!

Unless of course…

The parable was meant to hide.

If the parable was meant to hide, then the parable does not require an explanation. The parable then, is complete in itself without the use of an explanation, and therefore, it does fulfill the purpose for which it was created.

In fact, if the parable was meant to hide, and an explanation is given that explains the mystery of the parable, then, the explanation is actually contrary to the very purpose of the parable.

The explanation is contrary to the purpose of the parable!

The explanation is meant to reveal the mystery.
But the parable was meant to hide.

Therefore, the parables are complete without the explanations.

The parables are complete without any explanations!

They are perfect in their purpose.
They were meant to hide!

The Parables

We will one day from the kingdom,
understand the mysteries of the parables.
But *we will never* from the parables,
understand the mysteries of the kingdom!

The mysteries of the kingdom are too deep and too wide.
If you want to know what these parables are for,

> *The parables are meant to hide!*

ACT 9 VIGNETTE

HE DID NOT SPEAK WITHOUT A PARABLE

J ESUS USED PARABLES WHEN SPEAKING TO THE PEOPLE, just how much though, we might be surprised.

Mark wrote this of Jesus,

> *With many such parables He was speaking the word to them, so far as they were able to hear it; and He did not speak to them without a parable*
>
> *Mark 4:33-34 NASB*

He did not speak without a parable!

Welcome to Act 9 – He Spoke to Them a Parable

Act 9

He Spoke to Them a Parable

He Said He Spoke a Parable

WHEN JESUS SPOKE TO THE PEOPLE, there were times He specifically said He was speaking a parable. Here are a few examples.

Jesus said,

> *"Now learn this parable from the fig tree: ..."* Matthew 24:32 NKJV par.
> *"Therefore hear the parable of the sower: ..."* Matthew 13:18 NKJV par.
> *"Hear another parable: ..."* Matthew 21:33 NKJV par.

There were times when Jesus said He was speaking a parable, but there were other times Jesus did not. During some of these times, the people nevertheless recognized the parable.

Here is one example where the people did recognize the parable.

Jesus said to His disciples and to the crowds,

> *"Hear and understand: Not what goes into the mouth defiles a man; but what comes out of the mouth, this defiles a man."*

Peter afterwards said to Him,

> *"Explain this parable to us."*

> *So Jesus said,*
> *"Are you also still without understanding? Do you not yet understand that whatever enters the mouth goes into the stomach and is eliminated? But those things which proceed out of the mouth come from the heart, and they defile a man.*
> Matthew 15:10-11, 15-18 NKJV

In this passage, Jesus *did not say* He was speaking a parable. However, Peter recognized it and asked Jesus to, *"Explain the parable."*

Here we see,

> *They recognized the parable.*

There were times when the people recognized the parable. However…

There were times when the people did not.

"Son of Man" Is a Prophetic Title

As we have seen, Jesus used the term, *"the Son of Man"* continually throughout His teachings. The term, *"Son of Man"* is a prophetic title spoken of in the book of Ezekiel. When Jesus said, *"the Son of Man"* He was using a prophetic term with which the people should have been familiar.

However, Jesus never said there was anything special about His use of the term, *"the Son of Man."* He did not say, "I am the Son of Man," or tell them the Son of Man is a prophetic title. He did not tell them what the term, *"the Son of Man"* meant.

Jesus simply said, "the Son of Man."

The fact that Jesus did not tell the people *"the Son of Man"* was a special or prophetic title indicates He was hiding its meaning.

A parable or riddle has a hidden meaning. Therefore, because the term, *"the Son of Man"* has a hidden meaning, it too, is a type of parable or riddle.

"The Son of Man" is a parable.

"The Son of Man" Is a Parable

Jesus did give indications there was something special about *"the Son of Man"* when He would speak of the Son of Man coming in great glory and power. However, He never said there was anything special about *"that name."* He was using *the name*, without saying what *the name* meant.

Jesus used the term, *"the Son of Man"* as a parable, but *did not say* it was a parable. If He had said to the people, *"The term, 'the Son of Man' is a parable,"* He would have revealed there was something special about *that name.* Yet, He did not. He kept the parable hidden.

He spoke a parable, that He did not say was a parable.

>*The parable, was not known to be, a parable.*

The fact that the term, *"the Son of Man"* was not known to be a parable, was actually part of the parable of, *"the Son of Man."*

For if they had known it was a parable,
they would have known what *"the Son of Man"* meant.

That the parable was not known to be a parable,
was part of the *mystery of the parable.*

The parable being hidden, was part of the parable itself.
The parable being hidden, is part of the mystery.

Here is another critical detail and insight.

Jesus spoke a parable to the people saying,

> *"The kingdom of heaven is like a man who sowed good seed in his field; but while men slept, his enemy came and sowed tares among the wheat and went his way. But when the grain had sprouted and produced a crop, then the tares also appeared. So the servants of the owner came and said to him, 'Sir, did you not sow good seed in your field? How then does it have tares?' He said to them, 'An enemy has done this.' The servants said to him, 'Do you want us then to go and gather them up?' But he said, 'No, lest while you gather up the tares you also uproot the wheat with them. Let both grow together until the harvest, and at the time of harvest I will say to the reapers, "First gather together the tares and bind them in bundles to burn them, but gather the wheat into my barn."'"*

After the crowds had left, the disciples asked Jesus,

> *"Explain to us the parable of the tares of the field."*

And Jesus said to them,

> *"He who sows the good seed is the Son of Man. The field is the world, the good seeds are the sons of the kingdom, but the tares are the sons of the wicked one. The enemy who sowed them is the [fallen angel], the harvest is the end of the age, and the reapers are the angels.*
>
> *Therefore as the tares are gathered and burned in the fire, so it will be at the end of this age. The Son of Man will send out His angels, and they will gather out of His kingdom all things that offend, and those who practice lawlessness, and will cast them into the furnace of fire. There will be wailing and gnashing of teeth. Then the righteous will shine forth as the sun in the kingdom of their Father.*
>
> *Matthew 13:24-30, 36-43 NKJV par.*

Did you notice what just happened?

Jesus spoke a parable about the kingdom of heaven. The disciples asked Jesus to explain the parable, and when Jesus *"explained"* the parable, He said,

> *"He who sows the good seed is the Son of Man."*

Notice what Jesus did:
He used the term, *"the Son of Man,"*
to explain the parable of, *"the kingdom of heaven."*

Or, if said another way,

Jesus used *the parable* of, *"the Son of Man,"*
to explain *the parable* of, *"the kingdom of heaven."*

Jesus did say,

> *"He who sows the good seed is... the Son of Man."*

However, Jesus *did not* say,

> *Who the Son of Man is... that sows the good seed.*

Jesus used one parable, to explain another parable.

> *"Explain to us the parable"*

> *"He who sows the good seed is (the Son of Man)."*
> *"He who sows the good seed is (a parable)."*

They Did Not Recognize the Parable

Neither the people nor the Jewish leadership recognized who Jesus was.

> *They did not recognize (the Son of Man).*
> *They did not recognize (the Parable).*

> *"If you had known in this day, even you, the things which make for peace!* ***But now they have been hidden from your eyes.***
>
> *because* ***you did not recognize*** *the time of your visitation."*
>
> *Luke 19:42, 44 NASB e.a.*

Because they did not recognize *"the Parable,"*

> *He has now been hidden from their eyes!*

A Parable Does Not Need to Be Called a Parable

As we continue, we will see more things of which Jesus spoke that He did not say were parables. We will also see more instances of parables being used to explain parables.

And just as we saw from Act 1,

A prophecy does not need to be called a prophecy, to be a prophecy.

Even so, it is the same with the parables,

A parable does not need to be called a parable, to be a parable.

A parable is still a parable, regardless if anyone ever recognizes it or not! The parables were hidden and the Jewish people did not recognize them.

They did not recognize the Parable!

"(Son of man), pose a riddle, and speak a parable to the house of Israel
"(Parable), pose a riddle, and speak a parable to the house of Israel
See Ezekiel 17:2 NKJV par.

As we continue, remember this,

Something is a parable, which was not said to be a parable!

ACT 10 VIGNETTE

Faith

Faith
the final frontier
to boldly go where no one has gone before!

To quote a couple of lines from a popular science fiction series,[6] that's what faith is to us.

We use faith,

> *To boldly go, where no one has gone before.*
> *To boldly do, what no one has done before.*

What is faith?

In basic terms, it is defined as belief, or trust. We tend to use the words faith, belief and trust interchangeably yet, there are slight differences with each.

What did Jesus teach about faith?

Jesus spoke about the importance of having faith. He made quite an impressive case for faith and all that could be accomplished through faith.

Jesus taught that things which seemed impossible, were indeed possible with faith.

When Jesus spoke of faith,
He spoke of those who had faith,
and spoke of those who had no faith.

Jesus commended those with great faith,
and reproved those with little faith.

We will look at each of the verses on faith and see exactly what Jesus taught about faith, the importance of faith, and most importantly of all, we will finally see...

> *What faith is truly for.*

Welcome to Act 10 – What Faith Is For

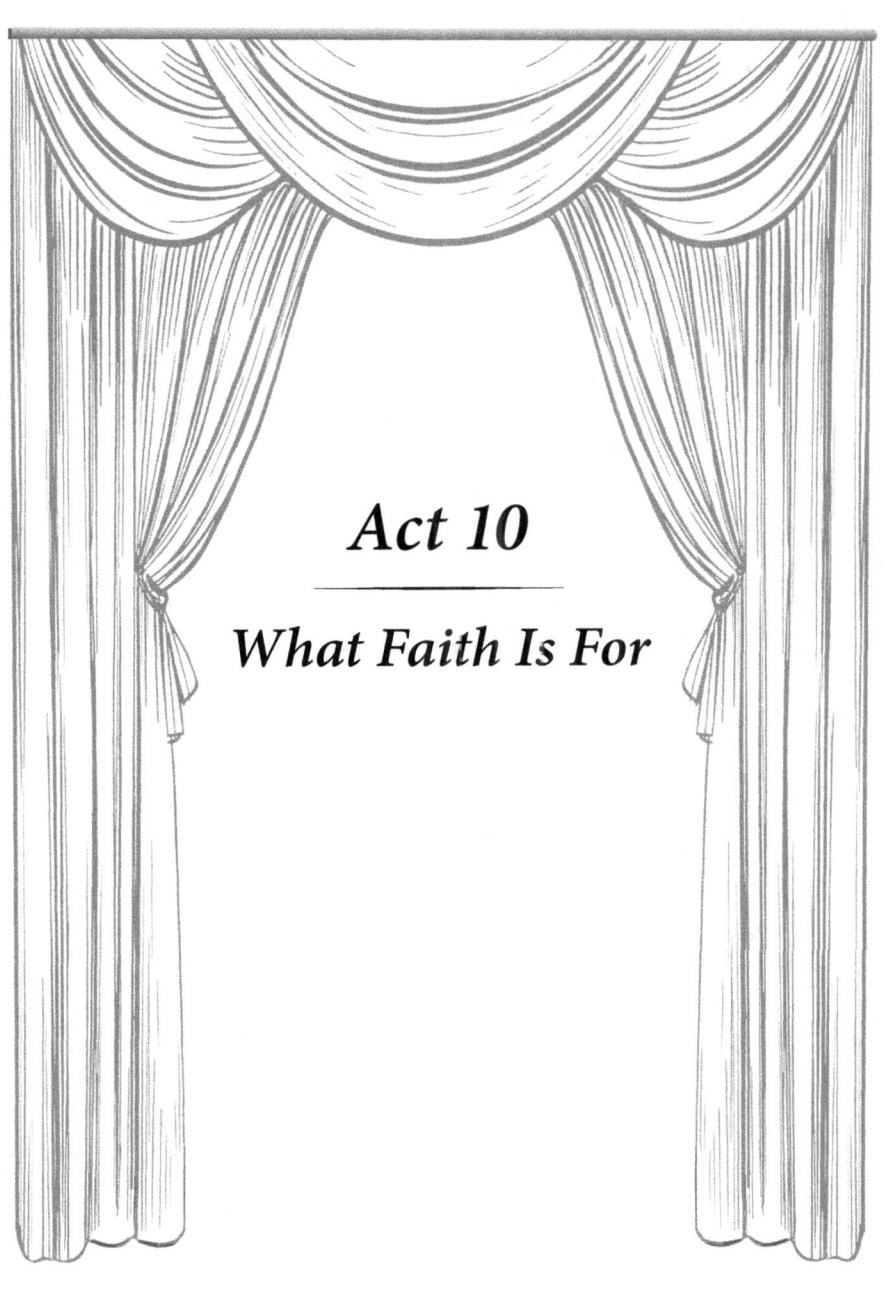

Act 10

What Faith Is For

What He Said

JESUS SPOKE OF THOSE WHOSE FAITH MADE THEM WELL. He also spoke of those whose faith saved them.

There was a woman who had been bleeding for twelve years. When she saw Jesus, she pressed herself through the crowd surrounding Him. It says,

> [She] came from behind and touched the hem of His garment.
>
> For she said to herself,
> "If only I may touch His garment, I shall be made well."

Jesus then said to the woman,

> "Be of good cheer, daughter; your faith has made you well."

And it says,

> And the woman was made well from that hour.
>
> See Matthew 9:20-22 NKJV par.

This woman pressed her way through the crowd to get to Jesus because she believed He could heal her.

Jesus said it was this woman's faith that healed her.

> "Your faith has made you well."

There was a man who was blind, sitting by the side of the road begging. When he heard Jesus was passing by, he cried out to Him saying,

> "Jesus, Son of David, have mercy on me!"

However, the people were telling him to be quiet. Refusing to be silent, he cried out all the more saying,

> "Son of David, have mercy on me!"

When Jesus saw the man, He said to him,

> "What do you want Me to do for you?"

And he said,

> *"Lord, that I may receive my sight."*

Jesus then said to the man,

> *"Receive your sight; your faith has made you well."*

And it says,

> *And immediately he received his sight, and followed Him,*
> *glorifying God.*
>
> See Luke 18:35-43 NKJV

Though everyone was telling this man to be quiet, he persisted and cried out for Jesus. He believed Jesus could heal him.

Jesus said it was this man's faith that healed him.

> *"Your faith has made you well."*

There was a group of ten men who had leprosy. When they saw Jesus coming near to them, they stood off at a distance because of their disease and called out to Him saying,

> *"Jesus, Master, have mercy on us!"*

Jesus spoke and told the men to go show themselves to the priests. The passage says as they were leaving the men were healed.

Now one of the men, after realizing he had been healed, turned and went back to Jesus. It says he was glorifying God with a loud voice and fell on his face at Jesus' feet giving thanks to Him.

When Jesus saw the man, He said,

> *"Were there not ten cleansed? But where are the nine? Were there*
> *not any found who returned to give glory to God except this*
> *foreigner?"*

(The man was a Samaritan.)

Jesus then said to the man,

> "Arise, go your way. Your faith has made you well."
>
> See Luke 17:12-19 NKJV

This man called out after Jesus because he believed Jesus could heal him. After being healed, with a heart of gratefulness, he fell before Jesus with his face in the dirt, thanking Him.

Jesus said it was this man's faith that healed him.

> "Your faith has made you well."

There was a woman known to be a sinner. When she heard Jesus was at a Pharisee's home eating a meal, the woman came in and began to anoint Jesus' feet with perfume. It says,

> when she knew that Jesus sat at the table in the Pharisee's house, brought an alabaster flask of fragrant oil, and stood at His feet behind Him weeping; and she began to wash His feet with her tears, and wiped them with the hair of her head; and she kissed His feet and anointed them with the fragrant oil.

Jesus said to the Pharisee, the owner of the house,

> "Do you see this woman? I entered your house; you gave Me no water for My feet, but she has washed My feet with her tears and wiped them with the hair of her head. You gave Me no kiss, but this woman has not ceased to kiss My feet since the time I came in. You did not anoint My head with oil, but this woman has anointed My feet with fragrant oil. Therefore I say to you, her sins, which are many, are forgiven, for she loved much. But to whom little is forgiven, the same loves little."

Jesus then said to the woman,

> "Your faith has saved you. Go in peace."
>
> See Luke 7:36-38, 44-47, 50 NKJV

This woman was not ashamed to use her own hair to wipe the feet of Jesus. She washed and anointed His feet with her tears and perfume.

Jesus said it was this woman's faith that saved her.

> *"Your faith has saved you."*

What was it Jesus said that healed these people?
He said it was their faith.

What was it Jesus said that saved the woman who anointed His feet?
He said it was her faith.

> *It was their faith that healed them.*
> *It was her faith that saved her.*

Jesus spoke of those who had great faith.

On one occasion there was a gentile woman whose daughter was possessed by a demon. The woman came to Jesus asking Him to heal her daughter. Yet, Jesus would not respond to the woman with a single word.

Despite this, the woman persisted and bowed herself before Jesus.

The woman said again,

> *"Lord, help me!"*
>
> *And He answered and said,*
> *"It is not good to take the children's bread and throw it to the dogs."*
>
> *But she said,*
> *"Yes, Lord; but even the dogs feed on the crumbs which fall from their masters' table."*

Then Jesus said to the woman,

> *"O woman, your faith is great; it shall be done for you as you wish."*

And it says,

> *And her daughter was healed at once.*

See Matthew 15:22-28 NASB

Even after Jesus had ignored her, then made reference to a dog (for she was not Jewish), this woman did not relent or take offense. Rather, she persisted all the more saying, *"But even the dogs feed on the crumbs!"*

This woman persisted after Him because she believed Jesus could do for her what she asked. Jesus commended this woman for her faith.

Jesus said this woman had great faith.

> *"O woman, your faith is great"*

A Roman centurion came to Jesus asking Him to heal his servant who was at home paralyzed and sick. Jesus told the man He would go and heal his servant.

However, the centurion replied,

> *"Lord, I am not worthy for You to come under my roof, but just say the word, and my servant will be healed. "For I also am a man under authority, with soldiers under me; and I say to this one, 'Go!' and he goes, and to another, 'Come!' and he comes, and to my slave, 'Do this!' and he does it."*

When Jesus heard this, He said to the people following Him,

> *"Truly I say to you, I have not found such great faith with anyone in Israel.*

Then He said to the centurion,

> *"Go; it shall be done for you as you have believed."*

And it says,

> *And the servant was healed that very moment.*
>
> *See Matthew 8:5-10, 13 NASB*

This centurion had such a strong belief in what Jesus could do that he felt there was no need for Him to travel to his home. Instead, he believed Jesus could simply say the word and his servant would be healed. Jesus commended this man for his faith.

Jesus said this man had great faith.

> *"I have not found such great faith"*

Jesus said we must believe. There is an account of two blind men following Jesus, who cried out after Him.

They said to Jesus,

> *"Have mercy on us, Son of David!"*

Jesus said to the blind men,

> *"Do you believe that I am able to do this?"*
>
> *They said to Him,*
> *"Yes, Lord."*
>
> *Then He touched their eyes, saying,*
> *"It shall be done to you according to your faith."*

Then it says,

> *And their eyes were opened.*
>
> *Matthew 9:27-30 NASB*

Jesus asked the men if they believed He was able to heal them, and they said, *"Yes."* Jesus then said their healing would be to them according to their faith.

The men believed, and they were healed.

> *"Do you believe?"*

There was a man named Jairus whose daughter was at home dying. He came and fell at Jesus' feet and begged Him to come to his home and lay His hands on his daughter so she would live. Yet, while Jesus was speaking, someone came and told the man his daughter had died.

The person said to Jairus,

> *"Your daughter has died; do not trouble the Teacher anymore."*

However, Jesus said to the man,

> *"Do not be afraid any longer; only believe, and she will be made well."*
>
> See Luke 8:41-42, 49-50 NASB

The man believed and brought Jesus to his home. Jesus took the girl (who was dead) by the hand and spoke to her, saying,

> *"Little girl, I say to you, arise."*
>
> Mark 5:41 NKJV

And the girl got up!

Jesus told the man to only believe and his daughter would be healed. The man believed, and his daughter lived.

> *"Only believe"*

There was a man named Lazarus who had died. Jesus came to raise him from the dead. However, Lazarus had already been buried and a large stone was sealing the tomb's entrance.

Jesus therefore, said,

> *"Remove the stone."*
>
> *Martha, the sister of the deceased, said to Him,*
> *"Lord, by this time there will be a stench, for he has been dead four days."*
>
> *Jesus said to her,*
> *"Did I not say to you that if you believe, you will see the glory of God?"*
>
> *So they removed the stone.*

And Jesus cried out with a loud voice,

> *"Lazarus, come forth."*

And it says,

> *The man who had died came forth, bound hand and foot with wrappings, and his face was wrapped around with a cloth.*

> *Jesus said to them,*
> *"Unbind him, and let him go."*
>
> John 11:39-41, 43-44 NASB

The man who had died came back to life; he was raised from the dead!

Jesus said to Martha if she believed, she would see the glory of God. Martha believed, and her brother lived!

"If you believe, you will see"

Jesus spoke to His disciples and said to them,

> *"And all things you ask in prayer, believing, you will receive."*
>
> Matthew 21:22 NASB

He also said,

> *"Therefore I say to you, all things for which you pray and ask, believe that you have received them, and they will be granted you.*
>
> Mark 11:24 NASB

Jesus told the disciples that anything they asked for in prayer, if they believed, they would receive it.

"Believe, and you will receive"

There was a man whose son was possessed by a demon. The man came seeking Jesus and asked Him to cast the demon out of his son.

The man said to Jesus,

> *if You can do anything, take pity on us and help us!*

Jesus replied to the man,

> *"'If You can?' All things are possible to him who believes."*
>
> *Immediately the boy's father cried out and said,*
> *"I do believe; help my unbelief."*

Jesus then said to the demon,

> *"You deaf and mute spirit, I command you, come out of him and do not enter him again."*

And it says,

> After crying out and throwing him into terrible convulsions, it
> came out; and the boy became so much like a corpse that most of
> them said,
>
> "He is dead!"
>
> But Jesus took him by the hand and raised him; and he got up.
>
> See Mark 9:22-27 NASB

Here Jesus makes one of the greatest statements regarding faith and
believing.

> "All things are possible to him who believes."

Jesus said to His disciples,

> "If you had faith like a mustard seed, you would say to this
> mulberry tree, 'Be uprooted and be planted in the sea'; and it
> would obey you.
>
> Luke 17:6 NASB

He also said,

> truly I say to you, if you have faith as a mustard seed, you shall say
> to this mountain, 'Move from here to there,' and it shall move; and
> nothing shall be impossible to you.
>
> Matthew 17:20 NASB

Jesus tells the disciples, if they have faith nothing will be impossible to
them. Again, here is one of the most significant statements Jesus makes
about having faith.

> "If you have faith as a mustard seed, nothing will be impossible!"

Here are two versions of the same account. Jesus earlier had cursed a fig
tree because it was found without fruit. Later, the disciples saw this same
tree completely withered.

The disciples therefore questioned Jesus about the tree, saying,

> "How did the fig tree wither all at once?"

Jesus said to them,

> *"Truly I say to you, if you have faith and do not doubt, you will not only do what was done to the fig tree, but even if you say to this mountain, 'Be taken up and cast into the sea,' it will happen.*
>
> Matthew 21:20-21 NASB

In the book of Mark, Peter says,

> *"Rabbi, look, the fig tree which You cursed has withered."*

And Jesus said to them,

> *"Have faith in God. "Truly I say to you, whoever says to this mountain, 'be taken up and cast into the sea,' and does not doubt in his heart, but believes that what he says is going to happen, it will be granted him.*
>
> Mark 11:21-23 NASB

Jesus tells the disciples if they have faith and do not doubt, even if they say to the mountain, *"be cast into the sea,"* it will happen.

> *"If you have faith and do not doubt, it will happen."*

Jesus spoke of those who had little faith.

On one occasion the disciples were in a boat at night. Jesus was not with them; He had remained behind. During the night Jesus came to them walking on the water. When the disciples saw Him, they were terrified.

But Jesus spoke to them and said,

> *"Take courage, it is I; do not be afraid."*
>
> *And Peter answered Him and said,*
> *"Lord, if it is You, command me to come to You on the water."*

And Jesus said to Peter,

> *"Come!"*

And it says,

> And Peter got out of the boat, and walked on the water and came
> toward Jesus. But seeing the wind, he became afraid, and beginning
> to sink, he cried out, saying,
>
> "Lord, save me!"
>
> And immediately Jesus stretched out His hand and took hold of him,

Then Jesus said to Peter,

> "O you of little faith, why did you doubt?"
>
> See Matthew 14:25-31 <u>NASB</u>

Although Peter saw Jesus walking on the water, and although Jesus had
told Peter to come out onto the water, Peter doubted and began to sink.

Jesus reproved Peter for doubting and said he was a person of little faith.

> "You of little faith, why did you doubt?"

On another occasion, the disciples came to Jesus after having failed at
trying to cast a demon out of a young boy.

The disciples asked Jesus,

> "Why could we not cast it out?"

Jesus said to them,

> "Because of the littleness of your faith; for truly I say to you, if
> you have faith as a mustard seed, you shall say to this mountain,
> 'Move from here to there,' and it shall move; and nothing shall be
> impossible to you.
>
> Matthew 17:19-20 <u>NASB</u>

Jesus said they were unable to cast the demon out because of their little
faith.

> "Because of the littleness of your faith"

Jesus came to His home town and began teaching the people in their synagogue.

It says the people were astonished and said,

> *"Where did this man get this wisdom, and these miraculous powers? "Is not this the carpenter's son? Is not His mother called Mary, and His brothers, James and Joseph and Simon and Judas? "And His sisters, are they not all with us? Where then did this man get all these things?"*
>
> *And they took offense at Him.*
>
> *But Jesus said to them,*
> *"A prophet is not without honor except in his home town, and in his own household."*

And it says,

> And He did not do many miracles there because of their unbelief.
>
> Matthew 13:54-58 <u>NASB</u>
>
> *Because of their unbelief, He did not do many miracles.*

With all these things Jesus taught about faith, it should now be abundantly clear just how important it is that we have faith.

By their faith, people were healed.

> *"Your faith has made you well."*

Because they believed, they were healed.

> *"Do you believe that I am able to do this?"*
> *They said to Him, "Yes, Lord."*
>
> *And their eyes were opened.*

Because they believed, the dead came back to life.

> *"Lazarus, come forth!"*
> *"Little girl, I say to you, arise."*

With faith, all things are possible.

"All things are possible to him who believes."

With faith, nothing is impossible.

"If you have faith as a mustard seed, nothing will be impossible."

However, with little faith, Peter could not walk on the water.

"Lord, save me!"
"You of little faith, why did you doubt?"

With little faith, they could not cast out the demons.

"Why could we not cast it out?"
"Because of the littleness of your faith."

With unbelief, Jesus could not do many miracles.

And He did not do many miracles there because of their unbelief.

Jesus commended those with great faith,

"O woman, your faith is great."

Jesus reproved those with little faith,

"O you of little faith."

Quite a powerful case for faith!

Jesus continuously emphasized the vital importance of having faith. And not merely having faith, but having great faith; faith that will move mountains.

"All things are possible to him who believes."

With great faith,

We can do anything.

This all seems straightforward enough,

> *Have faith,*
>> *Do not doubt,*
>>> *Only believe,*
>>>> *And we can do anything.*

> *With faith anything is possible!*

And yet...

> *Remember how He spoke.*

Sometimes, things are not always as they seem.

It's Not as It Seems

Jesus has been telling us something about faith from the very beginning and we did not hear what He was saying. We were not listening *carefully*.

> *It's not as it seems!*

At one point the disciples came to Jesus and asked Him to increase their faith.

The disciples said to Jesus,

> *"Increase our faith!"*

This request of the disciples was a direct result of Jesus teaching them about having great faith. The disciples wanted to have more faith; they wanted to have great faith. Yet, notice how Jesus responds to them.

Jesus replied,

> *"If you had faith like a mustard seed, you would say to this mulberry tree, 'Be uprooted and be planted in the sea'; and it would obey you.*
>
> Luke 17:5-6 NASB

Notice, Jesus did not tell the disciples how to increase their faith. He only told them what they could do *if they had faith*.

> *"If you had faith ..."*

This then raises a question. If it was so important that they have great faith, why didn't Jesus tell the disciples how to increase their faith? Again, this request of the disciples was a direct result of Jesus' teachings on faith.

The answer to this question will be shown later in the chapter.

Let's look at precisely what Jesus said.

He said,

> *"If you had faith like a mustard seed, you would say to this mulberry tree, 'Be uprooted and be planted in the sea'; and it would obey you."*

> *"If you had faith... **like a mustard seed...**"*

If we need to have faith like a mustard seed, we therefore, need to ask the question, exactly how much faith is, *"faith like a mustard seed"*?

It would be reasonable to assume from what Jesus taught, *"faith like a mustard seed,"* must be more faith, than the *"littleness of faith"* the disciples had when they could not cast the demon out of the young boy.

When the disciples asked Jesus,

> *"Why could we not cast it out?"*

He said to them,

> *"Because of the **littleness of your faith**;*

Then He said,

> *for truly I say to you, **if you have faith as a mustard seed**, you shall say to this mountain, 'Move from here to there,' and it shall move; **and nothing shall be impossible to you.**

Matthew 17:19-20 <u>NASB</u> e.a.

Therefore, *"faith like a mustard seed,"*
    must be more faith,
than the disciples' *"littleness of faith."*

But again, exactly how much faith is, *"faith like a mustard seed"*?

Jesus spoke a parable about the kingdom of heaven and said it too, was like a mustard seed.

He said,

> **"The kingdom of heaven is like a mustard seed,** which a man
> took and sowed in his field; and this is smaller than all other seeds,
> but when it is full grown, it is larger than the garden plants and
> becomes a tree, so that the birds of the air come and nest in its
> branches."
>
> Matthew 13:31-32 NASB e.a.

There is a companion verse to this account in the book of Mark, in it,
Jesus said,

> "To what shall we liken **the kingdom of God**? Or with what
> parable shall we picture it? **It is like a mustard seed** which, when
> it is sown on the ground, is smaller than all the seeds on earth; but
> when it is sown, it grows up and becomes greater than all herbs,
> and shoots out large branches, so that the birds of the air may nest
> under its shade."
>
> Mark 4:30-32 NKJV e.a.

"The kingdom of heaven is like a mustard seed."

Therefore, if the kingdom of heaven is *"like"* a mustard seed,
and, we are supposed to have faith that is *"like"* a mustard seed,
then what exactly, is a mustard seed *"like"*?

What is a mustard seed like?

When we hear this parable of the kingdom of heaven, we tend to focus
on how large the mustard seed becomes *after* it has been planted.

After the mustard seed has been planted,

> "It grows up and **becomes larger than all the garden plants and
> becomes a tree, and forms large branches** so that the birds of the
> air come and nest in its branches."

Yet, look closely at the description of the mustard seed *before* it has been
planted, while it still is, *"a mustard seed."* For the only time a mustard
seed is a mustard seed, is before it has been planted. After a mustard seed
has been planted, it grows and becomes, *"a mustard plant."*

Jesus said,

> "*The kingdom of heaven is like a mustard seed,*
> *and this is* **smaller than all other seeds**"

He also said,

> "*It is like a mustard seed,*
> *it is* **smaller than all the seeds**"

So, what then is a mustard seed "*like*"?

A mustard seed is "*smaller than all other seeds.*"
A mustard seed is the smallest of all other seeds.
There is no seed smaller than the mustard seed.

Therefore, if a mustard seed is,
"*a seed*" that is, "*smaller than all other seeds,*"
then, faith that is "*like*" a mustard seed must be,
"*a faith*" that is, "*smaller than all other faiths.*"

How is it "*like*" a mustard seed?

It is the smallest faith of all other faiths,
just "*like*" the mustard seed,
is the smallest seed of all other seeds.

Therefore, there is no faith smaller, than faith that is "*like*" a mustard seed.

And because there is no faith smaller than "*faith like a mustard seed,*" it can therefore be said, "*faith like a mustard seed*" is the very smallest amount of faith there is.

And...

Since it is the very smallest amount of faith there is, it can therefore also be said, if you have any amount of faith, if you have *any faith at all,* then you must already have faith that is at least equal to, faith that is like a mustard seed.

If you have any faith at all, then you already have,

> "*faith like a mustard seed*"

That, my friends, is exactly how much faith,

"faith like a mustard seed" is.

Wait – Selah

Any Faith at All

Because *"faith like a mustard seed"* is the smallest amount of faith you can have, when Jesus said,

> *if you have (**faith as a mustard seed**), you shall say to this mountain, 'Move from here to there,' and it shall move; and **nothing shall be impossible to you**.*
>
> *Matthew 17:20 <u>NASB</u> e.a.*

what Jesus was actually saying is,

> *"If you have (**any faith at all**), nothing shall be impossible to you!"*

However, we now have a problem if we use this interpretation. The disciples asked Jesus why they could not cast the demon out of the boy.

And Jesus said to them,

> *"Because of the **littleness of your faith**;*

If our interpretation is correct and Jesus was saying,

> *for truly I say to you,*
> *if you have (**even the smallest amount of faith, any faith at all**), nothing shall be impossible to you.*

then there is an inconsistency and our interpretation does not make sense. Jesus states they could not cast the demon out because the faith they had was too small; they had too little of faith.

These two statements do not agree; there is a contradiction.

The answer to this contradiction is found in one of the original manuscript versions used for the verse, *"Because of the littleness of your faith."* Here is another version that recorded an entirely different reply.

When the disciples asked Jesus,

> *"Why could we not cast it out?"*

this manuscript records Jesus as saying,

> *"Because of your **unbelief**, ..."*
>
> Matthew 17:19-20 NKJV e.a. par.

The original Greek words being translated here as *"littleness of faith"* and *"unbelief,"* are two different Greek words.

The word being used for *"littleness of faith"* is the Greek word *'Oligopistos'* which means *'little faith or of little faith';*[7] it means *'to have little faith.'*

The word being used for *"unbelief"* is the Greek word *'Apistia'* which means *'faithless or unbelief';*[8] it means *'to have no faith or no belief.'*

These two words have two completely different meanings.
These two words are not interchangeable.

With *'Oligopistos,'* we have a *"little faith."*
With *'Apistia,'* we have *"no faith."*

One has *"little faith."*
One has *"no faith."*

One of these manuscript versions is correct, the other is not; they cannot both be right. How can we determine which is correct?

Except for this one word of *"unbelief"* or *"littleness of faith"* everything else Jesus said in this conversation is consistent <u>between the different versions</u>, and is not in dispute. We can look to see which of these two words is consistent with everything else Jesus said.

If we re-ask the question, *"Why could we not cast it out?"* and use the *'Apistia'* or *"unbelief"* version as Jesus' answer, we see this version is consistent with what He said next.

> *"Why could we not cast it out?"*
> *"Because of your (Apistia) **unbelief**, (because you have **no faith**);*
>
> *for truly I say to you,*
> *if you have faith as a mustard seed, (**any faith at all**),*
> *nothing shall be impossible to you."*

The *"unbelief"* version is consistent in the text with *"faith as a mustard seed."* They could not cast out the demon because they had *"no faith"*; they had *"unbelief."* Faith as a mustard seed does represent at least some faith.

Is there anything else Jesus said that can also be used to determine which version is correct? Look at what He said to the people when they first brought the boy to Him.

The father of the boy said to Jesus,

> *"Lord, have mercy on my son, for he is a lunatic, and is very ill; for he often falls into the fire, and often into the water. "And I brought him to* **Your disciples, and they could not cure him.**"
>
> *And Jesus answered and said,*
> *"O* **unbelieving** *and perverted generation, how long shall I be with you? How long shall I put up with you? Bring him here to Me."*

Matthew 17:15-17 <u>NASB</u> *e.a.*

Observe what Jesus says; He calls them an *"unbelieving generation."* The word being translated here as *"unbelieving"* is the Greek word *'Apistos'* which means *'to be unbelieving or faithless.'*[9]

The use of this word *'Apistos'* is not in dispute. All of the other manuscript versions and accounts of what Jesus said here use this same word *'Apistos'* and it is translated as either, *'faithless'* or *'unbelieving.'* It is another form of the word *'Apistia.'*

Therefore, when they brought the boy to Jesus, He called them *'Apistos,'* faithless or *"unbelieving."* When the disciples asked Jesus why they could not heal the boy, He admonished them that it was because of their *'Apistia,'* *"unbelief."*

So, we see the version, *"Because of your unbelief,"* is consistent with all that Jesus said; the *"littleness of faith"* version is not.

Why could they not cast out the demon? Because they did not believe.

> *They had no faith!*

If they would have had even a small amount of faith, they would have been able to cast out the demon.

> *If you have **any faith at all**, (**faith as a mustard seed**),*
> *nothing shall be impossible to you.*

Now, let's revisit the verse where the disciples asked Jesus to increase their faith, and this time we will use our interpretation of *"faith like a mustard seed"* there as well.

The disciples said to Jesus,

> *"Increase our faith!"*

Jesus replied,

> *"If you had faith like a mustard seed, (**any faith at all**), you would say to this mulberry tree, 'Be uprooted and be planted in the sea'; and it would obey you.*
>
> *Luke 17:5-6 NASB par.*

If we look back at the question asked earlier,

> *Why didn't Jesus tell the disciples how to increase their faith?*

It was because, they did not need great faith. It was only necessary they have some faith, *(any faith at all)*.

> *You do not need to increase your faith.*
> *"If you have **any faith at all**, nothing will be impossible to you."*
>
> *We only need just a little faith!*

This however raises another question. If we only need just a little faith, why then did Jesus teach about having great faith?

> *Why teach great faith?*

The answer to this question will be shown later in the chapter.

We were told to remember how He spoke, so let's examine exactly what Jesus said.

Notice, Jesus only said,

> *"If you have... **faith like a mustard seed** ..."*

If it is true, we only need just a little faith, any faith at all,
then, why didn't Jesus simply say, *"If you have... (any faith at all) ..."*?

Not once, did Jesus ever say,

> *"If you have (any faith at all), nothing will be impossible to you."*

He only said,

> *"If you have (faith like a mustard seed), nothing will be impossible to you."*

Twice Jesus said this,
once when the disciples asked Him to increase their faith,
and,
once when the disciples asked Him why they could not cast out the demon.

On both occasions Jesus' response was the same.

He said,

> *"If you have faith like a mustard seed ..."*

So, we need to ask the question again.

If, *"faith like a mustard seed"* does in fact mean *"any faith at all,"* why
then didn't Jesus simply say,

> *"If you have any faith at all..."*?

The answer is this:

> *Because something was being hidden!*

Hidden behind the phrase *"faith like a mustard seed,"*
is the truth that only *"just a little faith"* is needed.

By using the phrase, *"faith like a mustard seed,"* Jesus was able to say how much faith was needed so *"nothing would be impossible,"* without revealing how much faith that was.

It was hidden.

Remember how He spoke!

You of Little Faith

Jesus rarely spoke of little faith. The only times He ever spoke the two words, *"little faith,"* were when He said, *"You of little faith."* Jesus used this phrase four times. Each time, it appears He is reproving the people.

In using this expression, Jesus was saying they had little faith. The phrase *"You of little faith"* does in fact mean, *"You have little faith."*

However, if Jesus said the disciples needed to have *"faith like a mustard seed,"* and, *"faith like a mustard seed"* is truly the smallest amount of faith one can have, why then would He reprove them for having *"little faith"*?

Why would Jesus reprove them?

When Peter tried to walk on the water, Jesus reproved him for his little faith. Let's look again at this story.

Why Did You Doubt? You of Little Faith!

On a certain night the disciples were alone in a boat, in the middle of the sea, when Jesus came towards them walking on the water. When the men saw Jesus in the midst of the water, they were terrified.

Jesus therefore, called out to His disciples and said to them,

> *"Take courage, it is I; do not be afraid."*
>
> *And Peter answered Him and said,*
> *"Lord, if it is You, command me to come to You on the water."*

And Jesus said to Peter,

> "*Come!*"

And it says,

> *Peter got out of the boat, and walked on the water and came toward Jesus.* **But seeing the wind, he became afraid, and beginning to sink,** *he cried out, saying,*
>
> "*Lord, save me!*"
>
> *And immediately Jesus stretched out His hand and took hold of him,*

Then Jesus reproves Peter, saying,

> "*O you of little faith, why did you doubt?*"

See Matthew 14:25-31 <u>NASB</u> e.a.

Jesus reproves Peter for having little faith. Yet, Jesus twice before, told His disciples if they had any faith at all, "*faith like a mustard seed,*" nothing would be impossible to them.

Something is not right with this story.

The little faith Peter had must have been, at the very minimum, equal to "*faith like a mustard seed*" or, "*any faith at all.*" Jesus did say Peter had some faith.

> "*O you of little faith*"

If Peter therefore, did have "*faith like a mustard seed,*" why then did Jesus reprove him, saying,

> "*You of little faith, why did you doubt?*"

Again, why did Jesus reprove Peter?
The answer to this question will be shown later in the chapter.

Jesus said to His disciples,

> "*If you have faith like a mustard seed, nothing will be impossible.*"

Peter did have "*faith like a mustard seed.*"

So, the question is this:

If nothing will be impossible, if you have *"faith like a mustard seed,"* or as we interpret it, if you have just a little faith, any faith at all, and Peter did have a little faith, why then couldn't Peter walk on water?

Should Peter have been able to walk on water with the little faith he had?

The answer is absolutely, *Yes!*

Therefore, if Peter should have been able to walk on water with the little faith he had,

> *Why couldn't Peter walk on water?*

Jesus had also said to His disciples, *"Do not doubt."*
Jesus said,

> *"Truly I say to you, if you have faith and **do not doubt**, you will not only do what was done to the fig tree, but even if you say to this mountain, 'Be taken up and cast into the sea,' it will happen.*
>
> Matthew 21:21 NASB e.a.

Another version of this account says,

> *"Truly I say to you, whoever says to this mountain, 'Be taken up and cast into the sea,' and **does not doubt** in his heart, but believes that what he says is going to happen, it will be granted him.*
>
> Mark 11:23 NASB e.a.

Jesus told His disciples, if they have faith and *"do not doubt"* then, if they say to the mountain, *"be taken up and cast into the sea,"* it would happen. The impossible would be possible; the mountain would move.

So, the question now becomes:

Would Peter have been able to walk on water with his faith, if he had not doubted?

The answer is absolutely, *Yes!*

> *If you have faith and do not doubt, nothing will be impossible.*

The common understanding of this story of Peter walking on the water is he began to sink because he doubted. However, was it really because he doubted that he began to sink? Was it really because of Peter's doubt that he could not walk on water?

If it was because he doubted, we then need to ask the question,

> *Why did Peter doubt?*

After all, that is the very question Jesus asked him.
Jesus said to Peter,

> *"Why did you doubt?"*

Why did Peter doubt he could walk on water?
The answer is this:

> *Because men can't walk on water!*

The reason Peter doubted he could walk on water is simply because,

> *Men can't walk on water.*

If we are looking for an explanation of *Cause and Effect,*

> *It was not because he doubted, that he could not walk on water.*
> *It was that he could not walk on water, that caused him to doubt.*

Peter could not walk on water long before he ever doubted that he could.

As a result, we see doubting did not make Peter unable to walk on water; Peter could not walk on water anyway.

Therefore, if men can't walk on water,
and Peter could not walk on water,
how then did Peter walk on the water?

The passage most certainly says Peter actually did walk on the water, if only for a short time.

In Matthew it says,

> *And Peter got out of the boat, and **walked on the water** and came*
> *toward Jesus. But seeing the wind, he became frightened, and*
> *beginning to sink, he cried out,*
>
> *"Lord, save me!"*
>
>

Matthew 14:29-30 NASB e.a.

It does say Peter actually did walk on the water. What then made Peter able to walk on water for that short period of time? Was it because he did not doubt?

Is it possible, for a brief period of time, Peter was able to have no doubts, and that is why he was able to walk on water?

The answer is absolutely, *No!*

If the *presence of doubt* was not the reason why Peter was not able to walk on water (men can't walk on water), can the *absence of doubt* be the reason why he was able?

Or, said another way,
if the *existence of Peter's doubt* was not the reason why he could not walk on water, can the *non-existence of that same doubt* be the reason why he could?

If there is *"no doubt,"* how can *"it"* make him able?
There is *"no doubt"* to be responsible.

Where there is no doubt, there is nothing; there is no-thing. There is therefore, nothing that could have made him able.

> *There is nothing to make him able.*
> *There is nothing that could make him able.*

Therefore, in the same way that Peter's *"doubts"* did not make him not able to walk on water, neither then, did Peter having *"no doubts"* make him able.

Once more then, if it was not because Peter had no doubts, what exactly was it that made Peter able to walk on the water?

Was Peter able to walk on the water because of his faith? Peter did have a little faith, Jesus said he did.

> *"You of little faith"*

So, was it because of Peter's faith that he was able to walk on the water?

There was a point in time, while Peter was still in the boat, a time when Peter had never before walked on water. It was the point in time, just before taking his first step out of the boat.

Peter, seeing Jesus walking on the water, said to Him,

> *"Lord, if it is You, command me to come to You on the water."*

And Jesus said to him,

> *"Come!"*

It was at this point right here that it says,

> And **Peter got out of the boat,** *and walked on the water*
>
> *Matthew 14:28-29 NASB e.a.*

Right up until this very point and moment in time, the point just before taking his first step out of the boat, Peter had never walked on water.

And after Peter got out of the boat, it says,

> *He walked!*
>
> *Peter got out of the boat,* ***and walked on the water.***

However, it then says, while Peter was walking on the water, he began to sink.

> *But seeing the wind, he became frightened, and **beginning to sink,** he cried out,*
>
> *"Lord, save me!"*
>
> *Matthew 14:30 NASB e.a.*

Therefore, we see it is actually while Peter is walking on the water, that he begins to sink.

When did Peter have the most faith he could walk on the water?

Was it while he was standing in the boat?
Or,
Was it while he was standing on the water?

When did Peter have the most faith he could walk on the water?

Was it before he ever had?
Or,
Was it while he was?

When did Peter have the most faith he could walk on water?

It was... while he actually was walking on the water!

Peter had more faith that he could, while he actually was,
than the faith that he could, before he ever had.

Therefore, we see Peter had more faith not less, while he was walking on the water. Yet, while Peter is walking on the water (having more faith now than the faith he had when he first stepped out of the boat), he begins to sink.

Peter began to walk with less faith, than the faith he had when he began to sink.

Peter walked with less and sank with more!

Therefore, seeing that Peter walked with less faith and sank with more, it could not have been Peter's faith that made him able to walk on water.

If it was not Peter's faith, what then made Peter able?

Jesus Made Him Able

It was Jesus Christ that made Peter able. This is an extremely important truth. Jesus is able to walk on water and He made Peter able to walk on water.

Jesus made him able!

It could be said, because Peter had faith, Jesus made him able.
It could also be said, because Peter did not doubt, Jesus made him able.

Yet, these are not what made Peter able.
It was not faith, nor the absence of doubt, that made him able.

These, at their very best, would only be reasons why Jesus made him able.
Regardless of any reasons why, it was only Jesus Christ that made Peter able to walk on the water.

It was not anything Peter himself did that made him able to walk on water.
It was not that Peter had faith.
It was not that Peter had no doubts.
It was not anything Peter himself did that made him able.
It was Jesus Christ that made Peter able.

> *Jesus made him able!*

Seeing now that it was not Peter's faith that made him able to walk on water, then, it could not have been any lack of Peter's faith that made him sink.

So, this brings us to a question. If it was Jesus who made Peter able to walk on water, why then did Peter sink?

Peter sank because, what had made him able, no longer made him able. And no longer being able, he sank because,

> *Men can't walk on water!*

It was Jesus that made him able.
It was also Jesus that no longer made him able.

Consequently, Peter sank because Jesus stopped making him able to walk on water.

This of course creates an obvious question. If it was Jesus who made Peter able, why then did Jesus stop making Peter able?

The answer to this question will be shown later in the chapter.

We have now come back full circle to a question we had asked earlier. Why did Jesus reprove Peter for having little faith? If it was only because of Jesus that Peter was able, why did Jesus subsequently reprove him?

If men can't walk on water, and it is completely normal to doubt that you could, why did Jesus ask Peter,

> *"Why did you doubt?"*

If all you need to have is just a little faith, and Peter did have a little faith, why did Jesus say to Peter,

> *"O you of little faith!"?*

Why did Jesus reprove Peter?

The answer is, Jesus did not reprove Peter; it only sounded as though He did. What sounded like a reproval, was no reproval at all.

> *Remember how He spoke!*

We will come back to this point later in the chapter. First however, let's look at the other instances of Jesus using this phrase, *"You of little faith."*

Why Are You Worried? You of Little Faith!

Jesus spoke to His disciples and the people telling them they do not need to worry about the things of life.

Jesus said,

> **do not be worried** about your life, as to what you will eat or what you will drink; nor for your body, as to what you will put on. Is not life more than food, and the body more than clothing? "Look at the birds of the air, that they do not sow, nor reap nor gather into barns, and yet your heavenly Father feeds them. Are you not worth much more than they? "And who of you by being worried can add a single hour to his life?
>
> "And **why are you worried** about clothing?

> *Observe how the lilies of the field grow; they do not toil nor do they spin, yet I say to you that not even Solomon in all his glory clothed himself like one of these.* "*But if God so clothes the grass of the field, which is alive today and tomorrow is thrown into the furnace, will He not much more clothe you?*
>
> ***You of little faith!***
>
> "***Do not worry*** *then, saying, 'What will we eat?' or 'What will we drink?' or 'What will we wear for clothing?'* "*For the Gentiles eagerly seek all these things; for your heavenly Father knows that you need all these things.* "*But seek first His kingdom and His righteousness, and all these things will be added to you.*
>
> "*So **do not worry** about tomorrow; for tomorrow will care for itself. Each day has enough trouble of its own.*
>
> Matthew 6:25-34 NASB e.a.

This same account is also found in the book of Luke, chapter 12, starting at verse 22.

Jesus tells the people they do not need to worry about important things of life such as what they will eat or what they will wear. He tells them if God feeds the birds and clothes the grass of the field, how much more will He feed and clothe them.

This entire message is one of encouragement. Jesus tells the people how valuable they are. God will take care of all their needs.

All of it is hopeful and uplifting, except for one small thing…

Right in the middle of this message of encouragement, Jesus stops to reprove them and says,

> *"You of little faith!"*

Then, He continues on as before with His message of encouragement, saying,

> "Do not worry then, saying, 'What will we eat?' or 'What will we drink?' or 'What will we wear for clothing?'"

> "Your heavenly Father knows that you need all these things."

The account in Luke also adds one other tender word.

> "Do not be afraid, little flock, for your Father has chosen gladly to give you the kingdom.
>
> Luke 12:32 NASB

There was absolutely nothing in His message that had even the slightest hint of disapproval, except for this one statement,

> "You of little faith!"

Right in the middle of Jesus telling them they do not need to worry, He reproves them because they do worry.

This raises a question. If Jesus was teaching the people because they did not understand, why would He reprove them as though they did understand?

It certainly *sounds like*, Jesus is reproving them because they worry. It certainly *sounds like*, Jesus is saying they worry because they have little faith.

> "Why are you worried? You of little faith!"

It certainly does sound as though Jesus is reproving them.

Still, remember this, *"You of little faith!"* is the only statement in His entire message that sounds like a reproof.

And most of all…

> *Remember how He spoke.*

What Does "You of Little Faith" Mean?

Let's take a closer look at what Jesus said.

Remember now, Jesus rebuking them saying, *"You of little faith!"* does not appear to be consistent with the rest of His message.

Therefore, when He says, *"You of little faith"* what does that actually mean?

The Greek words being translated here as, *"You of little faith"* are *'Humas'* and *'Oligopistos,'* with *'Humas'* meaning *'You.'*[10] The word *'Oligopistos'* is comprised of *'Oligos'* which means *'little, small or few'*[11] and *'Pistis'* meaning *'faith.'*[12] *'Oligopistos'* means, *'little faith or of little faith.'*[13]

> *"(Humas) You (Oligopistos) of little faith"*
> *"You of little faith"*

To be *"of little faith"* is to be one whose faith is little or small. Jesus is saying they *"have little faith."*

> *"You of little faith"* means, *"You have little faith."*

That seems to be clear and straightforward enough. It certainly fits with our current understanding of its meaning as a reproval.

> *"Why are you worried? You have little faith!"*

If it is accurate to say *"You of little faith"* means, *"You have little faith,"* then it is also just as accurate to say it means,

> *"You have 'a' little faith"*

In fact, the word *'Oligos'* translated here as *"little"* is translated numerous other times in the Bible as, *"a little"* and *"a few."*

Therefore, when Jesus said to the people, *"You of little faith!"* He was in fact saying,

> *"You have a little faith!"*

Now let's look again at what Jesus said. This time however, we will use what *"You of little faith"* actually means and…, notice how it sounds!

Instead of,

> *"Why are you worried? You of little faith!"*

we now have,

> *"Why are you worried? You have a little faith!"*

The contrast between these two statements is so stark, the perceived meanings so different, it is startling to see. Yet, they mean exactly the same thing!

It no longer sounds like a reproof!

By taking what *"You of little faith"* actually means, we can see Jesus is not reproving them at all, but is continuing to encourage them just as He had before. Jesus is giving them another reason why, they do not need to worry.

> *You do not need to worry* **because...**,
> *"You have a little faith!"*

"You of little faith" and *"You have a little faith"* sound different; we interpret them differently. Yet, both of them are saying precisely the same thing;

> *"You – have – little – faith"*

So, what is Jesus really saying here?

> *"Do not be worried about your life, as to what you will eat or what you will drink;... Look at the birds of the air, ... your heavenly Father feeds them."*

> *"Are you not worth much more than they?"*

> *"And why are you worried about clothing? If God so clothes the grass of the field, ...*

> *will He not much more clothe you?"*

> *"Do not worry then, saying, 'What will we eat?' or 'What will we drink?' or 'What will we wear for clothing?' "For the Gentiles eagerly seek all these things; for your heavenly Father knows that you need all these things."*

If God so feeds and clothes the Gentiles, (who do not believe),

How much more will He feed and clothe you?

"You have a little faith!"

No Reproof at All

What sounded like a reproof for their little faith, was no reproof at all. It was in fact, an encouragement.

If Jesus says they can be assured God will care for the Gentiles, who do not believe, how much more then, can they be assured God will care for them, because they do believe?

God will provide especially for them, because they are a people who have a little faith.

You do not need to worry.
You have a little faith!

Why Do You Reason? You of Little Faith!

Here is another instance of Jesus using the phrase, *"You of little faith!"*

In contrast to the previous story, the way *"You of little faith"* is being used in this next account, it does seem to be in the same context as the rest of Jesus' message. He does seem to be reproving the disciples this time.

There are two similar accounts of this story, one is found in the book of Matthew, the other in the book of Mark. Rather than combine and paraphrase the two accounts, we will review both in full.

Jesus had told the disciples to beware of the leaven of the Pharisees. Yet, the disciples thought Jesus was referring to the fact they had brought no bread.

Jesus had previously fed over four thousand people with only seven loaves of bread and a few small fish. Jesus multiplied the bread and fish to such an extent that not only was He able to feed all the people, but when all had finished eating the disciples picked up seven large baskets full of the leftovers.

The account in Matthew reads,

> *And the disciples came to the other side of the sea, but they had forgotten to bring any bread.*
>
> *And Jesus said to them,*
> *"Watch out and beware of the leaven of the Pharisees and Sadducees."*
>
> *They began to discuss this among themselves, saying,*
> *"He said that because we did not bring any bread."*
>
> *But Jesus, aware of this, said,*
> ***"You men of little faith, why do you discuss among yourselves that you have no bread?*** *"Do you not yet understand or remember the five loaves of the five thousand, and how many baskets full you picked up? "Or the seven loaves of the four thousand, and how many large baskets full you picked up?*
>
> *"How is it that you do not understand that I did not speak to you concerning bread? But beware of the leaven of the Pharisees and Sadducees."*
>
> *Then they understood that He did not say to beware of the leaven of bread, but of the teaching of the Pharisees and Sadducees.*
>
> Matthew 16:5-12 NASB e.a.

There is another version that says, *"Why do you reason?"*

> *"O you of little faith,* ***why do you reason*** *among yourselves because you have brought no bread?*
>
> Matthew 16:8 NKJV e.a.

The account in Mark reads as follows.

> *And they had forgotten to take bread; and did not have more than one loaf in the boat with them.*

And He was giving orders to them, saying,
"Watch out! Beware of the leaven of the Pharisees and the leaven of Herod."

And they began to discuss with one another the fact that they had no bread.

And Jesus, aware of this, said to them,
"Why do you discuss the fact that you have no bread? *Do you not yet see or understand? Do you have a hardened heart?*
"Having eyes, do you not see? And having ears, do you not hear? And do you not remember, when I broke the five loaves for the five thousand, how many baskets full of broken pieces you picked up?"

They said to Him,
"Twelve."

"And when I broke the seven for the four thousand, how many large baskets full of broken pieces did you pick up?"

And they said to Him,
"Seven."

And He was saying to them,
"Do you not yet understand?"

Mark 8:14-21 <u>NASB</u> *e.a.*

The disciples were discussing or reasoning among themselves what they would do since they had no bread.

When Jesus says,

> *"You men of little faith, why do you discuss among yourselves that you have no bread?"*

it sounds like He is saying,

> *"You discuss that you have no bread* **because…** *you are men of little faith!"*

Jesus then goes on to say,

> *"Do you not remember the bread I multiplied?"*
> *"Having eyes, do you not see and having ears, do you not hear?"*
> *"Do you have a hardened heart?"*
> *"Do you not yet understand?"*

This unquestionably sounds like Jesus is reproving them for their little faith, especially after they had witnessed Him feed thousands with only a few loaves of bread.

Consequently, with Jesus saying *"You of little faith!"* and it sounding as a reproof, it does seem to be in context with the rest of His comments. This does seem to fit with the overall intent of His message.

Yet, there is again more to this story than meets the eye. Jesus asked His disciples one last question.

Jesus asked them,

> **"How is it that you do not understand…**
> *that I did not speak to you concerning bread?*
> *But beware of the leaven of the Pharisees and Sadducees."*

This question seems to be another reproof from Jesus that the disciples should have understood. Yet, look at what Jesus is asking. He is asking how it is, or why it is, they do not understand.

There is a reason *"why"* they do not understand and Jesus is giving them a clue to the answer. Listen to the question when broken down and paraphrased.

> **Why do you think it is,** *that you do not understand,*
> *that I did not speak to you **concerning bread,***
> *when I spoke to you **concerning leaven?***

The obvious answer is, because Jesus spoke of leaven, the disciples thought He spoke of bread. There is more to see however.

Notice, Jesus did not say what He spoke of;
Jesus only said what He *did not* speak of.
Jesus only said He did not speak of bread.

Jesus did not explain the meaning of His reference to leaven.
He only explained what it *did not* mean.

> *"I did not speak to you concerning bread."*

This is not all, there is yet still more to see.

He Said It the Same Way Twice

Jesus started this conversation, saying,

> *"Beware of the leaven of the Pharisees and Sadducees."*

The disciples did not understand this statement. Jesus then asks them why they did not understand. However, instead of explaining His meaning, He says precisely the same thing again.

> **"Beware of the leaven of the Pharisees and Sadducees."**

> *"He said that because we did not bring any bread."*

> *"How is it that you do not understand*
> *that I did not speak to you concerning bread? But...*
> **beware of the leaven of the Pharisees and Sadducees."**

After Jesus said the same thing, the second time, we are told the disciples then understood His reference to leaven.

It says,

> **Then they understood...**
> that He did not say to beware of the leaven of bread,
> but of **the teaching** of the Pharisees and Sadducees.

The disciples, *as it is written*, believed they now understood and thought He was speaking about *"the teaching of the Pharisees."*

They thought they understood.

Now this raises a question. If the disciples did not understand the first time Jesus spoke of leaven, why would they understand the second time He spoke of leaven? He never did explain His reference to leaven.

He said the same thing both times; He said nothing different.

Jesus knew His disciples did not understand this statement. Yet, although He knew this,

> *He said it the same way twice!*

He Said It Yet Once More

On a separate occasion, Jesus once more made this same statement to His disciples for what would now be a third time. On this occasion, however, Jesus followed with an explanation.

Jesus said,

> *"Beware of the leaven of the Pharisees, **which is hypocrisy**.*
>
> *Luke 12:1 NASB e.a.*

This time, Jesus clearly tells the disciples what He is referring to. Jesus is speaking of the "*hypocrisy*" of the Pharisees.

Jesus said to His disciples and the crowds,

> *"The scribes and the Pharisees have seated themselves in the chair of Moses; **therefore all that they tell you, do and observe**, but do not do according to their deeds; **for they say things and do not do them**.*
>
> *Matthew 23:2-3 NASB e.a.*

Jesus told His disciples to do and observe everything the Pharisees told them to do.

Or, said another way,

> *"Do everything they **teach you to do**,*
> *but do not do (as they do); for they say things and do not do them."*

Then seven times Jesus spoke directly to the Pharisees themselves and called them *hypocrites*.

> *"But woe to you, scribes and Pharisees, **hypocrites**,*
> *because you shut off the kingdom of heaven from people; for you do*
> *not enter in yourselves, nor do you allow those who are entering to*
> *go in.*

> *"Woe to you, scribes and Pharisees, **hypocrites**,*
> *because you devour widows' houses, and for a pretense you make*
> *long prayers; therefore you will receive greater condemnation.*

> *"Woe to you, scribes and Pharisees, **hypocrites**,*
> *because you travel around on sea and land to make one proselyte;*
> *and when he becomes one, you make him twice as much a son of*
> *hell as yourselves.*

> *"Woe to you, scribes and Pharisees, **hypocrites**!*
> *For you tithe mint and dill and cummin, and have neglected the*
> *weightier provisions of the law: justice and mercy and faithfulness;*
> *but these are the things you should have done without neglecting*
> *the others. "You blind guides, who strain out a gnat and swallow a*
> *camel!*

> *"Woe to you, scribes and Pharisees, **hypocrites**!*
> *For you clean the outside of the cup and of the dish, but inside they*
> *are full of robbery and self-indulgence. "You blind Pharisee, first*
> *clean the inside of the cup and of the dish, so that the outside of it*
> *may become clean also.*

> *"Woe to you, scribes and Pharisees, **hypocrites**!*
> *For you are like whitewashed tombs which on the outside appear*
> *beautiful, but inside they are full of dead men's bones and all*
> *uncleanness. "So you, too, outwardly appear righteous to men, but*
> *inwardly you are full of **hypocrisy** and lawlessness.*

> "Woe to you, scribes and Pharisees, **hypocrites!**
> For you build the tombs of the prophets and adorn the monuments
> of the righteous, and say, 'If we had been living in the days of our
> fathers, we would not have been partners with them in shedding
> the blood of the prophets.' "So you testify against yourselves, that
> you are sons of those who murdered the prophets. "Fill up, then,
> the measure of the guilt of your fathers. "You serpents, you brood of
> vipers, how will you escape the sentence of hell?
>
> Matthew 23:13-15, 23-33 NASB e.a.

When Jesus said, *"beware of the leaven of the Pharisees and Sadducees,"*
He was not telling the disciples to beware of the Pharisees' *"teachings."*

He was saying to beware of their *"hypocrisy"*!
He told us this Himself.

> *"Beware of the leaven of the Pharisees, **which is hypocrisy.**"*

> *"Therefore all that they (**teach**) you, do and observe,*
> *but do not do according to their deeds;*
> ***for they say things, and do not do them.*"**

So, did the disciples understand what Jesus meant by *"the leaven of the
Pharisees"*? No, apparently they did not!

Therefore, let's examine what He said a little closer.

On one occasion, when Jesus said, *"Beware of the leaven of the Pharisees,"*
He explains the statement and says, *"which is hypocrisy."* Everyone understood His meaning, because He explained His meaning.

However, on this occasion, when Jesus said, *"Beware of the leaven of the
Pharisees and Sadducees,"* His disciples did not understand the reference
to leaven. Jesus knew this, yet, He did not explain Himself.

This time, He simply repeats what He already had said.

> *He said it the same way twice.*

So, look at the question again. *"How is it that you do not understand?"*

Why did the disciples not understand? It was because Jesus did not speak plainly or explain His meaning. To answer Jesus' own question then, it was because of,

> *How He spoke.*

What we have is a question that sounded like a reproof, but was actually hiding a clue.

Consequently, if this question, which sounds like a reproof, was actually a clue into why they did not understand, what then was the purpose of the rest of the message, that also sounds like a reproof?

If this question is a reproof, the entire message is as well. However, if this question is not a reproof, that means the entire message is not a reproof either.

Looking back on everything, what specifically, did Jesus say?

Jesus *only asked* if the disciples did not understand or remember the bread that was multiplied.

> **"Do you...** *not yet understand or remember the five loaves of the five thousand, and how many baskets full you picked up?"*

He only asked if they had a hardened heart.

> **"Do you...** *have a hardened heart?"*

He only asked if they did not see or hear.

In fact, when Jesus said, *"having eyes, do you not see?"*
He was saying, *"having eyes, (you do have eyes to see)!"*

And when He said, *"Having ears, do you not hear?"*
He was saying, *"Having ears, (you do have ears to hear)!"*

There was one time only in which Jesus said the disciples did not understand, and it was here, in a question.

> *"How is it that you do not understand that I did not speak to you concerning bread?"*

The only thing Jesus said the disciples did not understand was the way in which He was speaking to them.

> *"How is it that you do not understand what I did not speak of?"*
> *"How is it that you do not understand what I did not say?"*

They did not understand…

> *How He spoke.*

Finally, back again to what Jesus initially said.

> *"You of little faith,*
> *why do you discuss among yourselves that you have no bread?"*

When Jesus said, *"Why do you discuss (this)?"*
He was saying there is no need to discuss this.

> *Do you not remember the bread that was multiplied?*
> *Why do you discuss this?*
> *You do not need to discuss this.*

And when Jesus said to them, *"You of little faith!"*
He was saying, *"You have a little faith!"*

Therefore, what Jesus was actually saying is,

> *"You have a little faith!*
> *You do not need to discuss that you have no bread!"*

So, listen again to what Jesus said.

> *And Jesus said to them,*
> *"Watch out and beware of the leaven of the Pharisees and Sadducees."*
>
> *They began to discuss this among themselves, saying,*
> *"He said that because we did not bring any bread."*
>
> *But Jesus, aware of this, said,*
> **"You men have a little faith,**
> *why do you discuss among yourselves that you have no bread?*
> **You do not need to discuss that you have no bread.**

"Do you not yet understand or remember the five loaves of the five thousand, and how many baskets full you picked up? "Or the seven loaves of the four thousand, and how many large baskets full you picked up?

Remember and understand that the loaves were multiplied for you.

"Do you have a hardened heart? **Do not have a hardened heart.**
"Having eyes, do you not see? **You do have eyes to see!**
"And having ears, do you not hear? **You do have ears to hear!**
"How is it that you do not understand
that I did not speak to you concerning bread?"

You do not understand what I said…, because of how I spoke!

Jesus was the initiator of this conversation. This entire discussion had one purpose, which was to teach the disciples (and us), all we need to have is *"just a little faith."* Yet, Jesus intentionally said it in such a way as to hide this truth by making it sound as though they were discussing their lack of bread because of their little faith.

He hid the truth that they only needed, *"just a little faith."*

It was said in this manner,
so those who did not see, would not see,
and, those who did not hear, would not hear.

Or, said another way,
it was said so only those who see, would see,
and only those who hear, would hear.

> *For there is nothing hidden which will not be revealed, nor has anything been kept secret but that it should come to light.*
>
> *If anyone has ears to hear, let him hear.*
>
> Mark 4:22-23 NKJV

You do not need to discuss that you have no bread.
You have a little faith!

Why Are You Afraid? You of Little Faith!

Here is one final story of Jesus using the phrase, *"You of little faith!"*

In this story, Jesus is in a boat with His disciples, when a severe storm arises and the disciples become terrified.

It says,

> When [Jesus] got into the boat, His disciples followed Him. And behold, there arose a great storm on the sea, so that the boat was being covered with the waves; but Jesus Himself was asleep.
>
> And they came to Him and woke Him, saying,
> "Save us, Lord; we are perishing!"
>
> He said to them,
> **"Why are you afraid, you men of little faith?"**
>
> Then He got up and rebuked the winds and the sea, and it became perfectly calm.
>
> The men were amazed, and said,
> "What kind of a man is this, that even the winds and the sea obey Him?"
>
> *Matthew 8:23-27 NASB e.a. par.*

The Sound of Reproof

Notice, it sounds as though Jesus is reproving them for their little faith. It might seem easy to conclude that Jesus is reproving them for being afraid during the storm. However, if you look at the whole story, the only part that even closely sounds disapproving, is when He says, *"You of little faith!"*

When Jesus asks them, *"Why are you afraid?"* He is clearly telling them they do not need to be afraid.

> *Why are you afraid?*
> *You do not need to be afraid.*

There is nothing else in this story that would make us think Jesus had any kind of disapproval of the disciples, except for this one statement. There is nothing else, except when He says,

> *"You of little faith!"*

With this in mind, let's take a closer look and examine the details of this story.

This was a violent storm. It is recorded that this was a *"great storm."*

The words translated here as *"great storm"* are *'Megas'* and *'Seismos.'* *'Megas'* means *'great or fierce'*[14] and *'Seismos'* means *'a shaking or commotion.'*[15] *'Seismos'* is the same word we get our word seismic from, meaning *'shaking of the earth.'*

This storm was also recorded in the books of Luke and Mark as a *"fierce gale of wind."* The word translated as *"fierce gale"* is *'Lailaps'* which means *'a violent attack of wind, or hurricane.'*[16] And the word translated as *"wind"* is the word *'Anemos'* which means *'a very strong wind or violent agitation of wind.'*[17]

See Luke 8:23 and Mark 4:37 NASB

They wrote that this was a great shaking, a violent attack of wind.

> *It was a violent storm!*

In the midst of this violent storm, it says the boat began to be swamped with water. The account in Matthew says, **the boat was being covered with the waves.**

The account in Luke says,

> and **they began to be swamped** and to be in danger.

Luke 8:23 NASB e.a.

In Mark it says,

> and **the waves were breaking over the boat** so much that **the boat was already filling up**.

Mark 4:37 NASB e.a.

Here we have a storm so violent, the boat was filling with water and became in danger of sinking.

We know at least three of the disciples, Peter, James and John were all experienced at sea, being fishermen by trade. These, along with at least one other person, the captain of the boat, means there were at the very least, four experienced seamen on board.

These men knew the sea. These men knew how to manage a boat. Yet, look at what they said to Jesus,

> *"Save us, Lord; we are perishing!"*

These experienced seamen knew they were in extreme danger, and were likely going to perish in this storm.

> *"We are perishing!"*

Notice what Jesus was doing during this storm.

> *Jesus Himself was in the stern, asleep on the cushion*
>
> *Mark 4:38 NASB*

During this violent storm, Jesus happens to be sleeping through it all.
With fierce wind and waves, Jesus sleeps.
The boat being tossed about, and Jesus sleeps.
Water rushing in, crashing over the bow, and Jesus sleeps.

Men frantically bailing water, yelling to each other above the roar of the storm in an attempt to save their boat.

And all the while…

> *Jesus sleeps!*

Doesn't it seem odd, Jesus is the only person on the boat sleeping during this storm?

Doesn't it seem odd, Jesus would sleep with all the noise and commotion going on around Him?

Doesn't this seem to be just a little bit odd?

Take note of what the disciples themselves say to Jesus.

> *they woke Him and said to Him,*
> *"Teacher,* ***do You not care that we are perishing?"***
>
> Mark 4:38 NASB e.a.

The disciples questioned why Jesus was just lying there "sleeping" when the boat was about to sink.

> *"Do You not care?"*

There was another occasion when the disciples were again in the midst of the sea with strong winds and waves.

The passage says,

> *The sea began to be stirred up because a strong wind was blowing.*
>
> John 6:18 NASB

The story is also recorded in Matthew.
It says,

> *But the boat was already a long distance from the land, battered by the waves; for the wind was contrary.*
>
> Matthew 14:24 NASB

Observe the similarities between this event and the previous event:

Both are in the midst of the sea.
Both have the wind and sea against them.

This time however, Jesus is not with them in the boat. This time, Jesus comes to them, walking on the water.

It says,

> *And in the fourth watch of the night He came to them, walking on the sea. When the disciples saw Him walking on the sea,* ***they were terrified****, and said,*
>
> *"It is a ghost!"*
>
> *And they cried out in fear.*
>
> Matthew 14:25-26 NASB e.a.

The text says the disciples were terrified and, *"cried out in fear."*

The disciples were again terrified, although this time, it is not because of the wind and the waves. And, it is not because their boat is about to sink, nor because they are about to die.

This time the disciples are afraid, because they thought they saw… a ghost!

> *"It is a ghost!"*

Notice how Jesus responded to them.

> *And they cried out in fear.*
>
> *But immediately Jesus spoke to them, saying,*
> *"Take courage, it is I; **do not be afraid.**"*
>
> *Matthew 14:26-27 NASB e.a.*

This time, simply because they thought they saw a ghost, Jesus said to His disciples,

> *"Take courage, **do not be afraid.**"*

This time, in complete contrast to how He spoke to them during the violent storm, Jesus encourages His disciples and tells them not to be afraid.

Yet, during the violent storm, a storm that is sinking their boat, Jesus says,

> *"**Why are you afraid**, you men of little faith?"*

Jesus does not encourage His disciples or tell them not to be afraid. Instead, He reproves them for being afraid.

It Was All an Act!

If we think, these men should have somehow known what was going on,
if we think, they should not have been frightened,
if we think, they should have known Jesus could calm the storm,
look at their reaction when Jesus finally does calm the storm.

> *Then He got up and rebuked the winds and the sea, and it became perfectly calm.*

And it says,

> *The men were amazed, and said,*
> **"What kind of a man is this***..., that even the winds and the sea obey Him?"*

Matthew 8:26-27 NASB e.a. par.

The disciples were amazed at what Jesus had done. Never had they seen Jesus do anything like this before. They said to themselves,

> *"What kind of a man is this?"*

With this being the case, doesn't it seem odd, that Jesus should reprove them for being afraid when He had not yet demonstrated His power over the wind and sea?

Jesus first said to them,

> *"Why are you afraid, you men of little faith?"*

And it says,

> *Then, He got up and rebuked the winds and the sea, and it became perfectly calm.*
>
> *Then..., He rebuked the winds and the sea!*

For Jesus to reprove them might possibly seem warranted if He had first demonstrated His power to control the wind and sea and they were still frightened. However, it would be completely unreasonable that Jesus should reprove them when He had not yet demonstrated this power.

Jesus reproved them first, and demonstrated His power second.

> *Something is not right!*

In the previous story, Jesus intentionally spoke of leaven, knowing the disciples were discussing they had no bread.

Jesus used the situation and circumstance of that event to teach the disciples a lesson about faith. Yet, He spoke of it in the form of a parable, hiding what He was truly saying by making it sound as though He was reproving them for their little faith.

Just as it was then, so it is now.

Jesus is using the situation and circumstance of this storm, to teach His disciples a lesson about faith. Again, He is teaching in a hidden form. Jesus is actually saying one thing, yet making it sound as though He is saying something else.

This time however, Jesus demonstrates the lesson not only by what He says, but also by what He does. He intentionally sleeps during the storm and acts as though this storm is of no significance.

Jesus acts as though, there is no reason for them to be afraid in this storm. Jesus acts as though, they are afraid because of their little faith.

"Why are you afraid, you of little faith?"

Jesus was literally acting out a parable.

It was all an act!

In Act 1 - Hidden Things, we read where the Lord told Moses to speak to the rock, but Moses struck the rock instead. The Lord was having Moses act out a prophecy. It was a prophetic act Moses was performing. However, Moses was not aware it was prophetic.

Moses did not know he was acting out a prophecy.
Moses did not know he was acting.

Just as it was then, so it is now.

Just as Moses did not know, he was acting.
The disciples also did not know, He was acting.

The disciples did not know Jesus was acting.

Jesus was acting out a parable!

It's Not as It Seems!

It's not as it seems at first glance.

Just as it was then,
> with Jesus encouraging His disciples when He came to them
> walking on the water,
so it is now.

Jesus is also encouraging His disciples in the midst of this storm. Hidden behind this veil of a reproof, is Jesus' true message.

When Jesus said, *"Why are you afraid?"* His meaning was, they do not need to be afraid. This clearly is the intent of that question, which is in fact a rhetorical question.

Likewise, when Jesus said to them, *"You of little faith!"* He was saying,

> *"You have a little faith!"*

Therefore, hidden behind what sounded like a reproof, was actually no reproof at all. Jesus was teaching and encouraging His disciples.

> *You do not need to be afraid. You have a little faith.*

Jesus used this storm to teach the disciples (and us), something hidden about faith. It was something to be taught and understood yet, needed to remain hidden.

He could not say it out loud;
so He said it as it were... in a whisper.

> *"I will open My mouth in parables;*
> *I will utter things hidden since the foundation of the world."*
>
> Matthew 13:35 <u>NASB</u>

> *He will utter hidden things.*

It was how He spoke.

> *Remember how He spoke!*

"Little Faith" or "No Faith"

There is one other detail that needs to be addressed. There is a discrepancy between this version of the story found in the book of Matthew, and the other versions of the same story found in the books of Mark and Luke.

There is an inconsistency as to whether Jesus actually said, *"You of little faith!"* The two other versions do not have Jesus saying this.

So let's look at these two accounts.

The account in Mark reads,

> *Jesus Himself was in the stern, asleep on the cushion; and they woke Him and said to Him,*
> *"Teacher, do You not care that we are perishing?"*
>
> *And He got up and rebuked the wind and said to the sea,*
> *"Hush, be still."*
>
> *And the wind died down and it became perfectly calm.*

Mark then records Jesus as saying,

> *"Why are you afraid? Do you still have **no faith**?"*
>
> Mark 4:38-40 NASB e.a.

The account in Luke reads,

> *They came to Jesus and woke Him up, saying,*
> *"Master, Master, we are perishing!"*
>
> *And He got up and rebuked the wind and the surging waves, and they stopped, and it became calm.*

Luke then recorded that Jesus said,

> *"**Where is your faith**?"*
>
> Luke 8:24-25 NASB e.a.

One account says the disciples have no faith, *"Do you still have **no faith**?"* The other says there is no faith to be found, *"**Where is your faith**?"*

These two accounts are in effect saying the same thing.
Both are saying the disciples have *"no faith."*

One of these versions,

>   the account in Matthew,

>   or,

>   the two similar accounts in Mark and Luke,

is in error.

The version, *"You of little faith"* is stating they have, *"a little faith."*
The versions, *"Do you still have no faith?"* and *"Where is your faith?"* are stating they have, *"no faith."*

Jesus is either saying the disciples have *"a little faith,"* or *"no faith,"* but not both.

Either the account in Mathew is correct, and both Mark and Luke are in error. Or, the two accounts in Mark and Luke are correct, and Mathew is in error.

It is either one or the other; they cannot all be right.

I believe the *"You of little faith"* version that says the disciples have *"a little faith"* is correct. There is evidence that supports this point of view. Jesus elsewhere did say the disciples had *"no faith."* However, the question is…

>   *To whom was Jesus speaking?*

Let's take another look at the event when Jesus had just come off the mountain with Peter, James and John. This is the account where the other disciples had failed trying to heal a boy possessed by a demon. The disciples asked Jesus why they could not cast out the demon and Jesus replied,

>   *"Because of your unbelief."*

Here Jesus did say the disciples had no faith. The question is however, to which disciples, specifically, was Jesus speaking?

Or, perhaps a better way to ask this question would be,
to which disciples, specifically, was Jesus not speaking?

When Jesus came down from the mountain with Peter, James and John, it says,

> When they came to the crowd, a man came up to Jesus, falling on his knees before Him and saying,
>
> "Lord, have mercy on my son, for he is a lunatic and is very ill; for he often falls into the fire and often into the water. "**I brought him to Your disciples**, (not Peter, James or John), and **they** could not cure him."
>
> And Jesus answered and said,
> "You **unbelieving** and perverted generation, how long shall I be with you? How long shall I put up with you? Bring him here to Me."
>
> And Jesus rebuked him, and the demon came out of him, and the boy was cured at once.
>
> Then the disciples, (not Peter, James or John), came to Jesus privately and said,
> "Why could we not drive it out?"
>
> Matthew 17:14-19 NASB e.a. par.

> So Jesus said **to them**, (not to Peter, James or John),
> "Because of **your unbelief**
>
> Matthew 17:20 NKJV e.a. par.

Jesus said to them, "Because of your unbelief."
Jesus said this to the other disciples.
Jesus did not say this to Peter, James or John.

Jesus said some of the disciples had unbelief.
But He did not say this about all of them.

In fact, Jesus said this same thing on a number of other occasions.
Speaking to His disciples, Jesus said,

> It is the Spirit who gives life; the flesh profits nothing. The words that I speak to you are spirit, and they are life. But **there are some of you who do not believe**.

And it says,

> *For Jesus knew from the beginning **who they were who did not*** *
> **believe**, and who would betray Him.*
>
> John 6:63-64 NKJV e.a.

There were some disciples who did not believe.
It then says,

> *From that time many of His disciples went back and walked with*
> *Him no more.*
>
> John 6:66 NKJV

(It is interesting to note the *verse number* appears to match the *verse topic* in this case. John is also the disciple who told us of this number.)

Jesus had many disciples, not just the twelve. Of the twelve, there were some who did not believe. And of the many, there were more who did not believe.

> *Many of His disciples withdrew.*

We see Jesus did not say all the disciples had no faith, Jesus said only some of the disciples had no faith. Therefore, if only some had no faith, this then means, all the other disciples had at least, some faith.

> *All of the other disciples had faith.*

> *"Why are you afraid? You men have a little faith!"*

Here is further evidence that supports the *"You of little faith"* version, in contrast to Mark and Luke's *"no faith"* versions.

This phrase, *"You of little faith"* is a pattern of speech used by Jesus several times. We have seen four instances of Jesus using this phrase.

> *"Why did you doubt? You of little faith!"*   See Matthew 14:31 NASB
>
> *"Why are you worried? You of little faith!"*   See Matthew 6:28, 30 NASB
>
> *"Why do you reason? You of little faith!"*   See Matthew 16:8 NKJV

And lastly, this passage,

> *"Why are you afraid? You men of little faith!"*   See Matthew 8:26 NASB

The accounts just listed are all found in the book of Matthew. Yet, the story of *"Why are you worried?"* can also be found in the book of Luke.

"Why do you worry? You men of little faith!"   See Luke 12:26, 28 NASB

Therefore, Luke himself does confirm and attribute to Jesus that He elsewhere did use the phrase, *"You of little faith."*

Notice this also, of the three stories in Matthew it is an accepted fact Jesus used this phrase. Jesus saying *"You of little faith"* is consistent in all three stories; this is not in dispute.

It is only in this last story in Matthew of the severe storm, that there is a question as to whether Jesus actually said, *"You of little faith."*

It is only because of the two accounts in Mark and Luke which record Jesus saying something different, that brings the Matthew version into question. If it were not for the Mark and Luke accounts, there would be no dispute with Matthew's account at all.

The Mark and Luke accounts do not agree with the account in Matthew; this is an obvious discrepancy. Additionally, we find the Mark and Luke accounts do not agree with each other.

Mark quotes Jesus as saying,

> *"Why are you afraid? Do you still have no faith?"*
>
> Mark 4:40 NASB

However, Luke records Jesus as saying,

> *"Where is your faith?"*
>
> Luke 8:25 NASB

The account in Luke does not even mention Jesus saying, *"Why are you afraid?"* So, what did Jesus actually say?

Did He say, *"Do you still have no faith?"*
Or, did He say, *"Where is your faith?"*

Which one? These are quotes, are they not?

Although the quotation mark symbols are not used in the original Greek texts, the authors are in fact telling us these are the words Jesus spoke. The authors are actually quoting what Jesus said.

With these being quotes, a quote is supposed to accurately state what someone said. Yet, these two quotes, state something different.

So which is correct? Is it possible Jesus said a combination of these two quotes such as,

> *"Where is your faith, do you still have no faith?"*

If this is the case, then it must be noted, even at a minimum, that neither account accurately or completely quoted Jesus.

So, what do we really have?

We have one version, the *"You of little faith"* version, which is consistent with three other stories of Jesus also saying, *"You of little faith."* Or, we have two other versions that do not even agree with each other; they themselves are in dispute.

Therefore, we will continue with what is consistent, not with what is in dispute. We will continue with, *"You of little faith."*

So, what was Jesus really saying to His disciples in the midst of this storm?

> *You do not need to be afraid. You have a little faith!*

Jesus was not reproving His disciples; He was encouraging His disciples!

> *It was no reproof at all!*

Those Who Do Not Believe

Here is one other point to consider. Those who do not believe Jesus was encouraging His disciples by telling them, *"You have a little faith!"*

must then believe…

Jesus was in fact reproving His disciples for their fear and complete lack of faith in the midst of a storm so severe it threatened to sink their boat.

But of course, this is exactly what some believe,
and this is precisely what some teach.

They know Jesus to be a hard man and taskmaster.
Jesus spoke a parable regarding people like this.

> 'Lord, **I knew you to be a hard man**, *reaping where you have not sown, and gathering where you have not scattered seed.* **And I was afraid**,
>
> Matthew 25:24-25 NKJV e.a.

> *"Save us, Lord; we are perishing!"*
> *"You do not need to be afraid. You have a little faith."*

Hush, be still – Selah

Back to Peter

We left off the story of Peter walking on the water with it sounding as though Jesus was reproving Peter for having little faith and doubting.

> *"You of little faith, why did you doubt?"*

Observe one other detail about this story.

Except for Jesus Christ, Peter is the only other person known to ever have walked on water. Peter was the only person that night willing to get out of the boat and at least try to walk on the water. None of the other disciples had the faith to get out of the boat, only Peter did.

Yet, it sounds as though Jesus is reproving Peter.

Jesus did not reprove any of the other disciples, who stayed behind safely in the boat. Jesus reproved only Peter, who, in the dead of night, stepped out of the boat.

Doesn't this seem just a little strange?

Doesn't it seem strange, Peter should try to do something no one else has ever done before, and Jesus would reprove him for doubting he could?

Doesn't it seem strange, Jesus does not encourage Peter or tell him to try again?

There was no obvious encouragement or compliment given from Jesus. There was no, "Nice try!" or, "You almost did it!" There was only,

> *"You of little faith, why did you doubt?"*

Peter was reproved because he tried.
Yet, there was no reproof given to the other disciples who did not try.

Doesn't that seem to be just a little bit strange?

In the story of Jesus sleeping during the storm, He intentionally acted as though the storm was of no significance, then also intentionally made it sound as though He was reproving the disciples.

Jesus used the circumstance of the storm to teach them a hidden truth about faith.

Recall also the story of the leaven. Jesus, while teaching the disciples of the hypocrisy of the Pharisees, intentionally spoke of leaven knowing they had no bread; then He intentionally made it sound as though He was reproving them.

Jesus used the opportunity of the disciples being without bread to teach them a hidden truth about faith.

Therefore we see, as it was then,
>   that Jesus intentionally acted and spoke during those other
>   events to teach a hidden lesson about faith,
so it is now.

Jesus is intentionally acting and speaking here in such a way, as to use this as an opportunity to teach the disciples the same lesson about faith.

Remember, it was Jesus that made Peter able to walk on water. Peter then began to sink because Jesus no longer made him able. Jesus, using the opportunity of Peter becoming afraid, intentionally lets Peter begin to sink.

>   *Yes, Jesus intentionally let Peter begin to sink!*

If it is difficult to imagine Jesus would intentionally let Peter sink, take note of this:

Jesus did not let Peter sink;
Jesus only let Peter *begin* to sink.

It says as soon as Peter began to sink, Jesus caught him.

> and ***beginning to sink***, he cried out,
> "*Lord, save me!*"
>
> ***Immediately*** *Jesus stretched out His hand and took hold of him*
>
> Matthew 14:30-31 NASB e.a.

And they got back into the boat together.

This is no different than Jesus sleeping during the storm and intentionally letting the boat fill with water and begin to sink.

Jesus did not let the boat sink;
Jesus only let the boat begin to sink.

Jesus spoke to the wind and sea and said,

> *"Hush, be still."*
>
> *And the wind died down and it became perfectly calm.*
>
> *Mark 4:39 NASB*

The boat did not sink!

In the same way that Jesus did not let the boat sink,
neither did Jesus let Peter sink.

He only let the boat and Peter begin to sink to teach the disciples a lesson about faith.

> *He did not let them sink!*

When Jesus said to the people,

> *"Do not worry"* and *"Why are you worried?"*

He was saying,

> *You do not need to worry!*

Just as it was then, so it is now.
When Jesus said to Peter,

> *"Why did you doubt?"*

He was saying,

> *You do not need to doubt!*

And, when Jesus said to Peter,

> *"You of little faith"*

He was saying,

> *You have a little faith!*

Therefore, what Jesus was truly saying to Peter, yet keeping hidden was,

> *Peter, you do not need to doubt. You have a little faith!*

Jesus was not reproving Peter at all.

> *Jesus was encouraging Peter!*

To answer the question we had asked earlier, why did Jesus stop making Peter able to walk on water?

Jesus did this to create the appearance that Peter failed at walking on water because of his little faith. He made it appear Peter needed more faith; He made it appear Peter needed great faith.

> *Jesus was hiding the truth about faith.*

Jesus used the circumstance of the storm, along with Peter's fear and doubt, to teach Peter (and us), we only need *"just a little faith,"* while keeping this truth hidden.

Notice now in all these things how Jesus spoke.

When Jesus said, *"Why are you worried? You of little faith!"* it sounded as though He was reproving them.

When in fact He was saying,

> *You do not need to worry. You have a little faith!*

When Jesus said, *"O you of little faith, why do you reason among yourselves because you have brought no bread?"* it sounded as though He was reproving them.

Yet, He was really saying,

> *You do not need to reason that you have no bread. You have a little faith!*

When Jesus said, *"Why are you afraid? You of little faith!"* it sounded as though He was reproving them.

Yet, He was in fact saying,

> *You do not need to be afraid. You have a little faith!*

And finally, when Jesus said, *"You of little faith, why did you doubt?"* it sounded as though He was reproving Peter, but He was not.

He was saying,

> *You do not need to doubt. You have a little faith!*

In each of these conversations Jesus was not reproving His disciples or the people. He was in fact saying to them,

> *You do not need to worry, or reason, or be afraid, or doubt.*

Because,

> *You have a little faith!*

What was made to sound like a reproof, was no reproof at all.
Instead, we find encouragement and praise from Jesus.

It was a secret being spoken; a hidden thing being uttered.
It was a mystery being spoken of while not revealing the mystery.
The hidden thing, remained hidden.

It remained hidden, so those to whom it had not been granted to know the mysteries of the kingdom of heaven, still would not know.

> *"To you it has been granted to know the mysteries of the kingdom of heaven, but to them it has not been granted.*
>
> Matthew 13:11 NASB

> *You only need just a little faith.*

If you listen closely, this is exactly what Jesus is saying.

Notice, I did not change what Jesus said,
I only changed what you heard.

> *"Take care how you listen"*
> *"Take heed what you hear"*
>
> See Luke 8:18 NASB and Mark 4:24 NKJV

Hush, be still – Selah

Something Is Hidden

Therefore, we see the phrase, *"You of little faith"* has a hidden meaning. It sounds like one thing, yet, means another.

Hidden behind the phrase, *"You of little faith,"*
is its true meaning, *"You have a little faith."*

By using the phrase, *"You of little faith,"* Jesus was able to speak to those who believed, teaching them about faith. Yet, speak in such a way that the truth regarding faith would remain hidden from those who did not believe.

> *"You have a little faith" was being hidden.*

Similar to riddles, parables will at times have hidden meanings. Therefore, because the phrase, *"You of little faith"* has a hidden meaning, it is a type of parable or riddle.

> *"You of little faith" is a parable.*

"You have a little faith" was not the only thing being hidden.

Take a look at the original phrase again. The phrase, *"You of little faith"* has a hidden meaning. It is a parable, which was never recognized as being a parable. Its meaning has always been understood to be, just as it sounds, a reproof.

Jesus did not say He was speaking a parable when He said, *"You of little faith."*

If Jesus had identified *"You of little faith"* as being a parable, it would have been known to be a parable. If it had been known to be *"a parable,"* it would have also been known what the parable meant.

The hidden meaning would no longer have been hidden.

Remember, the parable, *"You of little faith,"* was meant to hide, *"You have a little faith."* The meaning was to remain hidden because,

> *It had not been granted for others to know.*

So that the *meaning* of the parable might remain hidden,
it was necessary the *parable itself* also remain hidden.

Therefore, Jesus did not say He was speaking a parable.
The parable itself was being hidden.

Consequently, we now have a hidden parable, with a hidden meaning.

The parable being hidden, is part of the riddle of the parable.
The parable being hidden, is part of the mystery of the parable.

The hidden parable is part of the mystery.

So we see, during all this time that Jesus spoke and taught these things, He was speaking of a secret. He was speaking of a mystery, and all the while keeping the mystery hidden. He was hiding the truth we only need just a little faith.

When the disciples asked, Jesus did not tell them how to increase their faith. He only told them they can do anything if they have, *"faith like a mustard seed."*

Hidden behind the statement, *"If you have, (faith like a mustard seed) …"* is its true meaning, *"If you have, (any faith at all) …."*

The phrase, *"faith like a mustard seed,"* does translate to mean, *"any faith at all"*; it has a hidden meaning.

Because, *"faith like a mustard seed"* has a hidden meaning, it too is a type of parable or riddle.

"faith like a mustard seed" is a parable.

And, although *"faith like a mustard seed"* means, *"any faith at all,"* Jesus did not say, *"If you have any faith at all, nothing will be impossible to you."* Jesus was keeping this truth hidden.

Jesus was speaking a parable when He said, *"faith like a mustard seed."*
Jesus was speaking a parable when He said, *"You of little faith."*

Jesus was speaking in parables!

Whenever Jesus spoke of those with little faith, He would only say,

> *"You of little faith!"*

Jesus spoke of great faith as though it were required to do great things.
Jesus spoke of little faith as though it were not enough.

The main theme of Jesus' teaching on faith was:
With great faith you can do anything.
With little faith you can do nothing.

At least… that is what it sounded like.

You do not need great faith.
You only need,

> *"Just a little faith"*

To again revisit the question we had answered earlier, why didn't Jesus tell the disciples how to increase their faith?

It is because they did not need to have great faith; they needed only a little faith. This is exactly what Jesus said they already had, when He said to them, *"You of little faith."*

> *They already had all the faith they needed!*

However, if great faith is not needed, this raises another question we had also asked earlier,

> *Why teach great faith?*

Because something more was being hidden.

Your Faith Has Made You Well

Look at what Jesus said to these who came to Him for healing.

To the woman who said,

> *"If only I may touch His garment, I shall be made well."*

Jesus said,

> *"Be of good cheer, daughter; **your faith has made you well**."*
>
> *Matthew 9:21-22 NKJV e.a.*

To the man who said to Him,

> *"Lord, that I may receive my sight."*

Jesus said,

> *"Receive your sight; **your faith has made you well**."*
>
> *Luke 18:41-42 NKJV e.a.*

To the man with leprosy, who, when he saw he had been healed, fell on his face with a heart of gratefulness,

Jesus said,

> *"Arise, go your way. **Your faith has made you well**."*
>
> *Luke 17:19 NKJV e.a.*

To all these people, Jesus said it was "their faith" that healed them.

> *"**Your faith** has made you well."*

There was another event recorded when Jesus used this same pattern of speech. He said it to the woman who washed His feet with her tears.

Jesus said to her,

> *"**Your faith has saved you**. Go in peace."*
>
> *Luke 7:50 NKJV e.a.*

The words Jesus spoke to this woman are the same He spoke to the others. In the other instances it has been translated as *"Your faith has made you well."* The literal translation however, for all of these verses is, *"Your faith has saved you."* He is using the same pattern of speech, saying it was "her faith" that saved her.

Jesus clearly states it was faith, "their faith," that made them well; it was their faith that saved them. Such incredible faith is this. Faith that heals your sight, heals your leprosy, heals your sickness.

Faith that saves you!

Jesus identifies faith as the instrument of their healing.
Jesus declares *"faith"* is the source of their salvation.

> **"Your faith** has made you well."
> **"Your faith** has saved you."

However, was it really their faith that made them well?
Was it actually their faith that saved them?

Great Faith

Jesus spoke much about faith. But of faith He said was great, faith like this, He spoke of only twice. There are only two people of whom Jesus said had great faith; notice what He also said.

To the centurion who asked Jesus to heal his servant,

Jesus said,

> *I have not found such **great faith** with anyone in Israel.*
> *"Go; **it shall be done for you** as you have believed."*
>
> *Matthew 8:10, 13 NASB e.a.*

To the woman who pleaded with Jesus to cast the demon out of her daughter,

Jesus said,

> *"O woman, your **faith is great;***
> ***it shall be done for you** as you wish."*
>
> *Matthew 15:28 NASB e.a.*

To both He said,

> *"It shall be done for you."*

Although both had *"great faith,"* the greatest faith found,
it was not their faith that healed their sick.

> *It was done for them!*

If Jesus said *"it would be done"* for these with the *greatest of faith*,
why then did He say it was *"faith"* that healed the others?

If it was not *"the faith"* of those with the greatest faith, that healed their
sick, then it could not have been *"the faith"* that healed the sick to whom
Jesus said,

> *"Your faith has made you well."*

What was it then that made them well? Was it really their faith?
Was it actually their faith that saved them?

Consider this detail, at some point in time, something had to actually
engage their sickness and heal them. The sickness did not go away simply
because they had faith.

For they all had faith *before* they came to Jesus.
Yet, it was only *after* they came to Jesus they were healed and saved.

Therefore, something more than their faith, something greater than
their faith, engaged their sickness. Something greater than their faith,
saved them.

Something Greater Than Their Faith

We know they came to be healed by Jesus. It was Jesus who engaged
their sickness and healed them. Therefore, if it was not their faith, but
Jesus who healed them (if it was done for them), why then did Jesus say
it was their faith?

Because Jesus was speaking in parables!

Jesus wove a fine thread with the truth. He spoke with technical precision, but not for the purpose of clarity. Jesus was indeed truthful, technically speaking, when He said it was their faith that made them well. It was not however, as true as the meaning of this statement was intended to be perceived.

It was not true they were healed *"by their faith,"* as Jesus' statement would be interpreted. But it was true that *"their faith"* brought them to Jesus. Therefore, technically, it was their faith that brought them to their healing.

It was *"their faith"* that brought them to…

> *the One, by whom they could be healed.*

Consequently then, with just the slightest measure of truth,

> *It was their faith that made them well.*

Jesus intentionally spoke as though ascribing to their faith, the power to heal and save. The words Jesus chose to use created the perception that they, by their faith, made themselves well.

> **"Your faith** has made **you well."**

Yet, the reality is, it was Jesus who did it for them.

The statement, *"Your faith has made you well"* has a hidden meaning. It sounds like one thing, yet, means another.

This statement, *"Your faith has made you well,"* is another example of a parable Jesus spoke.

> *Jesus was speaking a parable!*

It Shall Be Done for You

Jesus used the phrase, *"It shall be done for you"* on another occasion. Two men who were blind came to Jesus asking to be healed.

Jesus said to them,

> **"Do you believe** that I am able to do this?"

> They said to Him,
> "Yes, Lord."
>
> Then He touched their eyes, saying,
> "**It shall be done to you** according to your faith."

Matthew 9:28-29 NASB e.a.

When Jesus said, *"It shall be done to you,"* notice the qualification He attached to that statement. He said it would be done for them,

    according to their faith.

This is the same qualification used when He spoke to those with great faith.

To the woman, He said, *"It shall be done for you **as you wish**."*
To the centurion, *"It shall be done for you **as you have believed**."*
And now, to these men, *"It shall be done to you **according to your faith**."*

    As you wish
    As you have believed
    According to your faith

    It shall be done for you.

Jesus said it was their faith, be it the quantity of their faith, or the quality of their faith, that would be the determiner of what would be done for them.

    "According to your faith, it shall be done for you."

Faith is the central figure. Faith stands out prominently in Jesus' teaching as being that which is attributable for their healing. Yet, in all these instances, Jesus Himself, was the instrument of their healing. Their healing can only be attributed to Jesus, not to faith itself.

Faith, the central pillar in Jesus' teachings of all things great and miraculous. Jesus is teaching faith; Jesus is speaking of faith. Jesus is teaching of the power of great faith.

Jesus spoke of faith that was great, twice.
Jesus spoke of faith that was little, "faith like a mustard seed," twice.

He spoke of both only twice.
He spoke of both equally.

For those with great faith, He said it would be done for them.
Yet, for those with little faith, faith like a mustard seed, He said it was
they, who would perform great miracles.

> *"If you had faith like a mustard seed, you would say to this*
> *mulberry tree, 'Be uprooted and be planted in the sea'; **and it***
> ***would obey you.***
>
> *Luke 17:6 NASB e.a.*

> *truly I say to you, if you have faith as a mustard seed, you shall say*
> *to this mountain, 'Move from here to there,' and it shall move; **and***
> ***nothing shall be impossible to you.***
>
> *Matthew 17:20 <u>NASB</u> e.a.*

With great faith, *"it shall be done for you."*
Yet, with little faith, *"nothing shall be impossible to you."*

These two statements on faith seem to disagree.

We have seen three instances of Jesus concealing the truth about faith.

Jesus concealed a truth when He said, *"You of little faith."*
Jesus concealed a truth when He said, *"Your faith has made you well."*

And, in using the phrase, *"faith like a mustard seed"* Jesus was concealing
the truth if we have *"any faith at all,"* nothing will be impossible for us.

If Jesus concealed a truth in, *"faith like a mustard seed,"* might He also
have concealed a truth when He said, *"nothing shall be impossible to you"*?

Jesus qualifies the type of faith required to perform great works.
Jesus said,

> *All things are possible to him who **believes**.*
>
> *Mark 9:23 NASB e.a.*

> *all things you ask in prayer, **believing**, you will receive.*
>
> *Matthew 21:22 NASB e.a.*

> *all things for which you pray and ask, **believe that you have***
> ***received** them, and they will be granted you.*
>
> *Mark 11:24 NASB e.a.*

Jesus tells His disciples, they will receive, if they believe they have received. He also said to them,

> *whoever says to this mountain, 'Be taken up and cast into the sea,'*
> *and **does not doubt in his heart, but believes** that what he says is*
> *going to happen, it will be granted him.*
>
> *Mark 11:23 NASB e.a.*

> ***if you have faith and do not doubt,** you will not only do what was*
> *done to the fig tree, but even if you say to this mountain, 'Be taken*
> *up and cast into the sea,' it will happen.*
>
> *Matthew 21:21 NASB e.a.*

Jesus tells His disciples, if they have faith and do not doubt, the mountain will move.

If you want to perform great works by faith, this is what you must be able to do.

You must not only believe the impossible is possible.
you must be able to believe the impossible *"will happen,"*
you must be able to believe, *"the mountain will move."*

This is not all however, there is more.

You must not only believe the impossible *"will happen,"*
you must also be able to believe the impossible *"has happened."*
You must be able to believe *"you have received."*
You must be able to believe *"the mountain has moved."*

> *You must be able to do this.*

If you are able to believe and have faith,
that what *"cannot happen, can happen,"*
and, what *"cannot happen, will happen,"*
and, what *"will happen, has happened,"*

and, if you are able to have no doubts,
that what *"has not happened, has already happened,"*
while you are still telling it *"to happen,"*
then, it will happen.

> *The mountain will move.*

This is what you must be able to do.

Making a mountain move is an impossibility. But what *you* must be able to do, to make the impossible happen, also borders on the realm of impossibility. What you must be able to do, to make the impossible happen, is also nearly impossible.

Regardless of whether this actually is impossible or not, it will most certainly be with great difficulty that anyone will be able to believe,

> *what has not happened, has already happened,*
> *while they are telling it to happen,*
> *and have no doubts it will and already has!*

This is what you must be able to do, to perform these great works by faith.

You must be able to do something that is very difficult to do.
You must be able to do something that is, quite possibly, impossible to do.
You must be able to do the impossible.

If you are able to do this, then, the impossible will happen.

> *The mountain will move!*

And yet…

Although you had the faith to tell the mountain to move,
and, although you had no doubts and believed the mountain would,
and, although it was you who spoke to the mountain,
it still was not you who made the mountain move.

> *whoever says to this mountain, 'Be taken up and cast into the sea,'*
> *and does not doubt in his heart, but believes that what he says is*
> *going to happen, **it will be granted him**.*
>
> *Mark 11:23 NASB e.a.*

"It shall be done for you."

Even with faith like this, even with *"such great faith,"* it still will not be by your faith the mountain will be moved. The mountain will be moved, but not *"by you"*; it will be moved *"for you."*

When you speak *"by faith,"* the mountain will move. But the mountain will not be moved *"by your faith"*; it will be moved by God.

Even with such great faith,

"It shall be done for you."

Why Teach Great Faith?

So why teach great faith?

If it shall be done for us, whether we have just a little faith or whether we have great faith, why then did Jesus teach about great faith?

So it might be shown to be *"by works."*

Jesus was teaching a way of works by faith. He was teaching a way of works for those who do not believe in His works, but rather, want to trust and believe in their own works.

This might seem a difficult thing to imagine that Jesus would be teaching a way of works by faith. Yet, we have already seen Jesus did indeed conceal the truth we only need a little faith. Now let me show you something more.

To perform these great works by faith, this is what Jesus said we really must be able to do.

Jesus said you must have faith and have no doubts.

> **if you have faith and do not doubt,** *you will not only do what was done to the fig tree, but even if you say to this mountain, 'Be taken up and cast into the sea,' it will happen.*
>
> Matthew 21:21 NASB e.a.

To do these great works you must, *"have faith"* and *"do not doubt."*
You must be able to, *"have no doubts"* and *"have faith."*

What does it mean then, to have faith and have no doubts;
to have no doubts (while at the same time) to also have faith?

If you have no doubts, where then is your faith?
If you have no doubts, why then do you need faith?

If there is no doubt the mountain will move, where then is the faith that it will?

To have absolutely *"no doubts"* something will happen, is to know with certainty it will; for there is *"no doubt."*

Therefore, if you *"have no doubt"* what you say will happen,
why then do you *"have faith"* it will?

If there is no doubt you are able,
where then is the faith you can?

When you doubt, it is because you do not know.
But when you know, you will not doubt.
When you know, there is no doubt.
And where there is no doubt,

> *There is no need for faith!*

It is not by faith when you speak by what you know.
It is not by faith when you do what you know you are able to do.

If you have no doubts, it is because you know.
And if you know, then it is not by faith.

So you see, you cannot, *"have faith,"*
and at the same time, *"have no doubts."*

> *It is impossible!*

Impossible Faith

Jesus told His disciples if they wanted to do what was done to the fig tree, or even cast a mountain into the sea, then they must have faith and have no doubts. What Jesus said the disciples had to do was impossible. Jesus was teaching a way of impossible works, by having a faith impossible to have.

Yet, even if it were possible, even if you somehow had this impossible faith, Jesus stated, *"it will be granted"* you. You may speak with impossible faith, yet, it will not be by your faith that the mountain moves. The mountain will be moved by God.

Even with impossible faith,

> *"It shall be done for you."*

Now we see, whether we have the smallest of all faiths or impossible faith,

> *It is not by faith at all!*

Yet, if it is not by faith at all, why then did Jesus teach us to have faith? If it is not by faith at all, why did Jesus teach we can do all things, if we believe?

Why did Jesus say,

> **"*if you have faith* as a mustard seed,
> nothing shall be impossible to you"**?

See Matthew 17:20 <u>NASB</u> e.a.

If not by faith, why did He say,

> *"If you have faith..."*?

And, if not by us (if it shall be done for us), why did He say,

> *"Nothing shall be impossible to you"*?

If it is not by faith at all, and not by us at all,
why did He even bother to tell us this?

He said this because, He was teaching us another way.

There is another way!

There are two ways.

There is a difficult way.

You can, by your faith, by your *"works of faith,"* do what is very difficult to do, and God will do the impossible for you. But there is another way.

There is a better way!

A Better Way

Jesus said to the man whose daughter had died,

> *"Do not be afraid; **only believe**, and she will be made well."*
>
> *Luke 8:50 NKJV e.a.*

There is a better way.

Only believe!

Jesus asked the blind men,

> *"**Do you believe that I am able** to do this?"*
>
> *Matthew 9:28 NASB e.a.*

There is a better way.

Believe that He is able.

Believe Jesus Christ is able and it shall be done for you. If you have faith like a mustard seed, if you have even the smallest of faith, it shall be done for you.

This is all you have to do.
This is all you have to be able to do.

You only have to believe!

And,

"It shall be done for you!"

However, this still does not answer the question of why Jesus said we would be able, when He said,

"Nothing shall be impossible to you"

He also said,

"It would obey you"

How will it *"obey you,"* if it shall be done *"for you"*?
How will nothing be impossible *"to you,"* if it shall be done *"for you"*?

Why did Jesus say we could?
He said this,

Because we can!

Notice what Jesus said of Himself,

> *"Truly, truly, I say to you, **the Son can do nothing** of Himself,*
> *unless it is something He sees the Father doing*
>
> *John 5:19 NASB e.a.*

Jesus also said of Himself,

> *"**I can do nothing** on My own initiative.*
>
> *John 5:30 NASB e.a.*

Jesus, speaking of Himself, said He can do nothing.

If Jesus can do nothing, how much *more nothing* can we do than He?
If Jesus can do nothing, how much *less* can we?

Yet, Jesus did not really say He could do nothing at all. He said He could do nothing, *"unless it is something **He sees** the Father doing."* He said He could do nothing, *"on His own initiative."*

Jesus could do nothing, unless it was something He saw the Father doing. Jesus did, as the Father did.

What was done *"by the Father,"*
was also done *"by the Son."*

Jesus, speaking to the Father, said,

> *I have glorified You on the earth. I have finished the work which*
> *You have given Me to do.*
>
> *John 17:4 NKJV*

Jesus did, what was given Him to do.
Jesus said to the Jews,

> *"I showed you many good works from the Father; for which of*
> *them are you stoning Me?"*
>
> *"If I do not do the works of My Father, do not believe Me; but if I*
> *do them, though you do not believe Me, believe the works, so that*
> *you may know and understand that the Father is in Me, and I in*
> *the Father."*
>
> *John 10:32, 37-38 NASB*

So, as a point of clarification, we see,
works that were done by Jesus,
are works that were done, *"by Jesus"* Himself.

It may seem excessive to overemphasize such an obvious point, yet this
is an extremely important truth. It is necessary that this truth be understood, so what Jesus said next may also be understood.

Jesus is the one who did what He did.
His works were performed *"by Him."*

Jesus said,

> *"Truly, truly, I say to you, **he who believes in Me, the works that***
> ***I do, he will do also**; and greater works than these **he will do**;*
> *because I go to the Father.*
>
> *John 14:12 NASB e.a.*

Who did Jesus say would do the works that He did?

>*You who believe!*

In the same way then, that it was Jesus, who did the works that Jesus did, so too, it will be you, who will do the works that only Jesus could do.

You who believe, will do *"the works that I do."*
You who believe, will do the works only Jesus could do.

The works you do, will be performed *"by you."*
And, it will be *"by you"* because,

>*You believe.*

Of all the great and wonderful works they saw Jesus do, even *"greater works than these"* will we do, because,

>*We believe.*

It will simply be,

>*Because we believe.*

Let me show you something more.

There were only two people of whom Jesus said had great faith:
One was the woman whose daughter was possessed by a demon.
The other was the centurion whose servant was paralyzed.

These are the only two people of whom Jesus said had great faith and notice what they both share in common.

The story in Matthew says the woman was a Canaanite, from the region of Tyre and Sidon. The same story in Mark says she was a Gentile (a Greek), of the Syrophoenician race.

See Matthew 15:21-22 and Mark 7:26 NASB

Luke records the Jewish elders said of the centurion,

>*"He is worthy for You to grant this to him; for he loves our nation and it was he who built us our synagogue."*

Luke 7:4-5 NASB

Neither the woman nor the centurion were from Israel. These are the only two of whom Jesus said had great faith. And,

> *They are both foreigners!*

Jesus said of these, *foreigners with great faith,*

> *"I say to you that many will come from east and west, and recline at the table with Abraham, Isaac and Jacob in the kingdom of heaven;*

Matthew 8:11 NASB

They were foreigners to the kingdom of heaven, yet…

> *They believed.*

They were,

> *Foreigners who believed.*

To these, foreigners who believed,
to these, foreigners with *"great faith,"*
Jesus said,

> *"It shall be done for you!"*

Let me show you something more.

Peter was a Jew and by Jesus' own definition, was a *"son of the kingdom."* Jesus said Peter had a little faith and because he had a little faith, he walked on the water.

Jesus made Peter able to walk on water; it was done for him.

> *"It shall be done for you."*

Thus we see, for foreigners with great faith, it shall be done for them. And, for sons of the kingdom who have just a little faith, it shall be done for them as well.

Therefore, whether you are a foreigner or a son,

> *"It shall be done for you."*

Yet wait, I will show you something more.

It was Jesus who made Peter able to walk on the water, therefore, it was done for him. Yet, notice this also, it was Peter himself, who actually walked on the water.

It was Jesus who made Peter able.
But it was Peter who actually walked.

Jesus did not walk on the water *for Peter*,
Jesus walked on the water *with Peter*.

Therefore, it was not done for him; it was done *"by him."*

Peter walked on the water himself.
It was *"by him"* because he was able.

It was Peter who walked on the water.
It was Peter who did *"the works"* that Jesus did.

Jesus walked on the water.
Peter also walked on the water.

As Jesus said,

> *"The works that I do, he will do also."*

In the same way, *"the works"* which Jesus did, were done by Jesus Himself, so too then, *"the works"* which Peter did, were done by Peter himself.

It was Peter who walked on the water.
It was not done for him,

> *It was done "by him"!*

It was by Jesus that Peter was able.
But it was not by Jesus that Peter walked on the water.

Peter walked on the water *"by himself."*
He walked,

> *Because he was able.*

It was not by faith that Peter was able.
It was by Jesus, who made him able.

Therefore, it was not by faith that Peter was able to walk on the water. But it was by faith,

> *He walked.*

Peter, not knowing with any certainty whether he could walk on the water, believed what Jesus said, and because he believed, he stepped out of the boat.

By faith, Peter got out of the boat.

> *By faith, Peter walked!*

Therefore we see, it is by faith after all.

It was by faith that Peter walked on the water, because it was by faith *he tried.* Peter had all the faith he needed to have.

> *He had the faith to try.*

Jesus said all you need to have is *"faith like a mustard seed."*

And since, the mustard seed is the smallest seed of all seeds,
then, faith *"like"* a mustard seed, is the smallest faith of all faiths.

Therefore, Jesus said, *all you need is just the smallest of all faiths.*
If you have the smallest of all faiths, if you have any faith at all,

> *"Nothing shall be impossible to you."*

When Jesus said to Peter, *"You of little faith,"* He was saying Peter only had, *"just a little faith."* However, the little faith Peter had proved to be enough. It was all the faith he needed to have, because with it,

> *He walked on the water.*

> *Peter had the faith to walk on water,*
> *Jesus said he did.*
> *"O you of little faith!" He said.*
> *And with it,*
>
> > *Peter did!*

Peter walked on the water because he had a little faith.

So we see, it is *"by faith."*
It is *"by faith like a mustard seed."*

All you need is just a little faith.
All you need to have is just the smallest faith of all faiths and it will be enough.

> *It will be enough!*

By Faith, Do What You Are Able to Do

By faith, you can do what you are able to do.

Peter did by faith what he was able to do;
Peter was able to step out of the boat.

By Faith, Do What You Are Not Able to Do

By faith, you can do what you are not able to do.

By faith, Peter did what he was able to do, (he stepped out of the boat), in an attempt to do, what he was not able to do, (he was not able to walk on water).

> *Men can't walk on water.*

So, by faith, Peter did what he was able to do; (he stepped out of the boat). Then, he did what he was not able to do; (he walked on the water).

Therefore, it was by faith, that Peter did what he was not able to do.

Thus we see, it is by faith,
when you do what you are able to do, (when you take a step),
so you might do what you are not able to do, (so you might walk!)

By Faith, Do What You Know

When Peter saw Jesus walking on the water, Peter said to Him,

> *"Lord, if it is You, command me to come to You on the water."*

And Jesus said to Peter,

> *"Come!"*

Matthew 14:28-29 NASB

Peter knew Jesus had told him to come out onto the water.

It was by faith, Peter did, what he knew Jesus had told him to do.
And it was by faith, Peter did, what he knew he was able to do;
Peter knew he was able to step out of the boat.

> *By faith, Peter stepped out of the boat.*

By Faith, Do What You Do Not Know

Peter did not know he was able to walk on water.
Yet, he stepped out of the boat.

Because Peter did not know he was able,
what he did, he did, by faith.

Because Peter did not know he was able to walk on water,
he stepped out of the boat, by faith!

> *By faith, Peter stepped out of the boat.*

This means then, Peter did not know he was able, until... he walked on water.

Until he walked on water, Peter did not know he was able.
Until he walked on water, Peter did not know.

By Faith, He Knew

For this reason, we now see, it was by faith that Peter did,
what he knew he was able to do.

> *Peter knew he was able to step out of the boat.*

And it was by faith that Peter did,
what he did not know he was able to do.

> *Peter did not know he was able to walk on water.*

But now we see, it was by faith,

> *He knew.*

Peter did not know he was able, until he walked on the water.
Peter did not know he was able, until he walked,

> *By faith!*

It was by faith that Peter stepped out of the boat,
because he did not know he was able to walk on water.

However, when Peter found himself standing on the water,
what he had not known before,
what he had never known before,
he – now – knew!

> *He knew he was able.*

Therefore, it was by faith, he knew.

> *By faith, he knew!*

Because We Do Not Know

It is because of what we do not know and what we do not understand,
that we need faith. Because we do not know that something can be,
because we do not understand, *"How can these things be?"* we need to
proceed by faith.

We need faith, because we do not understand.
We need faith,

> *Because we do not know.*

Jesus said to the Jews,

> *"I showed you many good works from the Father;*
>
> *though you do not believe Me, **believe the works,***
> ***so that you may know and understand** …*
>
> *John 10:32, 38 NASB e.a. par.*

Believe, so you may know and understand.

> *Believe…, so you may know.*

We need faith, so we may understand.
We need to believe,

> *So we may know.*

Because we do not know, we need faith.

We need faith, until we know.
And until we know, we will continue to need faith.

> *Until we know, we will need faith.*

But then once, *"by faith"* we know, we will no longer need faith.
And we will no longer need faith…

> *Because we will know.*

Once we know what faith was used to show, faith will no longer be needed.

Faith was used to teach us, so we might know.
Faith has done its job; faith has made us know.
Faith has done its job.

> *By faith, we know.*

By Faith, We Know

When Peter walked on the water, he then knew he was able.

It was not by faith he was able, but it was by faith he knew.
It is not by faith we are able, but it is by faith we know.

And once we know we are able, we will no longer need faith, because, we will know we are able.

Because Jesus gave us faith to know, we absolutely need to know.
Because we need this faith to know, it absolutely will be by faith that we know.

It is entirely *"by faith,"* we know.

> *By faith, we know.*

There will be no other explanations on what is by faith and what is not by faith. This is what faith does; this is the purpose of faith.

> *The purpose of faith is that we may know.*

God spoke so there would be faith and gave us faith so we may know.
Therefore, God spoke so we may know.

> *"Let them know!"*

We Still Need Faith

It is written, *we walk by faith, not by sight,* and this so far has been true.

See 2 Corinthians 5:7 NKJV

However, it is not intended to remain this way.

We should come to a place where, by faith we know.
And because we know, we no longer need faith.

I am not at all certain if we will ever be entirely without the need for faith; for there are so many things we do not know. This one thing I do know; I know what we do by faith, we can know, and what we come to know, we can then do without faith.

It is true, we do not need faith for what we already know. But we still need faith for all those things we still have yet to know.

We still need faith.

Abram

God spoke to Abram and told him,

> *"Go forth from your country,*
> *And from your relatives*
> *And from your father's house,*
> **To the land which I will show you**

Genesis 12:1 NASB e.a.

Abram knew God had told him to go,
but Abram did not know where.

Because Abram knew God spoke and told him to go, Abram went. Abram did what he knew to do. Yet, because he did not know where he was to go, Abram went, by faith.

Abram went by faith knowing God told him to go,
but still not knowing where he was to go.

Abram did by faith, what he knew,
so he might go, where he did not know.

When Abram arrived where God had sent him, he then knew. The faith that had brought him to that place was no longer needed. This faith was completed, it had brought him where he needed to go. He no longer needed this faith; he had reached his destination.

Faith is not our destination.

Faith is not our destination!

Our goal is to reach our destination, not, to walk by faith.
However, we cannot reach our destination, unless we walk by faith.

We cannot reach our destination without faith.

Faith, in the simplest of terms, is the tool or instrument we use to reach our destination. Once we have reached our destination, then faith has done its job; the work is complete. And once a job is finished, the tool is no longer required; the tool can be discarded.

Faith can be discarded!

Faith has done its work in us; its work is complete.

Now we know.

Therefore, because we have walked by faith, there should come a time in our lives where we no longer need faith for things that were once unknown.

There should come a time where we should be able to walk as a people, who have no need for faith. We should be able to walk, as it were, as a people who have no faith. We will have no faith, because we will not need faith, and we will not need faith,

Because we know.

Jesus said,

> *when the Son of Man comes, will He find faith on the earth?*
>
> *Luke 18:8 NASB*

This has always been understood that Jesus wants to find faith when He returns. However, remember how He spoke. Perhaps, it was meant the other way. Perhaps, Jesus wants to find a people, who no longer need faith.

Notice *how* He said this.
Jesus did not say He wants to find faith.
Jesus only asked, *"will He find faith?"*

So, when the Son of Man comes, will He find faith on the earth?

Will Jesus find us still walking by faith, because we do not know?
Or, will Jesus find us walking without faith, because *"by faith"* we know?

Will we still be walking by faith?
Or, will we be walking as a people *who know* their God?

Jesus said people would say to Him during the end times,

> 'Lord, Lord, did we not *(by faith)* prophesy in Your name,
> and *(by faith)* in Your name cast out demons,
> and *(by faith)* in Your name perform many miracles?'
>
> "And then I will declare to them,
> **'I never knew you;** depart from Me,
>
> Matthew 7:22-23 NASB e.a. par.

So, when the Son of Man comes,

> *Will He find faith?*

Where We Started

If we look back at where we started with Jesus' teachings on faith, we saw those of whom Jesus said had *"great faith"* showed they had little doubt.

> "Yes, Lord; but even the dogs feed on the crumbs which fall from their masters' table."
>
> "O woman, your faith is great
>
> Matthew 15:27-28 NASB

And those of whom Jesus said had *"little faith,"* showed they had great doubt.

> "Lord, save me!"
> "O you of little faith, why did you doubt?"
>
> Matthew 14:30, 31 <u>NASB</u>

And of those whom Jesus said had *"no faith"* were those He said had *"unbelief."*

> *"O faithless and perverse generation,*
>   *"Why could we not cast it out?"*
> *"Because of your unbelief*

Matthew 17:17, 19-20 NKJV

To summarize:

> Those with *"great faith"* had *"little doubt."*
> Those with *"little faith"* had *"great doubt."*
> And those with *"no faith"* had *"unbelief."*

Faith in Jesus

Now, let's look at faith in regards to what Jesus said about the faith we really need to have.

If we have a *"little doubt"* in what Jesus is able to do,
Jesus only requires *"us"* to have *"just a little faith"*
and *"He"* will overcome that *"little doubt"* for us.

> *Do not worry, you have a little faith.*
> *How much more will your heavenly Father feed and clothe you.*
>
> *It shall be done for you.*

If we have *"great doubt"* in what Jesus is able to do,
Jesus still only requires *"us"* to have *"just a little faith"*
and *"He"* will overcome that *"great doubt"* for us.

> *"Save us, Lord; we are perishing!"*
> *You do not need to be afraid. You have a little faith.*

He said to the wind and sea,

> *"Hush, be still."*
>
> *It shall be done for you.*

If we have *"no doubt"* in what Jesus is able to do,
then it requires *"no faith"* to overcome that doubt;
for there is no doubt to overcome.

> *Where there is no doubt, there is no need for faith!*

Now we see we have a complete reversal of what we understood before.
Now it is understood, with faith in Jesus:

> *Little doubt requires only a little faith.*
> *Great doubt requires only a little faith.*
> *And no doubt requires no faith at all.*

Where there was no faith before, it was understood this was bad.
It was bad because the people did not believe and did not know.

However, we see, now where there is no faith, the people no longer believe,
and they no longer believe,

> *Because they know.*

Now we see we can have no faith, but no faith now is good.
What once was seen as only bad, now has been turned to good.

Having no faith previously was bad, it showed our unbelief.
Having no faith now is good.

It is good in this sense only however, that you once *"had faith,"* but now
no longer need it.

> *Because now, by faith, you know.*

Faith in Ourselves

Now let's look at faith for a moment, not in regards to God and God's
abilities, but in regards to ourselves and in the realm of our own abilities.

Perhaps there is something that is very difficult to do. It is something that
is within human possibilities and within our own ability; nevertheless,
it is extremely difficult to do.

Let us say for just a moment we are able to do this thing. However, we do not know we are able, or we are not certain we are able.

We are still able; we just do not know it.

If we have *"great doubt"* we are able,
it will require a *"great faith"* on our part to overcome our *"great doubt."*
It will require *"great faith"* for us to try and do,
what we have *"great doubt"* that we can do.

However, if we have only a *"little doubt"* we are able to do this thing,
then it will only require just a *"little faith"* to overcome our *"little doubt."*
It only requires *"just a little faith"* for us to try and do,
what we have *"just a little doubt"* that we can do.

And, if we have *"no doubt"* we are able to do this thing, then it does not require any faith at all. There is no doubt to overcome. We are able and we know we are able.

So, to summarize faith in ourselves, it would be:

> *"great doubt"* requires *"great faith"*
> *"little doubt"* requires *"little faith"*
> And *"no doubt"* requires *"no faith"*

Faith and Doubt - Your Doubt

If we look again at faith in the realm of our own abilities and also examine the role doubt plays, we observe the following:

If there is something we are able to do, whether great or small, yet we doubt we are able, this does not change the reality of the fact that, we are able.

We are still able; we only doubt we are able.

The only role your doubt plays here is, it will attempt to keep you from trying to do, what *"you doubt"* you can do. If you are able, you will still be able, regardless of how great *"your doubt"* may be.

If you are able, you will still be able, because, *"you are able."*

Doubt has no power to make you either able or unable.
Just as having *"no doubts"* does not make you able,
neither does having *"doubts"* make you unable.
Your doubts can never make you unable to do, what you are able to do.

Doubts can only make you not try.

Also, if because of doubt you do not try, that ultimately is not because of doubt itself, it is because you do not believe you can.

Consequently, doubts cannot even make you not try.

> *Doubt has no power over you.*

Doubt has absolutely no power over you.
Though you doubt,

> *You will still be able.*

Faith and Doubt - Your Faith

The role your faith plays in the midst of all this is, faith will make you try to do, what *"you doubt"* you can do.

It is because of doubt that you will not try.
Therefore, it is because of doubt that God gave us faith.
And because you *"have faith"* you will try.

> *"Let them try!"*

So, what do we see then between these two things, doubt and faith?

Doubt will try to make you quit.
Faith will make you try.

Which will win?

Will you quit?
Or,
Will you try?

"Your faith" telling you, *"you are able,"*
> must be greater than,
"your doubt" telling you, *"you are not."*

If you have great doubt, then you must have an even greater faith.

> *"Your faith" must be greater than "your doubt."*

> *You must have great faith!*

But of course, this is only speaking of faith in the realm of our own abilities.

In Jesus Christ however, we only need just a little faith, because it is *"He"* who will make us able.

All you need is *"the smallest of all faith"* in Him,
though you may have *"the greatest of all doubt"* in you.

Though you may absolutely know, you are not able to do what He has told you to do, if He has told *"You"* to do it, then *"by God"* He will make you able.

> *By God He will make you able!*

> *What God has told you to do,*
> *He will make you able to do.*
> *And if He has made you able,*
> *then you will be able.*

And *"by God"* if He has made you able, there is not a power in this life or the next, that will ever be able, to make you unable.

> *You will be able!*

> *By God you will be able!*

And I will say it again.

> *By God you will be able!*

> *Oh, but how will you ever know*
> *What God has made you able to do*
> *If you only listen to your doubts*
> *Telling you what it is*
> *You can and cannot do?*

Your doubts will never be able, to make you unable. Your doubts will never be able, to make unable what God Himself has made able.

Your doubts have absolutely no power over you.

And I will say it again.

> *Your doubts have no power over you.*

Therefore, though it seems that we might need a *"great faith"* to overcome our *"great doubt,"* it is not faith which makes us able to do what we doubt we can do.

Our faith is only for our doubt.

Also, just as doubt has no power over us, there is no power in faith as well.

> *There is no power in faith!*

There is no power in faith, except the strength, power and ability which is already in you. There is no power in faith to make you able, except, that you are already able. Faith will help you know you are able. But faith will not make you able.

Faith has no power to make you either able or unable.

Just as having faith does not make you able,
neither does having no faith make you unable.

If you are able, but *"have no faith"* that you are, you still will be able. And, if you are not able, but *"have faith"* that you are, you still will not be able.

Unless of course… God says you are!

Faith has absolutely no power to make you either able or unable, but it does have the power to conquer your doubt. The only reason faith has any power at all, is because, *you* have used it for the purpose for which it was made.

It was made to conquer your doubt, so you might know!

Therefore, it was you who used *"your faith"* to conquer *"your doubt."* It was by your strength that you conquered your doubt, because you used *"the tool"* God gave to you.

You used your faith!

Faith and Doubt

Faith and doubt are tied together.
Faith and doubt are opposites.
Neither one has any power over us.
Neither one has any power to make us either able or unable.

Doubt will try to make you quit.
Faith will make you try.
Doubt will try to kill your faith.
But faith will remove all doubt.

Faith will remove all doubt!

It Is OK to Doubt

It is OK to have your doubts, that's what your faith is for.
Only make sure you give your faith the attention it deserves.

If you pay more attention to your doubts, than the attention you give your faith, it will be your doubts that continue to grow. But if you ignore your doubts, and tend to your faith, it will be your faith that is going to grow.

So, it is OK to have your doubts, just have your faith as well. It is by your faith you will overcome your doubts and by it, your faith will grow. And when you, by your faith, overcome your doubts, it is ultimately you who will be the one to grow.

So, it is OK to have your doubts, just have your faith as well.
It is OK to have your doubts.

> *That's what faith is for.*

Selah

It Is Written

"It is written," if we ask anything of God we must,

> *ask in faith without any doubting, for the one who doubts is like*
> *the surf of the sea, driven and tossed by the wind.*
>
> *James 1:6 NASB*

"It is written!"

> *For that man ought not to expect that he will receive anything from*
> *the Lord, being a double-minded man, unstable in all his ways.*
>
> *James 1:7-8 NASB*

I know, *"It is written."*
I know, what *"It"* says.
Yet, even though I know *"It is written,"*
this is what, *"I say."*

> *If I must have a perfect faith,*
> *Or believe a certain way*
> *If I must have this perfect faith,*
> *With no doubting in the way*
>
> *If I must have this absolute faith,*
> *Before I even ask*
> *If there is anything that I must do,*
> *Anything at all, but ask*
>
> *Then I say to you,*
> *It is not because of faith I receive*
> *It is because of how I ask*
> *It is by "the works of faith" I do!*
>
> *And if "by my works of faith"*
> *God gives to me those things I ask*
> *Then it was not because I asked that He gave,*
> *But because of what... I did!*

"It is written!"

Unless you have this perfect faith, you should not expect to receive anything from God.

"It is written!"

If you ask with any doubts, you cannot expect to receive.

That is *"what is written."*
But this is what *"I know."*
I know, if you have *"enough faith"* to ask,
then you have *"enough faith"* to receive.

I know, that *"It is written."*
I know, what *"It"* says.
And even though I know *"It is written,"*
this is what, *"I say."*

> *I say to you,*
>
> *If you have the faith to ask,*
> *you have the faith to receive.*
>
> *If you have the faith to ask,*
> *you have all the faith you need.*
>
> *And I will say it again,*
> *AS LOUD AS I CAN!*
> *Because it is something you need to hear.*
>
> *If you have the faith to ask,*
> *you have all the faith you need.*
>
> *You have what Jesus said to have;*
> *you have faith, like a mustard seed.*
>
> *Selah*

You Do Not Need to Doubt

Jesus said to Peter,

"You of little faith. Why did you doubt?"

What Jesus was saying to Peter is,

You have a little faith. You do not need to doubt.

If you have *"just a little faith"* you do not need to doubt.
If you have *"faith like a mustard seed"* there is no need to doubt.

If it is true, there is *"no faith"* where there is *"no doubt,"*
how then can it be, if we do have faith, there is no need to doubt?

How can there be no need to doubt, if we cannot have faith without doubt?

This appears to be a difficult question, but this is what I know. In the same way, where there is no doubt, there is no need for faith, even so, where there is faith, there is no need to doubt.

However, the reason there is no need to doubt is not because of faith itself. The reason you do not need to doubt is because of, *who your faith is in.* You do not need to doubt because of, *who you know.*

God is the focus of your faith. He is the reason you do not need to doubt. So, how can it be, you can have faith and have no need to doubt?

God is the reason how.

You do not need to doubt, if you have faith like a mustard seed.
If you have just a little faith,

You do not need to doubt.

Jesus Did Not Walk by Faith

It is written,

> *we walk by faith, not by sight.*

See 2 Corinthians 5:7 NKJV

This so far has been true. But we should seek to walk as Jesus walked and this is something Jesus did not do.

> *Jesus did not walk by faith!*

Jesus said He only did what the Father did, He only did what He *"saw"* Him do.

Jesus, speaking of Himself, said,

> *"Truly, truly, I say to you, the Son can do nothing of Himself,* **unless it is something He sees the Father doing;** *for whatever the Father does, these things the Son also does in like manner.*

John 5:19 NASB e.a.

> *The Son can do nothing, unless it is something that He sees.*

Jesus walked *"by sight"* not *"by faith"* and what He saw, He knew. Jesus did not walk by faith at all, He walked by what,

> *He knew.*

Of all the things Jesus did, not once, did Jesus say He did anything by faith. Not once did Jesus say, what He did, He did by faith.

In fact, *everything* Jesus did, He said He did because,

> *He knew.*

Jesus said,

> *"For I did not speak on My own initiative, but the Father Himself who sent Me has given Me a commandment as to what to say and what to speak. "***I know** *that His commandment is eternal life; therefore the things I speak, I speak just as the Father has told Me."*

John 12:49-50 NASB e.a.

> *"**I know** that His commandment is eternal life; therefore I speak"*
> *"**I know** His commandment; therefore I speak"*
> *"**I know**; therefore I speak."*

Because Jesus knew, He spoke.

Jesus said,

> *"If I glorify Myself, My glory is nothing; it is My Father who glorifies Me, of whom you say, 'He is our God'; and you have not come to know Him, but **I know Him**; and if I say that I do not know Him, I will be a liar like you, but **I do know Him** and keep His word.*
>
> *John 8:54-55 NASB e.a.*

He also said,

> *"**I know Him**, because I am from Him, and He sent Me."*
>
> *John 7:29 NASB e.a.*

Jesus knew His Father.

He knew what His Father told Him to do.

Jesus did not walk by faith at all.

He walked because,

> *He knew.*

That We May Know

Jesus, speaking to His Father, said,

> *"Father, the hour has come. Glorify Your Son, that Your Son also may glorify You, as You have given Him authority over all flesh, that He should give eternal life to as many as You have given Him. And this is eternal life, that they may know You, the only true God, and Jesus Christ whom You have sent.*
>
> *John 17:1-3 NKJV*

And this is eternal life; that they may know You,

This is eternal life, that we may know the Father.
This is eternal life, that we may know Jesus Christ whom He has sent.

> *This is life, that we know God.*

To know God, is to know Life itself.
To know God, *"is life"!*

Jesus, again speaking to the Father, said,

> *"Father, I thank You that You have heard Me. And **I know** that You always hear Me, but because of the people who are standing by **I said this, that they may believe** that You sent Me."*
>
> John 11:41-42 NKJV e.a.

> *"I said this, that they may believe"*
> *I spoke, so they may believe.*

Jesus spoke, so we may believe.

Jesus spoke because He knew,
and spoke so we may believe.
So when we believe, we too will know,

> *The One, of whom He spoke.*

Jesus spoke so we would believe,
and in believing, we would know God,
and in knowing God, we would have eternal life.

Jesus spoke so we may have faith and by that faith, we would know. And when we know, we will have eternal life, because it is God we know.

> *By faith, we will know God!*
> *This is eternal life, that we may know.*

There Are Those

There are those who have no faith,
those who do not believe.
There are those who know not God,
they do not believe.

There are those who will not believe
no matter what they see.
There are those, who, no matter what God does,
never will believe.

> *But though He had performed so many signs before them,*
> *yet they were not believing in Him.*
>
> *John 12:37 NASB*

No matter what some people hear,
or what they ever see,
some people never will believe.

But Jesus said,
they are blessed who have believed,
though they have never seen.

> *Blessed are they who did not see, and yet believed.*
>
> *John 20:29 NASB*

To Thomas, who would not believe unless he saw,
Jesus said,

> *"Reach here with your finger, and see My hands; and reach here*
> *your hand and put it into My side; and **do not be unbelieving, but***
> ***believing."***
>
> *John 20:27 NASB e.a.*

Do not be unbelieving, but believing.

Be believing.
Be one who believes!

> *You only need just a little faith.*

Sons of the Kingdom

There are those,
who are *"sons of the kingdom,"*
who have a right by birth.
And yet, they do not believe.

There are those,
who are *"foreigners of the kingdom,"*
who have no right at all.
And yet, they still believe.

There are foreigners, like those sons,
who simply will not believe.

But there are those,
both foreigners and sons,
who, no matter what God does,
always will believe.

> *Though He slay me, yet will I trust Him.*

Job 13:15 NKJV

These are the *"Sons of the kingdom."*
These are *"Those who believe."*

Those who believe.

Those Who Believe

Jesus said,

> *"I say to you that many (who believe) will come from east and west, and recline at the table with Abraham, Isaac and Jacob in the kingdom of heaven; but the sons of the kingdom (those who do not believe) will be cast out*
>
> Matthew 8:11-12 NASB par.

Those who believe,
though they may be foreigners,
will come into the kingdom of heaven.

Those who do not believe,
though they may be sons,
will be cast out.

The kingdom of heaven will be taken away
from those who do not believe,
and given to those who do.

Jesus said,

> *"Do not be afraid, little flock, for your Father has chosen gladly to give you the kingdom.*
>
> *"You have a little faith!"*
>
> See Luke 12:32, 28 NASB par.

The kingdom of heaven belongs to *"Those who believe."*

> *Those who believe.*

> *There is a place that belongs to them,*
> *it belongs to "Those who believe."*
> *It is called the kingdom of heaven*
> *and belongs to such as these.*

> *"Let the children alone, and do not hinder them from coming to Me; for the kingdom of heaven belongs to such as these."*
>
> Matthew 19:14 NASB

There is a place that belongs to us.
We are,

> *"Those who believe."*

You Who Believe

Because you believe what God has said
And believe His word is true
Jesus said He'd go away
And make a place for you

> *I go to prepare a place for you.*
> *John 14:2 NASB*

There is a place that belongs to you
It belongs to "You who believe"
It is a place made just for you
Because you had faith to believe

There is a place that belongs to you
You are "Those who believe"
Of all those who do not believe
You are of "Those who do"

Jesus said because you believe
There is a place for you

There is a place for you

You who believe!

You Only Need Just a Little Faith

Here is a review and summarization of all we have seen in this chapter.

Because we now understand what Jesus meant when He said we must have *"faith like a mustard seed,"* we now understand faith. We understand what is by faith, and what is not by faith. We now know what *"faith like a mustard seed"* means.

Everything in this chapter is predicated on the understanding that *"faith like a mustard seed"* is the absolute smallest faith there is. There is no faith smaller than *"faith like a mustard seed."*

Everything in this chapter is based on the understanding,
if you have *"just a little faith,"*
if you have *"any faith at all,"*
then you have *"faith like a mustard seed."*

If you have faith like a mustard seed, nothing will be impossible to you. And because, *"faith like a mustard seed"* is *"any faith at all,"* then, if you have any faith at all, nothing will be impossible to you.

> *You only need just a little faith.*

The Truth Was Hidden

Hidden within the phrase, *"faith like a mustard seed,"*
is the truth, *"You only need just a little faith."*

Because *"You only need just a little faith"* is *"a truth"* that was being hidden, it can be stated,

> *The truth was hidden.*

A parable or riddle is something that has a hidden meaning.

Because the phrase, *"faith like a mustard seed,"* has a hidden meaning, it also is a type of parable or riddle.

The phrase, *"faith like a mustard seed,"* is a parable.

> *It is a parable!*

Since the truth, *"You only need just a little faith,"*
was hidden within the phrase, *"faith like a mustard seed,"*
and since, *"faith like a mustard seed"* is a parable,
then, the truth was hidden in a parable.

> *The truth was hidden in a parable.*

The phrase, *"faith like a mustard seed,"* was not understood to be a parable. When Jesus said, *"If you have faith like a mustard seed …,"* it was not understood He was speaking a parable.

When the disciples asked Him, *"Increase our faith,"*
Jesus only said, *"If you have faith like a mustard seed …"*

Jesus did not answer them plainly.

> *He answered them with a parable.*

This is not all.

Not only did Jesus answer His disciples with a parable,
Jesus did not say He was speaking a parable.
Jesus did not reveal the parable, was a parable.

Remember,

> *A parable does not need to be called a parable, to be a parable.*

> *The parable was hidden.*

The truth you only need just a little faith is one of the *"mysteries"* of the kingdom of heaven of which Jesus spoke.

> *"To you it has been granted to know **the mysteries** of the kingdom of heaven, but to them it has not been granted.*
>
> *Matthew 13:11 NASB e.a.*

This truth was hidden because it had not been granted for others to know this mystery of the kingdom of heaven.

Because the *"truth,"* *"You only need just a little faith,"*
was hidden within the *"parable,"* *"faith like a mustard seed,"*
and, the truth might have been understood,
if the parable had been known to be a parable,
the parable itself needed to remain hidden.

Jesus therefore, did not say *"faith like a mustard seed"* is a parable.
Jesus hid the parable!

> *The parable was hidden, so the truth would remain hidden.*

The truth was hidden in a parable.
The answer to that parable, was hidden within another parable.

The *"answer"* to the parable of, *"faith like a mustard seed,"*
was hidden within the parable of, *"The kingdom of heaven is like a mustard seed."*

> *"The kingdom of heaven is like a mustard seed,*
> *which ..., **is smaller than all other seeds***

Matthew 13:31-32 NASB e.a. par.

> *A mustard seed is the smallest seed of all seeds.*
> *"Faith like a mustard seed" is the smallest faith of all faiths.*

> *The answer was hidden.*

If it had been known there was *"something hidden,"*
the *"answer"* that was hidden might have been seen.
If the *"answer"* had been seen,
then the *"truth"* would have been known.

Therefore, it was necessary that *"something was hidden,"* needed to be hidden as well.

In the same way, that the *"answer"* to the parable of, *"faith like a mustard seed,"* was hidden in the parable of, *"The kingdom of heaven is like ...,"*
so too, that *"something was hidden,"* was also being hidden,
in another parable of, *"The kingdom of heaven is like ..."*

That there was something hidden, was also being hidden in these parables:

> *"**The kingdom of heaven is like** a treasure **hidden** in the field,*
> *which a man **found** and **hid** again; and from joy over it he goes*
> *and sells all that he has and buys that field.*
>
> Matthew 13:44 NASB e.a.

> *"To what shall I liken **the kingdom of God? It is like** leaven, which*
> *a woman took and **hid** in three measures of meal till it was all*
> *leavened."*
>
> Luke 13:20-21 NKJV e.a.

These parables speak of what *"The kingdom of heaven is like,"*
and in both there is *"something hidden."*

> *What shall I say the kingdom of heaven is like?*
> *The kingdom of heaven is like something hidden.*

That there was *"something hidden"* was also being hidden;
it was hidden in a parable.

> *That something was hidden, was hidden as well.*

Therefore, we see the truth, *"You only need just a little faith,"*
was hidden in the parable of, *"faith like a mustard seed."*

This *"parable,"* because it was not said to be a parable, was hidden.
The *"answer"* to this parable, was hidden inside another parable.
And that *"something was hidden"* was hidden in yet other parables.

> *The truth was hidden.*
> *The parable was hidden.*
> *The answer to the parable was hidden.*
> *And that something was hidden, was hidden as well.*

All of these were hidden.

> *Jesus hid the truth.*
> *And He hid it very well.*
> *Jesus hid the truth.*
> *And He hid it, in a parable.*

It may seem hard to think Jesus would hide the truth, but this is exactly what He did.

> *Jesus hid the truth in parables.*

> *He opened His mouth in parables*
> *and He uttered "hidden things"*
> *Jesus hid the truth in parables*
> *and it remained a "hidden thing"*

> *"I will open My mouth in parables and I will utter hidden things."*
>
> See Matthew 13:35 <u>NASB</u> par.

> *Jesus hid the truth!*

Jesus did hide the truth, yet I will show you something more.

The Truth Was Revealed

Jesus told us there was something hidden in the kingdom of heaven parable.
He said,

> *"The kingdom of heaven is like a treasure **hidden** in the field,*
>
> Matthew 13:44 NASB e.a.

> *"There is something hidden."*

He used the *"Parable of the Kingdom,"* to reveal something is hidden.

> *Jesus revealed something is hidden, "in a parable."*

Jesus told us He was speaking a parable, when He said, *"The kingdom of heaven is like a mustard seed."*

> *"To what shall we liken the kingdom of God? Or **with what** **parable** shall we picture it? It is like a mustard seed ...*
>
> Mark 4:30-31 NKJV e.a. par.

Jesus told us He was speaking a parable,
when He said, *"The kingdom of heaven is like a mustard seed ..."*
So we might see He was also speaking a parable,
when He said, *"If you have faith like a mustard seed ..."*

> *"Faith like a mustard seed' is a parable."*

Jesus used the *"Parable of the Kingdom,"*
to reveal the *"Parable of Faith."*

> *Jesus revealed the parable, "in a parable."*

Jesus told us in the kingdom of heaven parable what a mustard seed is like.

> *"The kingdom of heaven is like a mustard seed,*
> *which ..., is **smaller than all other seeds***
>
> Matthew 13:31-32 NASB e.a. par.

He told us what a mustard seed is like,
so we might see what *"faith like a mustard seed"* is like.

> *A mustard seed is the smallest seed of all seeds.*
> *Faith like a mustard seed is the smallest faith of all faiths.*

Jesus used the *"Parable of the Kingdom,"*
to reveal the answer to the *"Parable of Faith."*

> *Jesus revealed the answer, "in a parable."*

Even though when the disciples asked Him, *"Jesus, increase our faith!"*
and Jesus did not plainly say, "You only need a little faith,"
this is in fact what Jesus did say, He just said it... *"another way."*

He said it *"in a parable."*

Jesus did say what kind of faith we need,
He said, *"If you have faith like a mustard seed ..."*
Jesus did in fact say, "You only need a little faith,"
He just said it another way.

He said it *"in a parable."*

> *"It is like a mustard seed, which is smaller than all other seeds."*

> *"If you have faith like a mustard seed ..."*
> *"If you have faith smaller than all other faiths..."*

> *Nothing shall be impossible!*

Jesus used the *"Parable of Faith"* to reveal the truth of faith.

> *Jesus revealed something is hidden, "in a parable."*
> *Jesus revealed the parable, "in a parable."*
> *Jesus revealed the answer, "in a parable."*
> *Jesus revealed the truth, "in a parable."*

> *He opened His mouth in parables*
> *and He uttered "hidden things"*
> *Jesus spoke the truth in parables*
> *and revealed a "hidden thing"*

> *"I will open My mouth in parables and I will utter hidden things."*
>
> See Matthew 13:35 <u>NASB</u> par.

> *Jesus revealed the truth!*

The Parable Was Part of the Mystery

The parable of faith was hiding a mystery of the kingdom of heaven. The parable of faith itself, was also hidden.

Since the parable was hidden, the parable being hidden, was part of the riddle which needed to be solved. The parable being hidden then, was part of the mystery of the parable.

The meaning is this:

To find the answer to the parable, you first must find the parable. If you do not know it is a riddle, you will not look for the answer to the riddle.

If you do not know it is a parable, you will not look for the answer to the parable.

Finding the parable, was key to solving the mystery of the parable. Solving the mystery of the parable, was key to solving the answer to the mystery of the kingdom.

The parable being hidden then, was part of the mystery.

The parable was part of the mystery.

A Treasure Was Hidden

Jesus used the parable of what *"the kingdom of heaven is like,"* that it may be understood what faith like a mustard seed *"is like."*

Jesus then used yet another parable of what *"the kingdom of heaven is like,"* that it may be understood *"it is like"* *"a treasure hidden."*

> *"The kingdom of heaven is like a treasure hidden in the field*
>
> *Matthew 13:44 NASB*

Since you need to have faith that *"is like"* a mustard seed, and, the kingdom of heaven *"is like"* a mustard seed as well, then, you need to have faith that *"is like"* the kingdom of heaven.

And, since you need to have faith that *"is like"* the kingdom of heaven, and, the kingdom of heaven *"is like"* a treasure hidden, then, you need to have faith that *"is like"* a treasure hidden as well.

The faith you need to have *"is like"* a treasure that was hidden. The kind of faith you need to have *"is a treasure that was hidden."*

> *It is a treasure hidden.*
> *You only need a little faith.*

Hidden from the Foundation of the World

> *"I will open My mouth in parables;*
> *I will utter things hidden since the foundation of the world."*
>
> Matthew 13:35 <u>NASB</u>

This truth, *"You only need a little faith,"* has been hidden from the very foundation of the world. It was hidden long before we came into being, long before we ever were.

It was hidden from the beginning and has remained hidden. There has not been a time since the foundation of the world when it has not been hidden.

It has been hidden from the very beginning.

As far as I know… no one has ever known this truth, *"You only need just a little faith."* No one has ever understood,

> *If you have any faith at all, nothing will be impossible to you.*

No one knew and no one understood, because,

> *It was hidden!*

It was hidden, has remained hidden and has always been hidden. It has always been hidden that is…

> *Until now.*

Until now, it had been hidden.

> *But now the truth is known.*

The Parables

Oh the parables!
Now that we understand the parables,
we now understand the truth.
Because we understand the parables,
we now know the truth.

But it was never intended to be this way.
It was never intended we would know the truth,
because we understand the parables.
It was intended we would understand the parables,

Because we know the truth.

Remember, the parables were not given to us,
they were given only to those who do not believe.

The disciples asked Jesus,

"Why do You speak to them in parables?"

Jesus replied,

"To you it has been granted to know the mysteries of the kingdom
of heaven, but to them it has not been granted.

Matthew 13:10-11 NASB

He also said,

those who are outside get everything in parables

Mark 4:11 NASB

It is granted to us who believe,

To know the mysteries of the kingdom of heaven.

It is granted to us who believe,

To know what the kingdom of heaven is like.

But to those who do not believe, *"It has not been granted."*
Those who do not believe, *"Get everything in parables."*

> *because while seeing they do not see,*
> *and while hearing they do not hear,*
> *nor do they understand.*
>
> *"Therefore I speak to them in parables;*

See Matthew 13:13 NASB

It was intended that *"we who believe"* would know and understand this truth. Yet, this was to remain hidden from *"those who do not believe."*

It was not given to them, *"to know the mysteries of the kingdom of heaven"*; this was given only to us. It was intended this should remain hidden from them, because they do not believe.

> *And it did remain hidden from them,*
> *because it was hidden very well.*
> *But not only did it remain hidden from them,*
> *it remained hidden from us as well!*
>
> *It should not have been this way!*

We should have understood.
And I will say it again,

> *We should have understood!*

Thus we see, even *"we who believe"* did not understand the truth of what Jesus spoke. Neither *"we who believe"* nor *"those who do not believe"* have ever understood this truth.

It was never intended that *"we who believe"* would know this truth by understanding the parables, for the parables were meant to hide.

It was intended that *"we who believe"* would understand the parables, because we know the truth.

It was never intended that we would know the truth *"by the parables."*
It has always been intended that we would know the truth *"by faith."*

For it is *"by faith"* in Jesus Christ, that we will know the truth.
It is *"by His Spirit only,"* that the truth will be revealed.

> *The truth will not be revealed by parables.*

And I will say it again,

> *The truth will not be revealed by parables!*

But now we see the truth has been revealed.
However, this is only because the parables have now been explained.

Yes, the truth was revealed, *"in the parables."*
But the truth was not revealed, *"by the parables."*
The truth was revealed, *"by the Holy Spirit."*

It was the Holy Spirit who revealed this truth.
It is the Holy Spirit who reveals the truth spoken of in the parables.

Jesus said to His disciples,

> *"I have many more things to say to you, but you cannot bear them now. "But when **He, the Spirit of truth**, comes, **He will guide you into all the truth***
>
> John 16:12-13 NASB e.a.

He also said,

> *"But **the Helper, the Holy Spirit**, whom the Father will send in My name, **He will teach you all things**, and bring to your remembrance all that I said to you.*
>
> John 14:26 NASB e.a.

It is the Holy Spirit who reveals the truth to us.
It is the Holy Spirit who teaches all things to us.

I believe, *"we who believe"* were supposed to have known this truth about faith.
I believe, we should have known this truth a very long time ago.
I really believe, we should have known this truth because we are those who say,

> *"We believe!"*

I believe, we really, really missed it.
And we missed it such a long time ago.

> Yet, even though "I believe" we missed it,
> and believe we should have known,
> even though we missed it then,
> now the truth is known.

> We did not miss it now!

Know this one thing too,

> Even though these things were hidden,
> though they were not seen,
> we were a people who still believed,
> though we did not see.

> | Blessed are they who did not see, and yet believed.
> John 20:29 NASB

Now the Truth Is Known

> So, now we see the truth is known,
> but not by us alone.
> Now the truth is known to others as well,
> because it has been written down.

> Because faith and the parables have been explained,
> and it has been written down,
> now even those who do not believe,
> know what has been found.

Now those who do not believe are able to read and know the things that were hidden from them.

> So we see, even though it was hidden from them,
> it remained hidden from us as well.
> And now that it is revealed to us,
> it is revealed to them as well.

Now those who do not believe can know the mysteries of the kingdom of heaven.

It should not have been this way!

However, even though it should not have been this way I will show you something more.

They still need faith to believe.

Though They Know, They Still Need Faith

Now that the truth, "You only need a little faith," is known, it would seem they would no longer need faith to know. However, we will see even though they know this truth, they still need faith to believe.

Though you know, you still need faith.

Even though all things may be explained to you,
So that you absolutely know,
Until you've walked it out yourself,
It's only something that you know.

There is a difference in the things you know,
Some are explained, some are read.
But the things you experience for yourself,
Are no longer what someone else has said.

You can know what is the truth,
But never know the Truth itself.
Until you take the truth you know,
And walk it out yourself.

Though God Himself says to you,
That you can walk on water,
You may know God spoke to you,
You may know what He said,
You may know because it was God,
It is absolutely true what He said.

You may know that you can walk on water,
Because God Himself has said you can,
But until it's you who walks on water,
You only know "you can."
Until it's you who walks on water,
You only know some facts.

You may know that you can walk on water,
But until you have the faith to try,
You will know that "you can" walk on water,
But you will never know "what it is like."

What is it like to walk on water?
It is like the kingdom of heaven.

Oh the mysteries of the kingdom of heaven!

> *"To [us] it has been granted to know the mysteries of the*
> *kingdom of heaven,*
> *but to them it has not been granted.*
>
> *Matthew 13:11 NASB par.*

It has not been granted to them to know what it is like to walk on water.

But it has been granted to us!

So we see, even though they know these things and these things have been explained,

They still need faith to believe!

So we see these things have been explained
Even to those who do not believe
But even if they know these things
They too need faith to believe

Though they do not believe
How wonderful it would be
If perhaps we could see
They too would believe
Because they see, we believe

But I know there will be
"Those who believe"
Who know the way it has been

They know "what they know"
And will tell you so
You can't tell them anything
Other than that

Come with us, we say
We are going this way
To a place that is not on the map

But they will say
We know where we are
We never travel too far
We will stay right here
Where we are at!

Despite what we say
They will continue to say

We know the earth is flat!

Selah

We Will See

We will see,
some of those *"who do not believe,"*
will believe.

And we will see,
some of those *"who do believe,"*
will not believe.

There will be some *"who do believe,"*
who will not believe,
and they will not believe,
"because they know."

However, there will also be some *"who do not believe,"*
who will come to believe,
and because they have believed,
"they will know."

It Has Been Explained

Now it has been explained.
Now you know the truth.
Now there is only one thing you must be able to do.
You must "be able to believe."
And the only thing you need to be able to believe is,

Just a little faith.

That is all you have ever needed.
That is all you need to have.
If you have any faith at all,
you have all you need to have.

You only need just a little faith.

From Now On

From now on, *"You of little faith"* will no longer be a criticism.
From now on, *"You of little faith"* will be a compliment.

> *You have a little faith!*

From now on,

> *When someone says to you,*
> *"O you of little faith!"*
> *Tell the one who said it,*
> *"Thank you for what you say."*
> *Then turn around and praise the Lord,*
> *You have a little faith!*
>
> *Exclaim, "I have a little faith!" to everyone you see.*
> *Shout it at the top of your voice,*
>
> *"I HAVE THE FAITH I NEED!"*

Nothing Will Be Impossible to You

> *Because you know that you have faith,*
> *then know this one thing too,*
> *it is God Himself who gave this faith to you.*
>
> *And Jesus said,*
> *"If you have just a little faith, nothing will be impossible to you."*
>
> *And since it was God Himself who gave you this faith,*
> *then there is nothing you will not be able to do!*

Peter

If we look back at Peter, it was Jesus Christ who made Peter able to walk
on the water.

It may have been, Peter did not walk on the water long enough to fully know he was able. But Peter certainly walked on the water long enough to know that it is possible.

Because Peter had the faith to walk on the water,
he knew what he had never known before;
he knew it is possible to walk on water.
And he knew it with,

> *Just a little faith.*

> *It is possible to walk on water!*
> *Nothing will be impossible to you who believe!*

Walking on Water

If there ever was an acronym that so perfectly conveyed the feelings for which the words meant, it is the acronym for walking on water.

Peter walked on water.

> *W.O.W!*

What more can we say about something like that except, WOW!

> *Peter walked on water!*

Although everyone else stayed behind in the boat, Peter had the faith to try. Now, because Peter was able to do it, we know it can be done.

> *You did it, Peter.*
> *Well done!*

And with all that is within me, I have to say it again.

> *WELL DONE, PETER!*
> *It is long overdue.*
> *WELL DONE!*

Abide in Him

Jesus said to His disciples (and says to us as well),

> *Abide in Me, and I in you. As the branch cannot bear fruit of itself, unless it abides in the vine, neither can you, unless you abide in Me.*
>
> *"I am the vine, you are the branches. He who abides in Me, and I in him, bears much fruit; for without Me you can do nothing.*

John 15:4-5 NKJV

If you abide in Jesus Christ and He abides in you,

> *You will bear much fruit.*

Though you may believe it is not possible for you to bear much fruit, yet, because you believe in Him,

> *You will bear much fruit.*

It is only by His Spirit, by the Spirit of God, that any of us are ever able to do anything. Apart from Jesus Christ we can do nothing.

Nevertheless, I know this:
I know I can do all things through Jesus Christ who will make me able. And because He has given me the faith to believe, I know,

> *He will make me able.*

> *I know this.*
> *By faith, I know!*

You too need to know, that because you have the faith to believe,

> *He will make you able.*

Men Can't Walk on Water

Men can't walk on water
Men can't calm the seas
Men can't cast aside mountains
And men can't curse the trees

But we can!
Because He will make us able.

Even greater works than these will we do, because He will make us able!

> "*Truly, truly, I say to you, he who believes in Me, the works that
> I do, he will do also; and* **greater works than these** *he will do;
> because I go to the Father.*
>
> *John 14:12 NASB e.a.*

Because we believe.

Abel

As Adam was the first of many
Jesus also is the first of many
Jesus is known as our second Adam

But now we also see
As Abel was the first son of many to die
Jesus is the first Son of many that died, to rise

Jesus, who is our second Adam
Is also our second Abel

Through the first Adam
There came a son who was Abel
But Abel was slain,
By his brother Cain
And no longer was there one who was Abel

But another Son came,
Born later than Cain
And this Son too was Abel

But like the first Abel we see
He too died,
But He was hung from a tree
And no longer was there one who was Abel

But the Son who had died
And was crucified
Said to those by whom He was slain

Though you hate Me you'll see
You take nothing from Me
I lay My life down for My friends

I have the power to lay it down
I have the power to take it up again
And by this you will see

I am Able!

The Abel that died
Is able to live
And now there is one who is Able!

So we see Jesus has become our second Abel. The first Adam was father to only one who was Abel. And now we see through the second Adam, Jesus Christ, there will come many more who also are able.

> *Jesus Christ will make us able.*

> *Though the first Abel died,*
> *and the second Abel crucified,*
> *those who are able thereafter shall live!*

> *"I am the resurrection and the life. He who believes in Me, though he may die, he shall live. And whoever lives and believes in Me shall never die.*
>
> John 11:25-26 NKJV

> *You only need to believe.*
> *You only need just a little faith.*

His Giving Was in Secret

Jesus said,

> *when you give to the poor, do not let your left hand know what your right hand is doing, **so that your giving will be in secret***
>
> Matthew 6:3-4 NASB e.a.

Jesus told us the kingdom of heaven is like a mustard seed and then went on to describe the mustard seed. He described it two ways, saying two different things about the mustard seed.

In one hand, *His right hand,*
Jesus told us briefly, *how small* the mustard seed is.

> *this is smaller than all other seeds*
>
> Matthew 13:32 NASB

Then in the other hand, *His left hand,*
Jesus told us in great detail, *how large* the mustard seed would grow. He wrapped both sides of His message of how small the mustard seed is, by talking about a man sowing the seed in his field, and what it is like when it is full grown.

He said,

> **"The kingdom of heaven is like a mustard seed,**
> **which a man took and sowed in his field;**

and this is smaller than all other seeds,

> **but when it is full grown, it is larger than the garden plants,**
> **and becomes a tree, so that the birds of the air come and**
> **nest in its branches."**

Matthew 13:31-32 NASB e.a.

When Jesus described how large the mustard seed would grow, He was creating a distraction and diversion away from how small the mustard seed is, and how small of faith we actually need.

Jesus drew our attention away from the smallness of the seed, by telling us how large the mustard seed could become.

Picture His left hand waving to the people, while He quietly slips His right hand back into His pocket. No one noticed what He held in His right hand.

Our attention and focus were on what was in Jesus' left hand, (how large the mustard seed became).

We had no interest in seeing what was in Jesus' right hand, (how small the mustard seed is).

Our interest was in how large we could become.
We had no interest in how small we only needed to be.

He Gave Gifts to Men

Earlier we had mentioned Jesus gave two different gifts to two different groups.

To one group, He gave *"the gift"* to know the mysteries of the kingdom of heaven. To the other group, He gave *"the gift"* of the parables.

Paul wrote of Jesus, that He gave gifts to men.

> *"When He ascended on high,*
> *He led captive a host of captives,*
> *And **He gave gifts to men**."*

Ephesians 4:8 <u>NASB</u> e.a.

The gift and truth He held in His right hand, was the smallness of the seed.
Though His gift was hidden, He held it high for all to see.
But we only saw what He held in His left hand, that is,

> *How great with faith we could be.*

Speaking of how large the mustard seed would become, was a diversion.

> *when you give to the poor,*
> ***do not let your left hand know what your right hand is doing,***
> *so that your giving will be in secret*

Matthew 6:3-4 NASB e.a.

> *"Look at My left hand, so you will not see the gift I hold in My right."*

His gift was hidden.

> *His giving was in secret.*

By Faith, You Will Speak

Of all the many times Jesus spoke of faith, not once, did Jesus say we could actually do impossible things *"by faith."*

The only thing Jesus said we could do by faith, is what we are already able to do.

The only thing Jesus actually said we could do by faith, *is speak…* speak to the mountains.

> *I say to you, if you have faith as a mustard seed,* **you shall say***…*
>
> **you shall say** *to this mountain, 'Move from here to there,' and it shall move; and nothing shall be impossible to you.*
>
> Matthew 17:20 <u>NASB</u> e.a. par.

If you have faith as a mustard seed, you will speak.

By faith, you will speak!

The Purpose of Faith

There is no power in faith to heal the sick, raise the dead, or cast mountains into the sea.

> *There is no power in faith!*

What then is the purpose of faith?

> *The purpose of faith is so we can know God,*
> *not so we can cast mountains into the sea.*
> *If that were all we used our faith for,*
> *oh, what a waste of faith that would be!*

Faith itself cannot move mountains.
But a man or woman with their faith in their God,
when God has spoken and they know what to do,
will speak to those mountains that cannot be moved,
and by faith they will say,

> *"Move aside, I am coming through!"*

Have faith in God, those mountains will move.

A Pearl of Great Value Has Been Found

> *the kingdom of heaven is like a merchant seeking fine pearls, and*
> *upon finding one pearl of great value, he went and sold all that he*
> *had and bought it.*
>
> *Matthew 13:45-46 NASB*

So, what shall we say the kingdom of heaven is like?

> *It is like a pearl of great value that has been found.*
>
> *You only need just a little faith.*

My friends, that is,

What Faith Is For

The Encore

Do Not Be Afraid Any Longer

Jairus had been told,

> *"Your daughter has died; do not trouble the Teacher anymore."*

But Jesus said to him,

> **"Do not be afraid any longer**; only believe, and she will be made well."

Luke 8:49-50 NASB e.a.

You do not need to be afraid any longer; only believe.
You do not need to be afraid any longer; you only need just the smallest of faith.

If Jesus is able to bring that which is dead back to life, how much more then…

How much more then, can He do with those who live.
How much more, can He do with those who believe.
How much more can He do…

> *With you.*

> *Oh, how much more!*

It is recorded that Jesus used the phrase *"You of little faith"* four times.
Jesus said it four times and four times only.
Jesus never used that phrase the same way twice.
In each of those times, Jesus stated something different about our lives.

> Once He said, *"Why did you doubt?"*
> Once, *"Why do you reason?"*
> Once, *"Why are you afraid?"*

And,

> Once, *"Why are you worried?"*

In each of these He was declaring to us,

> *We do not need to doubt, reason, be afraid or worry.*

These four things together cover every concern or issue we deal with in our lives.

These four things were given together, as a whole, in completeness for us.

These four things together are complete.

It is complete.

And I will say it again,

It is complete!

There is nothing else needed. We do not need to doubt, or reason, or be afraid, or worry any longer.

No more!

If you ever find yourself being impacted by any of these issues, draw upon the strength of Jesus and be assured that He will walk you through it.

If you ever find yourself losing the fight to any of these issues, encourage yourself with what He has promised you and speak these words out loud.

DRAW upon Jesus!
*I do not need to **Doubt**, **Reason**, be **Afraid**, or **Worry**.*
I have a little faith!

Angelia Barton

It shall be done for you.
You have a little faith.

Jesus said,

> *"These things I have spoken to you, so that **in Me you may have peace**. In the world you have tribulation, **but take courage; I have overcome the world**."*

John 16:33 NASB e.a.

Have peace in Jesus Christ; take courage in Him.
He has overcome all our troubles.

You do not need to be afraid any longer.

It has all been taken care of; it has all been done for you.
Just as Jesus said it would be.

> *It shall be done for you.*
> *It has been done for you.*

> *"Take courage, I have overcome the world."*

Knowledge Comes by Faith

Faith does not come by knowledge.
Knowledge and understanding come by faith.

When Peter trusted Jesus and by faith, stepped out of the boat, he then understood and knew something he had never known before.

By faith, Peter understood.

As Jesus was washing the disciples' feet, when He came to Peter, Peter refused Him.

Peter said to Jesus,

> *"Lord, do You wash my feet?"*
> *"Never shall You wash my feet!"*

But Jesus replied to Peter,

> *"What I do you do not realize now, but you will understand hereafter."*
>
> *John 13:6, 8, 7 NASB*

Jesus said to His disciples,

> ***"I have many more things to say to you, but you cannot bear them now.*** *"But when He, the Spirit of truth, comes, He will guide you into all the truth; for He will not speak on His own initiative, but whatever He hears, He will speak; and He will disclose to you what is to come.*
>
> *John 16:12-13 NASB e.a.*

There are many things we do not know, many things we do not understand, and we cannot bear them now; we cannot understand them now.

The Holy Spirit will teach us; the Holy Spirit will guide us.

When we follow the Holy Spirit by faith, when we follow the Holy Spirit through things which we do not understand, we will then come to a place where we understand those things which before could not be understood.

But if we try to understand these things first, *before,* we go by faith, we will never understand, and we will never go by faith.

For faith does not come by understanding; understanding comes by faith.

>   *Understanding comes by faith.*

You will never obtain faith by knowledge.
And you will never obtain knowledge without faith.

In this regard, apart from faith, there is no knowledge.

By faith, we will understand.
By faith, we will know.

>   *Knowledge comes by faith.*
>   *By faith, we know!*

If you want to know, you must believe.
If you want to understand, *"How can these things be?"* you must have faith.

Jesus promised, you will understand.

>   *"What I do you do not realize now,*
>   *but you will understand hereafter."*
>
>   *You will understand.*

Faith, Belief and Trust

As we said at the beginning, we tend to use the words faith, belief and trust interchangeably, but there are slight differences in each.

We need to have faith, we need to believe, and we need to trust.

If you want to trust, you must believe.
If you want to believe, you must have faith.
If you want to have faith, the only thing you need to do is ask God and He will richly give it to you.

But know this:
If you have the faith, to ask God for faith,
then God has already given this faith to you
before you have even asked.

> *You already have faith.*

We need to have faith, we need to believe, and we need to trust.
What Jesus was saying to Peter is,

> *"Though you do not understand,*
> **trust Me for now**
> *and you will understand hereafter."*

Trust Him for now, and you will understand later.
Trust Him, and you will understand.

> *Trust Him.*

We Are Going Away

Come with us.

We are going away, to a place we have never been. It will be an incredible adventure. As it was with Abram, so it will be with us. We may not know where we are going, but the Lord will show us the way. And once we have arrived, we will know. And then this faith of ours will no longer be needed.

But oh, how will you know, unless you go?

Come with us.

You only need to believe.

You only need just a little faith.

A Letter

What you are about to read is a message from the Lord.
It is a letter from the Lord Himself, written as it were,
personally to you.

From the Lord
To you

If I asked you to do something great,
would you not do it gladly?

If I asked you to do something difficult,
would you not do it with joy?

How much more then,
if I only ask you to believe?

How much more then,
if I only ask you to trust Me?

I have many things to say to you,
but you cannot bear them now.

I have many things to say to you,
but you cannot understand them now.

Trust Me for now,
and I will help you understand.

Trust Me for now,
and you will understand hereafter.

I am the Lord,
and there is no other God beside Me.

I am the Lord,
and there is no other God like Me.

I am the God of Abraham, Isaac and Jacob.
I am not the God of the dead.
I am the God of those who live.

Come away with Me now and rest awhile.
We will be leaving shortly.

God Has Spoken

Our faith to believe, is by God and because of God.
God is the initiator; God is the finisher of our faith.

God is the creator of our faith.
God is the fulfillment of our faith.

Moreover, because we have faith, God will do what He has said.
So that, by Him and through Him, our faith might be complete.

Our faith to believe that mountains can move, is only because
God has said they can.

Because God has spoken and said the impossible is possible, we
believe it is.

> *Because God has spoken, you believe.*
> *Because God has spoken, you now have faith.*

> *"Let there be faith!"*

What I have written, I have written!

Behold the Man!

Jesus Christ
The King of the Jews

Jesus Christ
The King of those who believe

It is the glory of God to conceal a matter,
But the glory of kings is to search it out.

"I praise You, Father, Lord of heaven and earth, that You have hidden these things from the wise and intelligent and have revealed them to infants."

Jesus Christ, the Son of God

It will never look the same again

Now that you have seen
What you were never able to see before
You will never be able to see again
What you were only able to see before

It will never look the same again
It will never be the same again

It's just a game of Hide and Seek
We need to learn how things are hidden
It's just a game of Hide and Seek

> *We need to learn… how to play!*

It's Not as It Seems

To Be Continued…

Just one more thing before you go your way.
There would not be a mystery, if it were not said there is a mystery.

Therefore, let it be known, this book is a parable.

Oh, but now that it is known, the parable is a parable,
now the meaning of the parable will be known.

Well, perhaps…

ENDING CREDITS

ENDING CREDITS

1   *Apokalupto - 'to uncover or make known'*
    The Strongest NASB Exhaustive Concordance, Zondervan Bible Publishers (Grand
    Rapids, MI) Greek Dictionary Reference number 601
    THAYER'S GREEK-ENGLISH LEXICON OF THE NEW TESTAMENT,
    Hendrickson Publishing, (Peabody MA)

2   *Paroimia -'Parable, Proverb or Dark saying'*
    The Strongest NASB Exhaustive Concordance, Zondervan Bible Publishers (Grand
    Rapids, MI) Greek Dictionary Reference number 3942
    THAYER'S GREEK-ENGLISH LEXICON OF THE NEW TESTAMENT,
    Hendrickson Publishing, (Peabody MA)

3   *Parrhesia - 'speak openly, without concealment or ambiguity'*
    The Strongest NASB Exhaustive Concordance, Zondervan Bible Publishers (Grand
    Rapids, MI) Greek Dictionary Reference number 3954
    THAYER'S GREEK-ENGLISH LEXICON OF THE NEW TESTAMENT,
    Hendrickson Publishing, (Peabody MA)

4   *Didomi - 'to give, to allow or to permit'*
    The Strongest NASB Exhaustive Concordance, Zondervan Bible Publishers (Grand
    Rapids, MI) Greek Dictionary Reference number 1325
    THAYER'S GREEK-ENGLISH LEXICON OF THE NEW TESTAMENT,
    Hendrickson Publishing, (Peabody MA)

5   *Chiydah (or Chidah) - 'a riddle or difficult, perplexing or hard question'*
    NEW STRONG'S EXHAUSTIVE CONCORDANCE OF THE BIBLE, Thomas
    Nelson Publishers (Nashville, TN). Hebrew Dictionary Reference number 2420
    The Strongest NASB Exhaustive Concordance, Zondervan Bible Publishers (Grand
    Rapids, MI)

6   *the final frontier*
    to boldly go where no one has gone before
    From the opening monologue of the Star Trek television series - Paramount Global

7   *Oligopistos - 'little faith or of little faith'*
    NEW STRONG'S EXHAUSTIVE CONCORDANCE OF THE BIBLE, Thomas
    Nelson Publishers (Nashville, TN). Greek Dictionary Reference number 3640
    The Strongest NASB Exhaustive Concordance, Zondervan Bible Publishers (Grand
    Rapids, MI) Greek Dictionary Reference number 3640b

8   *Apistia - 'faithless or unbelief'*
    NEW STRONG'S EXHAUSTIVE CONCORDANCE OF THE BIBLE, Thomas
    Nelson Publishers (Nashville, TN). Greek Dictionary Reference number 570
    The Strongest NASB Exhaustive Concordance, Zondervan Bible Publishers (Grand
    Rapids, MI)

9   *Apistos - 'to be unbelieving or faithless'*
    NEW STRONG'S EXHAUSTIVE CONCORDANCE OF THE BIBLE, Thomas
    Nelson Publishers (Nashville, TN). Greek Dictionary Reference number 571
    The Strongest NASB Exhaustive Concordance, Zondervan Bible Publishers (Grand
    Rapids, MI)

10 *Humas - 'You'*
    NEW STRONG'S EXHAUSTIVE CONCORDANCE OF THE BIBLE, Thomas
    Nelson Publishers (Nashville, TN). Greek Dictionary Reference number 5209

11 *Oligos - 'little, small or few'*
    The Strongest NASB Exhaustive Concordance, Zondervan Bible Publishers (Grand
    Rapids, MI) Greek Dictionary Reference number 3641

12 *Pistis - 'faith'*
    The Strongest NASB Exhaustive Concordance, Zondervan Bible Publishers (Grand
    Rapids, MI) Greek Dictionary Reference number 4102

13 *Oligopistos - 'little faith or of little faith'*
    NEW STRONG'S EXHAUSTIVE CONCORDANCE OF THE BIBLE, Thomas
    Nelson Publishers (Nashville, TN). Greek Dictionary Reference number 3640
    The Strongest NASB Exhaustive Concordance, Zondervan Bible Publishers (Grand
    Rapids, MI) Greek Dictionary Reference number 3640b

14 *Megas - 'great or fierce'*
    The Strongest NASB Exhaustive Concordance, Zondervan Bible Publishers (Grand
    Rapids, MI) Greek Dictionary Reference number 3173

15 *Seismos - 'a shaking or commotion'*
    The Strongest NASB Exhaustive Concordance, Zondervan Bible Publishers (Grand
    Rapids, MI) Greek Dictionary Reference number 4578

16 *Lailaps - 'a violent attack of wind'*
    The Strongest NASB Exhaustive Concordance, Zondervan Bible Publishers (Grand
    Rapids, MI) Greek Dictionary Reference number 2978
    THAYER'S GREEK-ENGLISH LEXICON OF THE NEW TESTAMENT,
    Hendrickson Publishing, (Peabody MA)

17 *Anemos - 'a very strong wind or violent agitation of wind'*
    THAYER'S GREEK-ENGLISH LEXICON OF THE NEW TESTAMENT,
    Hendrickson Publishing, (Peabody MA)
    The Strongest NASB Exhaustive Concordance, Zondervan Bible Publishers (Grand
    Rapids, MI) Greek Dictionary Reference number 417